Religious and Philosophical Aspects of the Laozi

SUNY Series in
Chinese Philosophy and Culture

David L. Hall and Roger T. Ames, editors

Religious
and
Philosophical
Aspects
of the
Laozi

Edited by
Mark Csikszentmihalyi
and
Philip J. Ivanhoe

STATE UNIVERSITY OF NEW YORK PRESS

Production by Ruth Fisher
Marketing by Patrick Durocher

Published by
State University of New York Press, Albany

© 1999 State University of New York

For information, address the State University of New York Press,
State University Plaza, Albany, NY 12246

Library of Congress Cataloging-in-Publication Data
Religious and philosophical aspects of the *Laozi* / edited by Mark
 Csikszentmihalyi and Philip J. Ivanhoe.
      p. cm. — (SUNY series in Chinese philosophy and culture)
   Includes index.
   ISBN 0-7914-4111-3 (alk. paper). — ISBN 0-7914-4112-1 (pbk. :
alk. paper)
   1. Lao-tzu. Tao te ching. 2. Taoism—China. 3. Philosophy,
Taoist. I. Csikszentmihalyi, Mark. II. Ivanhoe, Philip J.
III. Series.
BL1900.L35R46   1999
299'.51482—dc21   98–46708
                                                               CIP

10 9 8 7 6 5 4 3 2 1

For our teacher Albert Dien,

如時雨化之者

"One whose influence is like timely rain."

Contents

Romanization Conversion Table

Romanizations in this volume are according to the *pinyin* system recently adopted by the Library of Congress. The following table may be used to convert *pinyin* to the Wade-Giles romanization used in many English-language works on Daoism. Where a *pinyin* syllable does not appear, it is the same under Wade-Giles.

Pinyin	Wade-Giles	Pinyin	Wade-Giles	Pinyin	Wade-Giles
ba	pa	ce	ts'e	cong	ts'ung
bai	pai	cen	ts'en	cou	ts'ou
ban	pan	ceng	ts'eng	cu	ts'u
bang	pang	cha	ch'a	cui	ts'ui
bao	pao	chai	ch'ai	cun	ts'un
bei	pei	chan	ch'an	cuo	ts'o
ben	pen	chang	ch'ang	da	ta
beng	peng	chao	ch'ao	dai	tai
bi	pi	che	ch'e	dan	tan
bian	pien	chen	ch'en	dang	tang
biao	piao	cheng	ch'eng	dao	tao
bie	pieh	chi	ch'ih	de	te
bin	pin	chong	ch'ung	deng	teng
bing	ping	chou	ch'ou	di	ti
bo	po	chuo	ch'o	dian	tien
bu	pu	chu	ch'u	diao	tiao
ca	ts'a	chuan	ch'uan	die	tieh
cai	ts'ai	chuang	ch'uang	ding	ting
can	ts'an	chui	ch'ui	dong	tung
cang	ts'ang	chun	ch'un	dou	tou
cao	ts'ao	ci	tz'u	du	tu

Pinyin	Wade-Giles	Pinyin	Wade-Giles	Pinyin	Wade-Giles
duan	tuan	jue	chüeh	peng	p'eng
dui	tui	jun	chün	pi	p'i
dun	tun	ka	k'a	pian	p'ien
duo	to	kai	k'ai	piao	p'iao
er	erh	kan	k'an	pie	p'ieh
ga	ka	kang	k'ang	pin	p'in
gai	kai	kao	k'ao	ping	p'ing
gan	kan	ke	k'o	po	p'o
gang	kang	ken	k'en	pu	p'u
gao	kao	keng	k'eng	qi	ch'i
ge	ko	kong	k'ung	qia	ch'ia
gei	kei	kou	k'ou	qian	ch'ien
gen	ken	ku	k'u	qiang	ch'iang
geng	keng	kua	k'ua	qiao	ch'iao
gong	kung	kuai	k'uai	qie	ch'ieh
gou	kou	kuan	k'uan	qin	ch'in
gu	ku	kuang	k'uang	qing	ch'ing
gua	kua	kui	k'uei	qiong	ch'iung
guai	kuai	kun	k'un	qiu	ch'iu
guan	kuan	kuo	k'uo	qu	ch'ï
guang	kuang	lian	lien	quan	ch'üan
gui	kuei	lie	lieh	que	ch'üeh
gun	kun	long	lung	qun	ch'ün
guo	kuo	luo	lo	ran	jan
he	ho	mian	mien	rang	jang
hong	hung	mie	mieh	rao	jao
ji	chi	nian	nien	re	je
jia	chia	nie	nieh	ren	jen
jian	chien	nong	nung	reng	jeng
jiang	chiang	nuo	no	ri	jih
jiao	chiao	nüe	nüeh	rou	jou
jie	chieh	pa	p'a	rong	jung
jin	chin	pai	p'ai	ru	ju
jing	ching	pan	p'an	ruan	juan
jiong	chiung	pang	p'ang	rui	jui
jiu	chiu	pao	p'ao	run	jun
ju	chü	pei	p'ei	ruo	jo
juan	chüan	pen	p'en	shi	shih

Pinyin	Wade-Giles	Pinyin	Wade-Giles	Pinyin	Wade-Giles
si	ssu	xiao	hsiao	zha	cha
song	sung	xie	hsieh	zhai	chai
suo	so	xin	hsin	zhan	chan
ta	t'a	xing	hsing	zhang	chang
tai	t'ai	xiong	hsiung	zhao	chao
tan	t'an	xiu	hsiu	zhe	che
tang	t'ang	xu	hsü	zhen	chen
tao	t'ao	xuan	hsüan	zheng	cheng
te	t'e	xue	hsüeh	zhi	chih
teng	t'eng	xun	hsün	zhong	chung
ti	t'i	ye	yeh	zhu	chu
tiao	t'iao	yi	i	zhua	chua
tian	t'ien	yong	yung	zhuai	chuai
tie	t'ieh	you	yu	zhuan	chuan
ting	t'ing	yu	yü	zhuang	chuang
tong	t'ung	yue	yüeh	zhui	chui
tou	t'o	yun	yün	zhun	chun
tu	t'u	za	tsa	zhuo	cho
tuan	t'uan	zai	tsai	zi	tzu
tui	t'ui	zan	tsan	zong	tsung
tun	t'un	zang	tsang	zu	tsu
tuo	t'o	zao	tsao	zuan	tsuan
xi	hsi	ze	tse	zui	tsui
xia	hsia	zen	tsen	zun	tsun
xian	hsien	zeng	tseng	zuo	tso
xiang	hsiang				

Introduction

The third century B.C.E. Daoist classic known to many in the West as the *Tao-te ching* 道德經 (but here called the *Laozi* 老子)[1] is essential reading for anyone interested in understanding the religious and philosophical traditions of East Asia. A remarkably terse text, consisting of a mere five thousand or so characters in the original Chinese, the *Laozi* has generated a vast literature of commentary and exegesis throughout East Asia and well beyond. It has exerted a profound, pervasive, and persistent influence on world thought, literature, and art and remains the most often translated Asian work in Western languages. And yet, despite its undisputed significance throughout East Asian cultures and the broad and sustained interest it has generated in the West, there have been few serious studies concerning the religious and philosophical thought of the text. Secondary articles focused on such issues appear rarely, scattered throughout various professional journals, and are not easily available to the nonspecialist. Almost none of these articles take into account recent archaeological discoveries and many do not reflect contemporary advances in our general understanding of early Chinese thought and culture. As a result, this important text remains on the periphery of scholarly conversations in which it might, and, in some cases, rightfully should take center stage. The present volume is offered as a first step toward rectifying this state of affairs.[2]

1

The Origins of the Text

For more than two thousand years those engaged in reading and explicating the *Laozi* have scrutinized the small amount of information regarding its composition in the hope that an understanding of the circumstances and context of its origin would resolve some of its ambiguities. Although recent discoveries (to be examined in the following section) have shed some light on its historical origins, the traditional understanding of the text has always been inextricably intertwined with stories surrounding Laozi or the "Old Master," the putative author of the text.[3] While the traditions surrounding the figure of Laozi seem largely to have been derived by inferring personal characteristics from the contents of the *Laozi*, the paucity of reliable evidence makes any definitive statement regarding his historicity impossible. Despite modern skepticism about the existence of a person named Laozi, the authorship of the text has consistently been an important topic for commentators, and specific constructions of the character Laozi have influenced many a reader's understanding of the text.

Many of the traditions surrounding Laozi may be traced to the biography included in Sima Qian's 司馬遷 (145–90 B.C.E.) archetypal historical work, the *Shiji* 史記. Sima's account may be divided into several different segments. He begins with the standard data for a *Shiji* portrait: place of birth, names (with varying degrees of formality), and the office in which the subject served. Sima Qian identifies Laozi as a native of the state of Chu 楚, the prefecture of Ku 苦 ("Bitter"), the district of Li 厲 ("Cruel"), and the hamlet of Quren 曲仁 ("Bent benevolence").[4] His name was Li Er 李耳, and he styled himself Dan 聃. He was a historiographer in the Zhou 周 archives. The uniform connotations of the geographical names in the biography might suggest that their origin was somewhat fanciful, but by Sima Qian's time these details appear to have been taken seriously. Following the presentation of the standard biographical information, Sima Qian relates the story of Laozi's meeting with Confucius. This is only one of several different accounts of this encounter, and both Anna Seidel and A. C. Graham have suggested that it forms the original core of the Laozi tradition.[5] In this version of their meeting, Confucius seeks Laozi's advice on ritual protocol, an idea that may surprise those familiar with the *Laozi*. One reason this episode has been especially significant is that it has been used as the basis for the traditional dating of Laozi to the age of Confucius, the Spring and Autumn period (770–476 B.C.E.). The next item in the biography describes Laozi's journey to an unnamed mountain pass and the subsequent writing of his book. This story has Laozi leaving a declining state of Zhou, writing a two-section work at the request of a keeper of the pass, and then disappearing into the west. This episode has proven significant as the origin of later traditions that have Laozi journeying to India to found Buddhism. Following these two narratives, Sima Qian examines the tentative identifications of Laozi with historical figures named Lao Laizi 老萊子 and Taishi Dan 太史儋. Finally, Sima traces Laozi's descendants to a living contemporary, and ends with an appeal for intellectual pluralism.

An extremely significant aspect of the *Shiji* account is that it is clearly a composite of different traditions, since Sima Qian uses phrases such as: "some say . . . ," "in general . . . ," "it is said . . . ," and "no one of this generation knows whether or not this is true." Treatments of this chapter by later critics tend to overlook these caveats and attempt either to amend the text in order to make it internally consistent or to reject it on the basis of its inconsistencies. But appeals for strict consistency overlook the nature of Sima Qian's historical method. The form of the *Shiji* account of Laozi shows that Sima Qian's method of compilation was broadly inclusive. He was careful to qualify his use of sources and expressed doubts about the reliability of certain information. It is surprising that it took more than a millennium for the composite nature of this biography to be adequately appreciated. And it is more surprising that in this century there are sinologists in both China and the United States who are still struggling to find readings of the biography that render it internally consistent.[6]

Doubts about the *Shiji* biography and its implicit Spring and Autumn period dating of the *Laozi* first surfaced in the Song dynasty (960–1279), and were advanced more forcefully during the Qing Dynasty (1644–1912) by Wang Zhong 汪中 (1744–1794) and Cui Shu 崔述 (1740–1816). Liang Qichao 梁啟超 (1873–1929) used his considerable influence to promote the idea that the text of the *Laozi* actually dated to the late Warring States period (475–221 B.C.E.), and specifically to the third century B.C.E. With the benefit of the advances of the last century, it has become apparent that many of Liang's arguments are flawed. However, Liang made the crucial observation that the *Laozi* is nowhere quoted by any important Spring and Autumn or early Warring States period thinkers, e.g., Confucius, Mozi 墨子, or Mencius. Liang's acceptance of the thesis that there were fundamental inconsistencies in the *Shiji* account also changed the course of research on Laozi. Once the figure of Laozi and the text of the *Laozi* were separated, research into their respective origins became more fruitful.

Other traditions accrued around Laozi after the *Shiji* biography, often closely tied to the dominant interpretation of the text during subsequent historical periods. During the Han, when the text was associated with techniques involving the suppression of desires in an effort to attain longevity, the practice of special concentration designed to lead to preternatural perception, and the cultivation of a state of spontaneity that surpassed the mundane rules provided by ritual texts, narratives emerged crediting Laozi with just such techniques.[7] During this period, other texts and inscriptions, such as the *Wenzi* 文子, drew on the authority of the figure of Laozi. Anna Seidel's examination of the 166 C.E. *Laozi Inscription* [*Laozi ming* 老子銘] reveals that during the Eastern Han there was a tradition claiming that Laozi "transformed" himself nine times, and later traditions had him undergoing even more transformations.[8] Elaborations of the story of Laozi's journey to India became a center-piece of both debates between the Daoists and Buddhists as well as an important point for those who sought to reconcile the two religions.

If the figure Laozi is in part a projection of attributes derived from readings of the text of the *Laozi*, then where did the text come from? A growing consensus, based on archaeological data and textual analysis, sees the *Laozi* as fundamentally composite, assembled from existing writings or sayings. This was the conclusion of such scholars as Naitō Konan 內藤湖南 (1866–1934) and Kimura Eiichi 木村英一 earlier in this century, and increasing attention to hermeneutical method has brought recent translators like Victor Mair and Michael LaFargue to the same conclusion.[9] Recent archaeological evidence seems to support this idea (see the following section). While this conclusion is significant, it should not be construed to mean that there is no organizing principle or set of principles that might play the same role that authorial intent has played for those interpreting the text over the last two millennia.

The idea that the text may be composite does, however, mean

that it is difficult to speak of a single date of composition. If the text
was circulating in an oral tradition or accrued gradually, establish-
ing a *terminus a quo* or point of origin of the text may be impossible.
However, it is easy to come up with a *terminus ad quem* or limiting
point in time for the text. The earliest extant copy of the text,
roughly as we know it, was interred in 168 B.C.E. It is also fairly
certain that some parts of the text existed in 240 B.C.E., because
they are quoted and sometimes attributed in works like the *Han
Feizi* 韓非子 and *Lüshi chunqiu* 呂氏春秋. As Wing-tsit Chan has
demonstrated, many of the ideas in the text were circulating at the
Jixia Academy around 300 or 280 B.C.E.,[10] and recent archaeological
evidence (see below) indicates that selected sections of the text
were in circulation at that time. However, many scholars find it
doubtful that the language and terms in the text predate the
Mencius (c. 300 B.C.E.) or the Warring States period. Arthur Waley,
the British translator, using Karlgren's criteria for the dating of
particles and pronouns, concluded that the *Laozi* was a third century B.C.E. text, a conclusion reached earlier by Gu Jiegang 顧頡剛 on
the basis of a comparison with texts of that period.[11] These considerations strongly imply that the majority of the source material accrued between 300 and 240 B.C.E., that some version of the text
existed by 240 B.C.E., and that the version we have today existed by
168 B.C.E.

Recent Advances and Discoveries

Three recent archaeological discoveries have shed significant light
on the nature of the composition and arrangement of the *Laozi*,
and the circumstances and dating of its early circulation in China.
The first two finds both date to 1973. One consists of two silk
manuscripts of the *Laozi* buried in a Western Han dynasty (202
B.C.E.–9 C.E.) tomb under a hill that later became known as
Mawangdui 馬王堆 near the modern city of Changsha 長沙 in Hunan
province. The second is a set of bamboo slips similar to the *Wenzi*,
found in Ding 定 county in Hebei province. The third find, from
1993, consists of sets of bamboo slips containing material from 31 of
the 81 chapters of the *Laozi*, and was discovered at a village named
Guodian 郭店, near Jingmen 荊門 in Hubei province.

The Mawangdui *Laozi* texts, as noted earlier, have proven that the *Laozi* existed in a form very similar to the received text as early as the closing of the tomb in 168 B.C.E. The two silk manuscripts in question, now labeled A (*jia* 甲) and B (*yi* 乙), are the earliest known copies of the complete text. The taboo against using the character of an Emperor's given name, which seems to be followed in one of the manuscripts, has suggested to some that the A manuscript was copied even earlier, at the latest before the death of the first emperor of the Han Dynasty in 195 B.C.E.[12] Before the Mawangdui discovery, the earliest mention of the text was dated decades later, when a regional ruler died in 131 B.C.E. and King Xian 獻 of Hejian 河間 received a copy. The copy is described in the standard history of the Han dynasty, the *Hanshu* 漢書, as an "old text (*guwen* 古文)" from before the Qin Dynasty.[13] The existence of a text extremely close to the received version, copied before 168 B.C.E., thus moves the verifiable age of the text back almost forty years.

In addition, the Mawangdui texts do differ in some significant ways from the received copies of the *Laozi*. The texts are not attributed, and instead of having the chapter divisions (*zhang* 章) common since at least the time of Wang Bi 王弼 (226–249), they are simply divided into two parts, *de* 德 and *dao* 道. This division is common to most received versions of the text, with the important distinction that in all such complete versions these two parts are in the reverse order (hence the name *Daodejing*, "Classic of *dao* and *de*"). The Mawangdui texts, (sometimes called the *Dedaojing*) begin with the *de* half of the text, and the traditional eighty-one chapters appear in the following order: 38, 39, 41, 40, 42–66, 80, 81, 67–79, 1–21, 24, 22, 23, 25–37. Additionally, there are important textual variants in the Mawangdui texts, but while these change the understanding of some individual sections of the text, they are not generally seen to indicate major changes in our understanding of the themes of the texts.[14] Finally, the two silk scrolls on which the *Laozi* was written contain other texts. The A text is followed by four texts often characterized as "Confucian-influenced," and the B text is preceded by four texts seen as "Daoist" or "HuangLao" 黃老 in orientation. This says something important about the syncretic character of the period during which these scrolls were copied, and perhaps also about the time in which the text was created. There have been several new English translations based on the Mawangdui texts, notably by Robert Henricks, D. C. Lau, and Victor Mair.[15]

The second discovery has implications for the attribution of the *Laozi* to a particular historical figure. The Ding county slips contain fragments not from the *Laozi* but from the *Wenzi*, a text whose received version contains many dialogues between Laozi and his disciple Wenzi. It is worth noting that in the newly discovered version, some of the same dialogues are instead between Wenzi and others.[16] This might indicate that Laozi was only one of several early sages who over time eclipsed the others, and to whom the collective body of their wisdom came to be attributed. Although some passages in the *Laozi* might be difficult to imagine existing in an earlier dialogue format, others, such as chapter 75, appear to have originally been cast as a dialogue.

The newest discovery consists of 730 inscribed bamboo slips found in 1993 near the village of Guodian in Hubei province. Written in a script characteristic of the ancient Chu state, this find includes 71 slips with material that is also found in 31 of the 81 chapters that comprise the transmitted *Laozi*. As with the Mawangdui silk manuscripts, the Guodian slips were buried with a number of other texts, in this case texts primarily concerned with a discussion of various ethical virtues now associated with Confucius. The recently looted tomb containing all these texts has been estimated, on the basis of the tomb's formal features and the style of its artifacts, to have been originally interred at the beginning of the third century B.C.E.[17] In terms of dating the composition of parts of the text, this most recent find moves back the *terminus ad quem* of much of the current text of the *Laozi*.

Aside from the implications these slips have for the dating of the text, the discoveries at Guodian also raise some fascinating questions regarding its composition. In the first publication of the facsimiles of the Guodian *Laozi* slips (1998), the editors arrange them into three groups according to their dimensions and shape. Each group may be further divided into a several self-contained segments, running from the top of one slip through several others and ending with blank space at the bottom of the last slip, that contain passages from between one and ten chapters of the *Laozi*. These passages are arranged in a completely different order than in the Mawangdui and transmitted versions of the *Laozi*. In terms of the traditional chapter numbering, the content of these segments is as follows (an * indicates that the text does not include the whole chapter):

Group A (39 slips, 32.3 cm long)

> 19, 66, 46*, 30*, 15*, 64*, 37, 63*, 2, 32
> 25, 5*
> 16*
> 64*, 56, 57
> 55*, 44, 40, 9

Group B (18 slips, 30.6 cm long)

> 59, 48*, 20*, 13
> 41*
> 52*, 45, 54

Group C (14 slips, 26.5 cm long)

> 17, 18
> 35
> 31
> 64*

The formal aspects of the Guodian texts are notable in several respects. First, it appears that the current chapter divisions were either disregarded or did not exist at the time these texts were copied. While punctuation marks separate what are now known as chapters in some cases, in others (chapters 32 and 45) they appear in the middle of the chapter. On the whole, the arrangement of interspersed partial and full chapters in the Guodian texts matches more closely with the divisions between the conceptually independent "sections" that D. C. Lau presented as an alternative to chapters and that he felt "need not originally have belonged together."[18] Another difference is stylistic. The Guodian texts contain more significant textual variants than in the Mawangdui versions of the *Laozi*, but their frequency varies from segment to segment. There are few major deviations in content from those parts of the *Laozi* that are mirrored in this find. Among the omissions are the last lines of chapters 15 and 55, and the famous section of chapter 30; "Where troops have camped/Brambles will grow." Another point that is sure to be the subject of controversy is whether the order of the Guodian slips is clearer than the transmitted or the Mawangdui versions. Patterns like the common references to non-action (*wuwei* 無為) in the four consecutive chapters 64, 37, 63, and 2 might be taken to argue for the internal coherence of the Guodian order. The repetition of the last part of chapter 64 in two very different forms, however, might be seen to indicate that the Guodian texts were drawn from different sources, and as such might represent variable rather than fixed texts.

Finally, the Guodian texts' intriguing variation on chapter 19 will certainly elicit much comment. In the received text, that chapter contains one of several attacks on two important virtues associated with Confucius, benevolence and righteousness: "Eliminate benevolence and discard righteousness, and the people will return to filial piety and compassion (*jue ren qi yi, min fu xiaoci* 絕仁棄義民復孝慈). The Guodian slips have instead "Eliminate artiface and discard falsehood, and the people will return to being filial sons" (*jue wei qi cha, min fu xiaozi* 絕偽棄詐民復孝子). For whatever reason, this oldest version of this chapter of the *Laozi* does not include explicit criticisms of the virtues extolled in the other texts next to which it was buried.[19] The relationship of the three Guodian texts to the *Laozi* as it has been transmitted over the last two millennia is surely going to be a major issue in studies of the composition of the *Laozi* for decades to come.

The Text in the Chinese Tradition

Since at least the second century B.C.E., the honorific term "classic (*jing* 經)" has been attached to the *Laozi*, a sign of the important influence it would come to have on many different aspects of Chinese culture. The *Laozi* has been read by philosophers and political theorists, alchemists and seekers of immortality, members of Daoist religious traditions ranging from the second century C.E. messianic communities to the denizens of modern day temples, Buddhists and Confucians, military strategists, poets, recluses, and casual readers. Not only has the understanding of the *Laozi* varied according to the group reading the text, but it has also changed along with the intellectual and religious context against which it was read. The Yuan dynasty (1264–1368) scholar Du Daojian 杜道堅 observed that most commentators have followed the particular values of their age: "In the Jin dynasty the commentators created a Jin *Laozi*, and in the Tang and Song dynasties they created a Tang *Laozi* and a Song *Laozi*."[20] The hundreds of commentaries written through the dynasties have provided the backdrop against which modern readings of the *Laozi* take place.

The earliest commentators on the *Laozi* appear to have read the text alongside others produced by the "various masters" (*zhuzi* 諸子) of the Warring States period. These works constitute what is sometimes called the "Golden Age" of Chinese philosophy and include the writings of Confucius and Mozi among others. The earliest partial commentary to the text is the "Explaining the *Laozi*" ("*JieLao*" 解老) chapter of the *Han Feizi*, in which selections are used to support a Legalist theory of statecraft. The earliest references to full commentaries are three entries in the "*dao*" subsection of the "various masters" section in the bibliographic chapter of the *Hanshu*. Two of these entries are commentaries that are formally similar to commentaries on other "various masters" texts, and the third is an expository essay by the scholar-official Liu Xiang 劉向 *Exposition of the Laozi* [*Shuo Laozi* 説老子].[21] The majority of early commentaries on the *Laozi* appear not to have been written by members of a specific philosophical school of Daoists, and the text appears to have been part of the "various masters" corpus.

Commentaries dating to the second century C.E. begin to explicitly associate the text with ritual practice or other techniques. Much of the Heshanggong 河上公 ("the old man by the river") commentary to the *Laozi*, with its numerous references to longevity techniques, may date to the Han, although other parts may be as late as the third century C.E.[22] According to Pei Songzhi 裴松之, the *Laozi* was recited alongside ritual offerings of wine in the Five Bushels of Rice Movement during the late second century C.E.[23] This movement formed the basis for the Celestial Masters tradition, for whom Laozi was known as "Taishang Laojun" 太上老君, "Lord Lao, Most High."

These developments occurred at about the same time as the arrival of Buddhism in China, a development that was to have a profound impact on the way that the *Laozi* was read. Buddhist influence may be seen in the widely read and highly regarded third-century Wang Bi commentary, which emphasizes the concepts of *li* 理, "principle," and *wu* 無 "nothingness." This period also saw a renewal of interest in the *Zhuangzi* 莊子, influencing the reading of the *Laozi* and resulting in the amalgam known as LaoZhuang 老莊 thought.

By the time of the Tang dynasty (618–907), in groups like the Chongxuan 重玄 school of interpretation, led by Cheng Xuanying 成玄英 and Li Rong 李榮, the use of Buddhist terminology in commentaries on the *Laozi* was well established. Although an occasional commentator like the twelfth-century Kou Caizhi 寇才質 objected to the appropriation of Buddhist concepts like *śūnyatā*, the Buddhist influence on commentaries after Wang Bi cannot be underestimated.[24] During this period, the text was also read in more straightforward and practical ways. Since the Tang ruling house traced its descent to Laozi, the *Laozi* gained even more importance. In it were found lessons in diverse fields, including statecraft, as with the 735 commentary attributed to Emperor Xuanzong 玄宗, and even principles of military strategy.

From the Song dynasty (960–1127) onward, the *Laozi* was also increasingly interpreted in light of the Confucian tradition. Many Song commentators relied heavily on the *Yijing* 易經 (*Book of Changes*) to explain the text, and the Yuan dynasty commentator Du Daojian drew parallels with the writings of Confucius. The intellectual dominance of Neo-Confucianism further assured that commentaries following the Song incorporated the views and terminology of this type of Confucianism. This continued into the Qing (1644–1912), at which time the prevailing emphasis on textual research began to have a strong influence on commentarial writing.

The importance of the text in traditional China is attested by the many attempts by writers, of every persuasion and period, to appropriate the meaning of the text for their own purposes. This is a significant fact for the modern reader of the text, who should know that contemporary translations almost all draw on layers of competing intellectual influences.

Individual Contributions

The first contribution, "Mysticism and Apophatic Discourse in the *Laozi*," by Mark Csikszentmihalyi, challenges the widely held view that the *Laozi* is a mystical text. Csikszentmihalyi argues that whatever else mysticism might be, it is a form of religious experience that has as one of its defining characteristics a fundamental ineffability. Those who claim that the *Laozi* is a mystical text either insist that it describes mystical experience or practice, or hold that its apophatic or self-negating language creates an irresolvable tension that points beyond normal experience and helps evoke such experience in the reader. But through a careful analysis of the *Laozi*, Csikszentmihalyi shows that there is very little textual support for these kinds of claims. First of all, there simply are very few

passages that reasonably can be interpreted as references to mystical experience. This of course does not mean that the text necessarily denies the possibility of a mystical *Dao*. Quite the contrary, as
Csikszentmihalyi says, "the text advocates the *theoretical* possibility of the existence of a mystical *Dao* but it is not an *experiential*
description of mystical union."

Csikszentmihalyi presents a sympathetic and careful discussion
of contemporary interpretations of the text that advocate the mystical reading he opposes. Such interpretations rest on the view that
takes "union with the *Dao* to be the text's definitive mystical aspect." Csikszentmihalyi shows that such interpretations have become increasingly suspect as the study of different forms of
mysticism has undermined confidence in the idea that mystical
experience is a universal, natural kind of religious experience. He
argues that none of the more recent attempts to read the text as
a report of even a distinctively "Eastern" form of mysticism are
plausible.

Csikszentmihalyi also argues against those who reason that
because the text contains some of the special terminology from
traditions of medical and meditational practice, it in fact is a medical or meditational manual. This simply does not follow: "The similarity between the vocabulary of the *Laozi* and early medical or
meditation texts . . . does not make the *Laozi* one of these texts." As
further evidence for his view, Csikszentmihalyi presents a review of
early commentators, specifically those who wrote before Buddhism
became a dominant force within Chinese intellectual life, and argues that Chinese commentators did not understand the apophatic
language of the text as pointing to some ineffable mystical experience. Quite the contrary, these early commentators offered a variety
of explanations to resolve what they regarded as only the *apparent*
contradictions within the text. When properly viewed, such passages were thought to be quite accessible and did not require or
appeal to ineffable mystical states of consciousness.

In his concluding remarks, Csikszentmihalyi presents an
alternative understanding of the nature of this remarkable text.
He notes that the early historian Sima Tan associated the *Laozi*
with a group of thinkers who believed that there was a set of deeper
principles—the *Dao* 道—informing the various specialized traditions of learning at the time. On such a view, the individual disciplines were simply different manifestations of this underlying *Dao*.
Thus, rather than being some transcendent and ineffable entity, the

Dao was thought to be a set of principles that are manifested throughout our everyday experience and readily accessible to anyone who takes the time to pay attention to the world around them. Thus, the *Laozi* is more a collection of different descriptions of these underlying principles than a report of mystical contact with the transcendent. Drawing a contemporary analogy, Csikszentmihalyi suggests that the text might have more in common with scholars of religion attempting to describe phenomena like the "numinous" than religious practitioners seeking to embrace or evoke such experiences. Seen in this way, "the *Laozi* has more in common with Rudolf Otto's discussion of Meister Eckhart than with Eckhart's writing itself."

Hal Roth has contributed our second essay, "The *Laozi* in the Context of Early Daoist Mystical Praxis." Roth's central argument is that mystical praxis is at the heart of the *Laozi* and the political, social, and ethical philosophy one finds in the text are derived from experiences that arise out of such practice. He begins by offering a summary of his recent work on the history of early Daoist mysticism in order to provide a sketch of the beliefs and practices that formed the historical context from which the *Laozi* emerged. Next he presents a critical discussion of those aspects of mysticism theory that he has found most insightful and productive in his study of early Daoist beliefs and practices. Roth then proceeds to explain and analyze passages in the *Laozi* that provide evidence for his claim concerning the centrality of mystical praxis.

In his description of the historical context of the *Laozi* Roth claims that, ". . . particularly in the case of Daoism, the foundational texts of the tradition were produced within one or more closely related master-disciple lineages whose principle focus was on learning and practicing specific techniques." Thus, instead of being products of speculative philosophizing, Roth sees works such as the *Laozi* more as deriving from a meditation practice involving guiding and refining the flow of vital energy or vital breath. He goes on to argue that there are two distinct though possibly complementary forms of meditation within the early Daoist communities that produced these texts. The first is a more dynamic, moving form of meditation, "whose postures resembled modern positions in *taiji* 太極 and *qigong* 氣功." The second is a kind of seated meditation which involves regulation of and concentration on breathing. In other published work, Roth identifies this second form of meditation as "inner cultivation." According to Roth, the practice of such inner

cultivation lies at the heart of the *Laozi* and shares its distinctive
and characteristic features with other early seminal texts of Daoism
and in particular with the *Neiye* 內業 ("Inward Training") essay of
the *Guanzi* 管子.

From among the different approaches and conceptual resources
of mysticism theory, Roth singles out Walter Stace's distinction
between "extrovertive" and "introvertive" forms of mystical experience as particularly useful. Roth adapts this distinction to describe
what he calls a "bimodal" form of mysticism and claims that this is
the best way to describe the type of mysticism one finds in texts like
the *Zhuangzi* and *Laozi*. The first mode of bimodal mysticism concerns attaining a "unitive consciousness in which the adept achieves
complete union with the *Dao*." This is roughly equivalent to Stace's
"introvertive" form of mysticism. Stace's "extrovertive" mysticism
represents the second of Roth's two poles. In such experiences, the
practitioner "returns to the world and retains, amidst the flow of
daily life, a profound sense of the unity." Another of the resources of
mysticism theory that Roth singles out is recent work on the technical terminology employed by mystical practitioners. Special terms of
art that have application only within the practice of meditation, e.g.,
those that refer to extraordinary states of minds, constitute the
esoteric argot of meditation communities and are important keys
for identifying and understanding these communities and their
practices.

In the remaining sections of his essay, Roth draws upon his
sketch of the historical context that gave rise to the *Laozi* and
applies the various conceptual resources and approaches of mysticism theory he has described and developed in order to explicate a
number of critical passages in the text. He argues that these show
that the *Laozi* is centered on specific techniques of mystical praxis
which are part of "a greater tradition of lineages that shared a
common meditative practice as their basis." Roth provides a table
in the appendix to his essay in which he illustrates some of the
important similarities he has found among the various mystical
practices and experiences described in different Daoist source texts.
He concludes by noting that the practices and experiences he has
identified in early Daoism also share remarkable similarities to
mystical practices and experiences in many other cultural and religious traditions.

Our third essay, "Qian Zhongshu on Philosophical and Mystical

Paradoxes in the *Laozi*," by Zhang Longxi, is a lucid and informative presentation of the views of this important contemporary Chinese scholar. Qian's work unfortunately does not appear in translation and so has not received the attention it so richly deserves outside of China. But because of its form, content and, methodology, his work is not easily accessible even for the well-trained and determined Chinese scholar. Qian writes in elegant but difficult classical Chinese and often employs the terse style of traditional commentary. Moreover, as Zhang explains, his work is "deeply personal and related to his deep suspicion of systems and systematic argument." All of Qian's work is focused on ancient Chinese texts, which means that the content of his writings will not be widely familiar to those outside this specialty, and he employs a profoundly sophisticated intertextual approach that demands familiarity with not only the Chinese and Western traditions but contemporary literary theory as well. Despite these formidable obstacles, Qian's work represents some of the most insightful and impressive contemporary scholarship done on early Chinese literature and thought. Mastering his writings is not unlike climbing a mountain: a task that requires great skill, effort, and considerable courage but repays one with breathtaking views and deeper understanding. We should be thankful that Zhang has scaled this edifice for us and presented such an elegant and insightful account of his explorations.

Qian's work crosses a wide range of academic disciplines. For example, in arguing that the Wang Bi text of the *Laozi* is to be preferred over the Longxing Guan stone tablet version, he deploys philological, textual, philosophical, and sociocultural arguments to refute the claims of Qing Dynasty scholars regarding the latter's authenticity. A quite different example of Qian's intellectual range and depth is his discussion of the opening lines of the *Laozi*. He begins by challenging the Qing dynasty scholar Yu Zhengxie's 俞正燮 interpretation as anachronistic but then quickly moves from this point to a discussion of the philosophy of language represented by these lines. Zhang describes Qian as arguing that the real issue is distinguishing "naming as the act of signification from words as signifiers." The often poor fit between the words we use and the sense we are trying to express is used by Laozi to illustrate "the inadequacy of all verbal expression." Thus, these opening lines point toward the mystical philosophy that lies at the heart of the text. But Qian does not rest there, he goes on to relate the general theme of the inadequacy of language to a variety of traditional Chinese philosophers and literary figures. In so doing, he explicates this ancient text, relates it to other traditional texts, both Chinese and Western, and shows how their problems remain problems for us, in both contemporary philosophy and literary theory.

One of the many intriguing issues Qian explores is the way that mystics, poets, and other thinkers accommodate the challenge of talking about the ineffable. This is an issue Zhang himself has explored in some of his own work.[25] Qian introduces and explains various strategies, drawn from a wide range of thinkers both East and West and representing many distinct traditions and disciplines, for "circling around the inexpressible" and "speaking in non-words." Again he displays a stunning command of diverse traditions and a masterful control of a variety of scholarly disciplines and approaches.

Qian also offers an interesting discussion of Laozi's conception of sagehood. In particular, he examines the sense in which the sage is to "imitate heaven and earth in putting his body last" and how this in fact proves beneficial and leads to its being preserved. Qian is critical of what he sees as the later appropriation of this notion by "popular religion" in the form of longevity practices. He believes that the true import of this teaching is to advocate asceticism and he offers several examples, again from a range of traditions and times, that show that mystics display a general tendency to turn away from and even mortify the body.

His final major topic is a discussion of Laozi's teachings regarding the dialectical movement of things and events. Qian draws a number of interesting parallels between Laozi's dialectical views and those of Hegel. Hegel criticized Chinese language as an unsuitable medium for philosophizing because it could not accommodate dialectical movement. Qian disagrees; he argues that in the *Laozi* we see several concepts that simultaneously express opposite meanings, "just like Hegel's favorite term, the much-vaunted *Aufhebung*." Qian then goes on to discuss, in greater detail, the senses of Laozi's dialectic and its relationship to other philosophical, literary, and mystical writings.

Zhang closes with some fascinating thoughts on how Qian's methodology itself manifests the dialectical nature he so admires in Laozi's thought. The very project of understanding the *Laozi* through a comparative study in the context of Eastern and Western philosophy and mysticism is as Qian says, "not to reconcile differences, nor to claim false kinship relations." It is rather to note differences within the similarities and similarities within the differences. But to note the differences between things, they must be conceived as being in some way similar enough to be compared. And if one feels a need to point out the similarities between two things, one must already regard them as being different. As Zhang says, these concepts are "mutually defined and mutually implicated." In the hands of a master like Qian Zhongshu, this dialectical process of mutual contrast and comparison leads to a deeper understanding not only of the thinkers and texts being studied but of their significance for us in our own time and place. As Zhang concludes, "Once Qian Zhongshu has disclosed those connections and similarities, we can read the *Laozi* as we have never read it before. . . . It is hard to imagine a better way to introduce us to that little ancient book."

Isabelle Robinet's essay, "The Diverse Interpretations of the *Laozi*," explores a number of interesting issues surrounding the concept of *Dao*. She begins with a critical review of four contemporary scholars: Benjamin I. Schwartz, Angus C. Graham, Chad Hansen, and Michael LaFargue. Robinet explains the disagreements among these different interpreters of the *Laozi*. For example, she shows that Schwartz sees the text as representing a mystical attitude concerned with an eternal and unchanging "principle of organization" which underlies the apparent and accessible natural world. Since language arises in and concerns this latter, limited, and impermanent natural order, it proves almost wholly ineffective in describing the underlying *Dao*. This interpretation is quite different from what Graham offers. Graham sees language not so much as in principle inapplicable but as simply inadequate to the task of describing the *Dao*. Since it is the very nature of language to discriminate among things, the more successful it is the more it distorts and undermines the fundamental unity of the *Dao*. Graham sees Laozi as trying to defuse this harmful effect of language by advocating that we recognize the mutual interdependence of dichotomies, embrace these and thereby return to the unity of the *Dao*. Chad Hansen agrees with Graham in rejecting views that take the *Dao* to be some metaphysical entity. For Hansen, *Dao* means a prescriptive discourse, a way of carving up the world that serves to guide human activity. But Hansen parts company with Graham in holding that the text is primarily concerned with making the metalinguistic point that *all* such *Dao*s (and any we might propose) are equally ad hoc. None captures the true nature of reality better than any other and all drag us into greater, social purposes that often generate considerable trouble for us. For Hansen, the *Laozi* is not about THE *Dao*, but about the ways in which various *dao*s, i.e., different discourses, guide thought and behavior. Michael LaFargue joins Graham and Hansen in rejecting the metaphysical reading but he sees the text as a kind of manual on the arts of governing and prolonging life. Thus, he sees the text as representative of what is generally regarded as the core of the HuangLao movement. Since LeFargue believes the text to be a kind of manual for those within such a movement, he argues that it presupposes a general familiarity with the concepts and practices of such an informed audience.

Robinet then seeks to distill a general understanding of the term *Dao* by reviewing and relating a variety of traditional Chinese commentaries. She makes use of the work of more than twenty commentators and augments their opinions with references to Han apocrypha and works such as the *Zhuangzi, Huainanzi* 淮南子, *Liezi* 列子, and the *Yijing*. Robinet examines eleven related issues concerning the nature of the *Dao*: the degree to which it is amenable to human understanding, its relationship to things, the sense in which it is one, its concrete and ephemeral modes, its role as source or seed of the world, its named and nameless aspects, its characteristic spontaneity, its tendency toward reversal or turning back, its constancy, its role as the cause of order in Nature and its mystical character. In the course of her examination she often extends the analysis of traditional commentators in interesting and revealing ways and occasionally voices her disagreement with the modern Western interpreters mentioned above. Robinet argues that there is in fact a respectable degree of consensus among traditional commentators on most of the issues she explores. And while Robinet acknowledges that by its very nature the text lends itself and even encourages a multiplicity of interpretations, she argues for "a certain coherence in the general trend of interpretations" among Chinese commentators and cautions that a principled insistence on the validity of all interpretations leads to the absurd conclusion that, "the text itself signifies nothing."

In his intriguing meditation, "Re-exploring the Analogy of the *Dao* and the Field," Robert Henricks describes a memorable and instructive way to imagine and convey the nature of Laozi's *Dao*. Henricks begins by identifying three central and related characteristics of the *Dao*. First, the *Dao* is a "cosmic reality" in the sense that it is what existed before and gave rise to the various living things within the world, what the Chinese call "the ten thousand things." But the *Dao* is also a "personal reality" in that it remains present within each of the ten thousand things and plays a significant role informing their development and inclining them in certain directions. And so the *Dao* also describes a "way of life" for each of the ten thousand things, a way they will tend to go in the absence of interference. In this respect, the *Dao* describes a way that is in some sense normative.

Henricks goes on to describe a number of characteristic features of the *Dao* based on the content of the *Laozi*'s individual chapters. The *Dao* is a single, undifferentiated, and intangible reality. By this he seems to mean that because it is the all-encompassing pattern underlying and informing all phenomena, the *Dao* itself lacks any specific form. The *Dao* is also "still, tranquil, and empty" but within it are the "seeds" or "beginnings/essences of the ten thousand things." This set of features connotes not only the ideas that the *Dao* is the origin and source of order for all things in the world but also, in its stillness and tranquility, it displays no inclination for or against, no prejudice toward or favor for any particular part of the world. We are also told that the *Dao* is "inexhaustible." While the *Dao* itself is empty and intangible it works like a "bellows" breathing life and form into each of the ten thousand things. These various characteristics of the *Dao* are part of why the text often describes it as "feminine" in nature. For the *Dao* gives birth to, nourishes, and protects all of the ten thousand things; it shows each the unqualified love thought to be characteristic of a mother.

With this description of the *Dao* in hand, Henricks then draws an analogy between this cluster of characteristics and a field. He has in mind "an untended field, one that is left to grow on its own." This is an important point. For the Daoists employ such natural vegetative metaphors to convey their ideal state of being and this distinguishes them from the Confucians who use *agricultural* metaphors—i.e., carefully cultivated and tended fields—as symbols for their ideal. The riot of grasses and wildflowers that sprout up and bloom in this field are then, by analogy, the "ten thousand things." Unpacking this analogy, Henricks leads us to see that the field, in winter, appears to be "undifferentiated" and "empty" like the *Dao*. But this same field gives birth to the "ten thousand things" that grow out of it and supports each of them, showing favoritism to none.

Throughout this process, the field is largely "invisible"; it makes no show and claims no credit for its remarkable achievements. The process that unfolds upon the field occurs without purposive effort, i.e., through *wuwei* 無為 ("non-action"), and is so of itself, i.e., *ziran* 自然 ("naturally"). In these ways, again it is like the *Dao*. Henricks goes on to discuss some of the apparent limitations of his proposed analogy and some of the ways it captures other important features of Laozi's thought. He concludes his essay with a description of how he first developed this analogy, which reveals itself to be yet another example of the marvelous workings of the *Dao*.

Tateno Masami's essay, "A Philosophical Analysis of the *Laozi* from an Ontological Perspective," is not concerned with how the text was understood by early Chinese commentators but seeks to explicate a novel and intriguing interpretation of its own. In certain respects, Tateno's reading of the text bears some likeness to that of Csikszentmihalyi. He argues against those who understand the *Dao* as an abstract entity, something wholly beyond our everyday experience. While the *Dao* clearly cannot be adequately explained, it is something that can and must be experienced. In fact, the *Dao* can only be understood through a specific regimen of spiritual practice. Such practice begins with a kind of cognitive therapy. Confronting and contemplating the inescapably relativistic framework of human understanding is to lead to the realization that any purely rational approach cannot possibly yield absolute knowledge concerning the nature of the world and our proper place within it. This recognition of the limitations of rational thought purportedly marks the beginning of an enhanced understanding, for it encourages one to seek understanding through the alternative means of spiritual training.

This regimen of training begins with an active withdrawal of the senses, which are seen as a source of distraction and diversion, and an inward turn toward meditative cultivation. Such cultivation consists in "concentrating one's spirit," and this allows one to directly embody the "oneness" that is the defining characteristic underlying all of reality. This personal experience of oneness is in principle inexpressible since words rely on the very distinction between subject and object and the framework of time and space which such a state is thought to overcome. The experience of oneness facilitates a direct grasp of the true nature of the world. Tateno emphasizes that this state of consciousness in no way represents or advocates a rejection of the world. For as one experiences the oneness underlying the world one realizes that there is no real distinction between self and world. From an epistemological point of view, this means that the world is "nothing" in the sense that it is not an object distinct from the self that presents itself to understanding. At the same time, from an ontological perspective, we *are* the world and if we are to live in light of this truth we must live our lives in the world as embodiments of its underlying unity.

Tateno goes on to explore the relationship between the *Dao* 道 ("Way") and *de* 德 ("virtue"). Invoking an explanation with a long history in Chinese thought, he describes virtue as the phenomenal "manifestation of the *Dao*." In other words, virtue is what each actual thing receives from the *Dao* and this determines what kind of thing it is and what kinds of activities and powers it displays. While the *Dao* itself remains beyond description, the *de* of each thing presents it in various palpable and accessible forms. When one engages in the spiritual practice described above, one comes to appreciate the ways in which the *de* of each thing points to the underlying *Dao* which it represents. And through the completion or perfection of one's own virtue, one comes to see and embody the *Dao* in the actual world. As Tateno says, "In other words, through *practice* of the *Dao*, we can pass beyond the world of our ordinary relativistic way of thinking and directly embody the true nature of the world. When, in our own being, we exist as *de*, each of us is the *Dao*, and this *Dao*, just as it is, is the entire world."

In his essay, "Method in the Madness of the *Laozi*," Bryan W. Van Norden offers a philosophical critique and critical evaluation of the "core vision" of the *Laozi* and the ways in which this core vision informs the mystical, cosmological, and ethical views of the text. Van Norden argues that the core vision of the *Laozi* is motivated by a reaction to the corrupt and dangerous times in which it was written. This leads to a call for a return "to a kinder, gentler, and simpler era, before the corrupting influences of new ideas and new choices" could undermine the pristine nature of early society. Unlike some who advocate similar views, Laozi does not believe that "the corrupt state of society" to which we have fallen is "natural or inevitable." And so the text offers not only a diagnosis of society's ills but a prescription designed to restore it to health. The cure will take us back to a "primitive agrarian utopia" characterized by "a lack of curiosity, envy, reflection, higher culture, and self-consciousness," in which people will lead "simple but admirably contented lives." With a clear view of this core political vision in place, Van Norden then proceeds to relate it to Laozi's views on cosmology, mysticism, and ethics.

Since the *Laozi* insists that its ideal society requires the undoing and elimination of active and reflective efforts to improve people and their lot in life, Van Norden argues that it "owes us an explanation of how the universe is structured such that nonintervention will result in a well-ordered society." By way of example, he notes that Social Darwinists presuppose that survival of the fittest explains *why* the absence of governmental interference actually works for the long-range good of society. We should expect that there are similar beliefs underlying and justifying the Daoist political vision. Van Norden argues that Laozi's concept of the *Dao* ("Way") plays just such a role. He explains how the *Dao* is both "causally" and "normatively transcendent" and therefore how it serves as "a paradigm for the human sage."

Van Norden then turns to a discussion of how the core vision is related to mysticism in the *Laozi*. His goal is not to offer an account of the nature of Laozi's particular form of mysticism (for that, readers can turn to several of the other essays in this collection) but rather to show how this aspect of the work is informed by and related to some of the other important teachings one finds within it. So Van Norden employs a low-flying and uncontroversial definition of mysticism: "I shall mean by 'mysticism' the position that there is a kind of important, action-guiding 'knowledge' (in some broad sense of that term) of the nature of the universe that cannot adequately be expressed in words." Van Norden first notes that the *Laozi* advocates the view that most of society's problems arise from over-intellectualization and that therefore the learned intellectuals should be cast out of the Daoist utopia. And yet, at the same time the text espouses the need for Daoist sage rulers. We must therefore infer that there is a special, nonstandard and ineffable kind of knowledge that is needed, especially by those who would rule. Thus, in order to bring about the core political vision that is the ultimate goal of the *Laozi*, we need people with this special kind of mystical knowledge. Van Norden goes on to suggest that only those who possess such knowledge can both themselves be and bring the world into the particular state of unity represented by this core vision. Only they can bring about the perfect "harmonious whole" that it describes. Anything other than this ideal is something less and results in the disunity, alienation, contention, and conflict that mark contemporary society.

The core vision results in what Van Norden describes as "the ethics of paradox," which in turn is directly related to both the cosmology and mysticism of the text. The core vision asserts that "contemporary society is upside down." This leads to a paradoxical state of affairs in which most people regard as good what is actually bad and where their efforts to make things better inevitably produce the opposite effect of making things worse. This situation results in a paradox that Van Norden defines in terms of three essential features: *wuwei* ("non-action"), embracing the *yin* 陰, and reversal. *Wuwei* is the ideal Daoist mode of activity. It is "unpremeditated, nondeliberative, noncalculating, nonpurposive action." Thus the best action is paradoxically non-action. Embracing the *yin* is to prefer a soft, yielding "feminine" disposition and approach over one that is hard, assertive, "masculine." Again, paradoxically, the approach that appears to be weaker and less effective is the only sure way to assure strength and success. Embracing the *yin* is related to the third feature of the ethics of paradox, reversal. This is the view that over time, things and situations tend to change into their opposites. For example, something that is assertive and strong tends over time to become passive and weak. The idea here is again the paradoxical claim that straining to gain some fixed personal goal inevitably leads to one losing it and worse still injuring oneself in the bargain. Van Norden argues for the asymmetrical nature of reversal; this dynamic only operates in cases of characteristically *yang* 陽 activity. Those who embrace the *yin* do not end up reversing and undermining themselves, for they are acting according to the *Dao* and not for themselves. Thus, they are working within the harmonious mystical unity of the Way.

In our next contribution, "An Inquiry into the Core Value of Laozi's Philosophy," Liu Xiaogan argues that the concept of *ziran* ("naturalness") is the foundation of Laozi's ethical philosophy. This notion of "acting naturally" or "letting things happen of themselves" informs other central teachings in Laozi's philosophy such as *wuwei* ("non-action") and the *Dao* ("Way") and provides the underlying justification for them.

Liu begins with a discussion of *ziran* and *wuwei* by pointing out that both notions "cross into all of the various divisions of philosophy" (e.g., ontology, epistemology, and historiography) and also find more practical applications in fields such as "politics, military science, and self-cultivation." These notions have no clear correlates in Western philosophy and this, together with their protean nature and wide application, make them difficult to describe and analyze within the traditional framework of philosophy. These observations inform Liu's own study, which relies on a careful analysis of many different examples of the use of these terms. But he also presents his own interpretation of the meaning and significance of these concepts by offering a critique and critical assessment of both traditional and contemporary scholarship.

One common misunderstanding Liu identifies is the view that treats *ziran* and *wuwei* as two terms for a "single concept." Liu points out that though consistent, they are quite different concepts and *ziran* is the more basic ethical notion. Among the points he makes is that naturalness is a positive term used to describe "the progression of a certain state of affairs" while *wuwei* is a negative term which places "restrictions upon human activity." Moreover, naturalness can describe a larger class of phenomena; specifically, it can apply to both the human and nonhuman realm. Non-action, though, only restricts the proper range of *human* action. Summing up Liu's view on the relationship between these two concepts, we can say that *ziran* is "the central value in Laozi's philosophical system, while *wuwei* is the basic method or principle for action he recommends to realize or pursue this value."

Liu then proceeds to offer a careful explication and analysis of the notion of naturalness as found in the *Laozi*. Relying on a remarkable command of traditional and contemporary scholarship, Liu discusses a range of knotty interpretive problems. For example, there is a debate about how much if any "force" the ideal Daoist ruler can employ in governing his people. When is he acting to maintain a natural state of affairs? When do his actions cross the line and become interference in the natural life of his people? And how is one to make such judgments? Liu goes on to explore the notion of naturalness in regard to the relationship between the sage and the myriad things and the way in which it is to govern the interactions between humans, heaven, and earth. In each of these cases, he demonstrates how naturalness provides the guide and justification for how all things are to function.

Liu provides an illuminating discussion of other ways the ideal of naturalness is expressed in the *Laozi*. For example, *zihua* 自化 ("transforming of one's own accord") clearly is another way of expressing this normative ideal for how things and affairs are to progress. Things that are allowed to function naturally return to what is "normal" or "proper" for them. They are then *zheng* 正

("rectified") and this is another way of expressing the ideal of naturalness. Similarly, the word *chang* 常 ("constant"), which describes the enduring, regular, and proper state of things, the state to which they will tend in the absence of artificial interference, "also signifies naturalness." These are but a few of the many compelling examples Liu presents.

In another section of his essay, Liu explores the basis of Laozi's regard for the value of naturalness. He argues that it is easy to see why naturalness, particularly when understood as the absence of governmental interference, would have great appeal, especially in a largely agrarian society. The elimination of oppressive taxes, coercive regulations, and aggressive warfare would readily be appreciated as positive goods by those suffering such difficulties. Moreover, these afflictions could easily be understood as imposed, artificial interferences, the removal of which allows a return to a natural, constant, and proper state of affairs.

Liu also defends the *Laozi* against certain criticisms levelled by a number of different interpreters, e.g., that the text urges rulers to "keep the people in ignorance" or that it advocates "historical retrogression." He argues that such criticisms rest upon anachronistic or misguided understandings of the text and that these can be rectified by a proper understanding of the role of naturalness. Liu also offers his own thoughts on some ways we might reinterpret and modify Laozi's notion of naturalness so that it can contribute to contemporary ethical debates.

The final essay, "The Concept of *de* ('Virtue') in the *Laozi*," by Philip J. Ivanhoe, offers an ethical interpretation of Laozi's notion of "virtue." Ivanhoe argues that like his Confucian predecessors, Laozi used the word *de* ("virtue") to mean not a particular excellence of character, e.g., as we might say "prudence is a virtue," but rather, like the Latin *virtus*, to describe the natural activity and power of a given thing (hence Arthur Waley's translation of *daode* in *Daodejing* as "The Way and Its *Power*," emphasis added). When used to describe the characteristic activity and power of ideal human beings, this early sense of *de*, for both the Confucians and the Daoists, is defined by three features: its attractive power, its ability to affect others in distinctive ways and its relationship with *wuwei* ("non-action").

In other work, Ivanhoe has argued that among early Confucians, *de* had the sense of "moral charisma." This notion was often, though not exclusively, a quality associated with good rulers. *De* was the quality of character that enabled such rulers to attract and retain worthy ministers and subjects around them. Thus, it displays the first of Ivanhoe's three characteristics. In one memorable passage, Confucius remarks that "One who rules through *de* ('moral charisma') is like the Pole Star, which remains in its place while all the myriad stars pay homage to it." In addition to the ability to attract people, those with moral charisma influence others in distinctive ways. They move others to yield to and support them and they inspire others to emulate their virtuous example. The Confucian sage attracts and uplifts those who come under his influence. These first two features explain the relationship between *de* and *wuwei* ("non-action"). For those with virtue, and especially rulers, are able to carry out their work without having to coerce others. By drawing the people to him and inspiring them to higher levels of ethical development, he is able to reign—not rule—over his people.

Ivanhoe goes on to argue that one can find a related but distinct notion of *de*, displaying each of his three characteristic features, in the *Laozi*. Like his Confucian counterpart, Laozi's sage attracts others to him but in a different way. Instead of drawing people *upward* through the excellence of his moral charisma, he draws people to him and wins their allegiance by placing himself in the *lowest*, most humble position. Instead of being like the Pole Star, Laozi's sage is a valley, welcoming, accommodating, and nourishing all, according to their individual needs. Those who are drawn within the orbit of such an individual are affected in profound ways. Unlike the Confucian sage who inspires people to strive to emulate him and develop themselves ethically, the influence of the Daoist sage works to "empty, unravel, and settle" people. The natural ease of the Daoist sage has a "therapeutic effect" on those around him. It helps them to realize the harmful influences of socialization and over-intellectualization and allows them to slough off the social posturing and outright self-deception that plagues most people. This in turn allows them to better hear and heed their spontaneous tendencies and inclinations, which leads them to live in greater harmony and peace. Thus, those who develop this Daoist form of *de* not only are at peace and in harmony with the world, they settle others down as well and turn them away from the greedy and competitive activities that give rise to all the worst disasters a state might suffer. Thus, such individuals make ideal rulers. Like their Confucian counterparts, they too rule through *wuwei* but their "non-action" works in a different way. The Confucian sage-ruler reigns through the authority of his moral charisma, inspiring others to pursue their various functions and work on moral self-improvement. The Daoist sage-ruler influences people to "turn back" to a simpler, less centralized form of life, the "agrarian utopia" described throughout the text.

Ivanhoe supplements his study of *de* in the *Laozi* with a brief exploration of the concept of *de* in the other early Daoist classic, the *Zhuangzi*. He notes some of the distinctive features of Zhuangzi's notion of virtue and suggests that this concept deserves much greater attention in this and other texts of the period. Ivanhoe also argues that these different conceptions of *de* reflect deep and important differences between Confucian and Daoist views of human nature and its flourishing. In the remaining parts of his essay he suggests ways that each of these views can contribute to the contemporary understanding of "interpersonal moral psychology."

The variety of perspectives represented by the articles in this volume underscores the diverse ways in which the *Laozi* has been and may be read. Some may be disappointed that this collection does not present a unified view of the provenance or meaning of the text. But this diversity is an accurate reflection of the ambiguous history and polysemantic nature of the text. The origins and uses of the *Laozi* are simply not yet clear—and they may never be. One of the few approaches to the text that can with confidence be rejected as implausible is that which maintains there is but one way to read it. As the *Laozi* itself warns, "those who hold onto it, lose it" (chapter 64).

The range of different yet plausible approaches to and interpretations of the *Laozi* is a manifestation of its distinctive nature and an indication of the scope of its relevance. This remarkable text can and should play a much more prominent role in future conversations about such issues as the character of mystical experience, texts and praxis, the theory of interpretation, and the nature of paradox. The *Laozi* also has much to teach us about Chinese conceptions of reality, beliefs about human nature, and aspirations for utopia, as well as such basic philosophical concepts as *Dao*, *de*, *ziran*, and *wuwei*.

The contributions included in this volume not only offer diverse interpretations of the *Laozi*, they themselves represent a wide range of scholarly traditions and a variety of ways to engage, ponder and, evaluate the text. This shows that the *Laozi*, whether originally intended as a classic, scripture, poem, polemic, or manual, has become all of these things and more to an audience whose number must far exceed the expectations of those responsible for its creation. By collecting some of the finest contemporary scholarship on this important and fascinating text, we hope not only to enrich and challenge the understanding of specialists but also to invite and interest nonspecialists to join this ever-expanding hermeneutical circle and come to appreciate the text in new and edifying ways.

Mark Csikszentmihalyi
Philip J. Ivanhoe

NOTES

This collection contains translations of three essays originally written in languages other than English but which have not been published in any form prior to the present volume. Tateno Masami's essay, "A Philosophical Analysis of the *Laozi* from an Ontological Perspective," was translated from a Japanese version entitled *"Rōshi* ni okeru sonzaironteki kanten kara no tetsugakuteki bunseki 老子における存在論的観点からの哲学的分析," by Philip J. Ivanhoe. Mark Csikszentmihalyi translated Isabelle Robinet's article "The Diverse Interpretations of the *Laozi*" from a French original by the title of "Les diverses interprétations du *Laozi*," with help from Amelia Dockery. Liu Xiaogan's contribution, "An Inquiry into the Core Value of Laozi's Philosophy," was translated by Edward Gilman Slingerland III from an original essay in Chinese called, "Shilun *Laozi* zhexuede zhongxin jiazhi 試論老子哲學的中心價值."

1. The text is commonly referred to as the *Daodejing* (in the *pinyin* romanization used in mainland China), the *Tao-te ching* (in the Wade-Giles romanization still used in some academic circles), the *Laozi* or *Lao-tzu* (using the putative name of the author in each romanization, respectively), or even as the *Dedaojing* or *Te-tao ching* (reversing the traditional order of its two sections, again in each romanization). Because of the disagreement over the original order of the two sections, the title *Laozi* is used here. For the sake of consistency, the *pinyin* system is used exclusively in this volume. Chinese words in quotations have been converted into *pinyin*. A conversion table between *pinyin* and Wade-Giles is provided in the frontmatter to this volume.

2. While this manuscript was in press, Livia Kohn and Michael LaFargue's *Lao-Tzu and the Tao-te-ching* (Albany: State University of New York Press, 1998) was published. This new collection contains excellent essays on the myth and interpretation of the text and of the figure Laozi. It also explores a variety of different methodological approaches. We see the present volume, focused on the thought of the *Laozi*, as complimenting this new and important publication.

3. "Old Master" is only one of several ways that the characters *lao* and *zi* have been understood. One tradition, attested first in the third century C.E., reads the character *zi* as "child," citing the legend that Laozi's mother was pregnant for eighty-one years and the sage was born with white hair (see the preface *Laozi Daodejing xu* 老子道德經序 attributed to Ge Xuan 葛玄, *Sibu congkan* edition, 1b.) A Qing dynasty commentator has proposed that *lao* does not mean "old" but is instead a surname (Wei Yuan 魏源, *Laozi benyi* 老子本義, *Zhuzi jicheng* edition, 5).

4. See chapter 63 of the *Shiji* (Beijing: Zhonghua shuju, 1959), 2139 ff.

5. These modern scholars suggest that an existing tradition surrounding a teacher of Confucius named Laozi was utilized by the compilers or transmitters of the *Laozi* in order to privilege their text over those associated with Confucius. Anna K. Seidel makes this suggestion in *La divinisation de Lao Tseu dans le Taoisme des Han* (Paris: École Française d'Extrême-Orient, 1969), 12, and it is developed in more detail by A. C. Graham in "The Origins of the Legend of Lao Tan," in *Studies in Chinese Philosophy* (Albany: State University of New York Press, 1990), 111–124. On the authorship of the text, see also the appendix "The Problem of Authorship" by D. C. Lau, *Lao Tzu Tao Te Ching* (Harmondsworth: Penguin, 1963), 147–162.

6. A notorious iteration in the series of debates surrounding this issue was carried out in the United States in the 1940s by the eminent sinologists Homer H. Dubs and Derk Bodde. Dubs's main thesis is that Laozi can be dated to 300 B.C.E., a point that hinges on the identification of two historical figures with similar names. See H. H. Dubs, "The Date and Circumstances of the Philosopher Lao-dz," *Journal of the American Oriental Society* 61 (1941): 215–221, and "The Identification of the Lao-dz," *Journal of the American Oriental Society* 62 (1942): 300. Bodde's responses are "The New Identification of Lao Tzu," *Journal of the American Oriental Society* 62 (1942): 8–13, and "Further Remarks on the Identification of Lao Tzu," *Journal of the American Oriental Society* 64 (1944): 24–27. The possibility of rectifying the inconsistencies in Sima Qian's account of Laozi will likely remain a grail pursued by some sinologists, but the import of the very existence of such profound inconsistencies should not be overlooked.

7. For Han traditions surrounding the figure of Laozi see Mark Csikszentmihalyi, "The Tradition of Laozi," in "Emulating the Yellow Emperor: The Theory and Practice of HuangLao, 180–141 B.C.E." (Ph.D. Diss., Stanford University, 1994): 96–143.

8. Seidel, 92–102. Such transformations marked increasingly advanced states of spiritual achievement and were thought to entail profound physical as well as psychological transformations.

9. Victor Mair, *Tao Te Ching* (New York: Bantam, 1990); Michael LaFargue, *Tao and Method* (Albany: State University of New York Press, 1994).

10. Chan's valuable introduction to the antecedents of the *Laozi* may be found in his translation *The Way of Lao Tzu* (Indianapolis: Bobbs-Merrill, 1963), 61–71.

11. See Arthur Waley, *The Way and Its Power: A Study of the Tao Tê Ching and Its Place in Chinese Thought* (New York: Grove Weidenfeld, 1958): 127, and Gu Jiegang "Lüshi chunqiu tuice *Laozi* zhi chengshu niandai 呂氏春秋推測老子之成書年代," in *Gushibian* 古史辨, ed. Gu, et al., v. 4 (Shanghai: Kaiming, 1941): 462–520.

12. The fact that the character *bang* 邦 is systematically avoided and replaced with the synonym *guo* 國 in the Mawangdui *Laozi* B text indicates it was copied after Liu Bang's 劉邦 (the first emperor of the Han dynasty) reign began in 207 B.C.E. The *Laozi* A text has no such substitution, a fact taken by Tang Lan 唐蘭 to mean that it was copied in the late years of his reign or just after Liu Bang's death in 195 B.C.E. (Tang Lan, "Mawangdui chutu *Laozi* yiben juanqian guyishude yanjiu 馬王堆出土老子乙本卷前古逸書的研究," *Kaogu xuebao* 考古學報 (April 1975): 7). However, the practice of avoiding names does not appear to have been used consistently at this early date.

13. See chapter 53 of the *Hanshu* (Beijing: Zhonghua shuju, 1962), 2410.

14. Many of the changes are discussed in William G. Boltz, "Textual criticism and the Ma wang tui *Lao tzu*," *Harvard Journal of Asiatic Studies* 44, no. 1 (June 1984): 185–224.

15. Robert G. Henricks, *Lao-tzu Te-Tao Ching* (New York: Ballantine, 1989); D. C. Lau, *Chinese Classics, Tao Te Ching* (Hong Kong: Chinese University Press, 1982); Mair, *Tao Te Ching*. On this spate of translations, see also Stephen Durrant, "Packaging the *Tao*," *Rocky Mountain Review of Language and Literature* 45, no. 1–2 (1991): 75–84.

16. Guojia wenwuju guwenxian yanjiushi 國家文物局古文獻研究室, "Dingxian 40 hao Hanmu chutu zhujian jianjie 定縣40號漢墓出土竹簡簡介," *Wenwu* (August 1981): 11–12.

17. See Cui Renyi 崔仁義, "Jingmen Chumu chutude zhujian *Laozi* chutan 荊門楚墓出土的竹簡老子初探" in *Jingmen shehui kexue* 荊門社會科學 (May 1997): 31–35, and Jingmenshi bowuguan 荊門市博物館, *Guodian Chumu zhujian* 郭店楚墓竹簡 (Beijing: Wenwu, 1998).

18. D. C. Lau, trans., *Tao Te Ching* (Harmondsworth: Penguin, 1963), 51.

19. See slip 1 on p. 3, the transcription on p. 111, and Qiu Xigui's 裘錫圭 note 3 on p. 113 of Jingmenshi bowuguan, *Guodian Chumu zhujian*.

20. Du Daojian (fl. 1264–1306), *Xuanjing yuanzhi fahui* 玄經原旨發揮, 2.1a.

21. See chapter 30 of *Hanshu*, 1729.

22. For a detailed treatment of the Heshanggong and Wang Bi commentaries see Alan K. L. Chan, *Two Visions of the Way* (Albany: State University of New York Press, 1991).

23. Chapter 8 of *Sanguozhi* 三國志 (Beijing: Zhonghua, 1959), 264, n.1.

24. See Judith Boltz, *A Survey of Taoist Literature* (Berkeley: Institute of East Asian Studies, 1987), 216–217.

25. See Zhang Longxi, *The Tao and the Logos: Literary Hermeneutics, East and West* (Durham: Duke University Press, 1992).

Mysticism and Apophatic Discourse in the Laozi

Mark Csikszentmihalyi

It is impossible, therefore, to adduce any definite example,
for, as soon as anything is an example,
what I wish to show is already past.

—Schleiermacher, *On Religion*

Go up to it and you will not see its head;
Follow behind it and you will not see its rear.

—*Laozi*, chapter 14

W hat does it mean to describe a text like the *Laozi* as "mystical?" Mysticism, in common with other terms that derive from attempts to generalize particular historical phenomena, is used in a variety of senses that vary according to the "mystical" phenomenon that is consciously or unconsciously used as a model. The common understanding of mysticism as a variety of religious experience adds to the problems that arise from the term's ambiguity, especially in the context of a text like the *Laozi*, which contains little internal evidence to suggest that it is a direct expression of experience. The conflation of the categories of text and experience make it difficult to know what senses of mysticism and what practical contexts are assumed when the *Laozi* is compared to more canonical mystical texts. In this essay, I will examine some of the criteria according to which the *Laozi* has been classified as a mystical text, and focus particularly on one, its use of apophatic, or self-negating, language. I hope to show that there are justifiable readings of the text that undermine orthodox classification of the text as mystical, and that the text advocates the *theoretical* possibility of the existence of mystical experience but is not an *experiential* description of mystical union.

Current Debates on Mysticism(s)

It is a deceptively simple observation that the *Laozi* does not closely resemble accounts of mystic visions common in some Christian accounts. This is because the theoretical discussion of mysticism has evolved in complexity to the point where quite a bit is at stake in defining the degree and character of the resemblance between such phenomena. Not only does any such definition bear on the debate over the unity of mystical experience, it also has implications for the dichotomy between "Eastern" and "Western" mysticism, and the degree to which mystical experience is mediated by specific beliefs and attitudes. In turn, these contemporary debates define the parameters for the application of the term *mysticism* to specific phenomena, and locating the *Laozi* in the framework of these discussions must precede any attempt to examine its mystical qualities.

By examining the stages in the evolution of the theory of mysticism, the various definitions according to which the *Laozi* has been classed a mystical text may be examined against the theoretical background according to which they were formulated. The earliest attempts to define mysticism were based on a set of criteria that were little more than generalizations of aspects of particular archetypal experiences such as those of Teresa of Avila. In the influential account of William James (1842–1910), these criteria were (primarily) ineffability, noesis, (and secondarily) transiency, and passivity. The *Dao*, it has been argued, is both ineffable, which is to say that it cannot be expressed or communicated in words, and knowledge of it is noetic, that is, not theoretical but a form of insight, and so it satisfies the two most important canonical criteria for mysticism outlined by James.[1] Scholars soon found, however, that these criteria were too closely tied to particular religious traditions and increasing emphasis was placed on the more holistic picture of the "experience of mystical union or direct communion with ultimate reality" that Webster's and other general sources now use to define mysticism.

A good avenue to embark on to explore the relevance of these early definitions to the *Laozi* is the concept of the *Dao*, since many scholars have seen union with the *Dao* to be the text's definitive mystical aspect. On what basis have modern interpreters of the *Laozi* read passages such as "Therefore the sage embraces the One and is a model for the empire"[2] as evidence of an appeal to mystical union? For some of these interpreters, it is the One, usually read as a reference to the *Dao*, which plays a role similar to that of God in more archetypal forms of mysticism. John Koller identifies this goal of union with the *Dao* as the characteristic that defines the text as a mystical one:

> By giving up desires and letting the *Dao* enter and pervade oneself, life will rise above the distinctions of good and evil. All activity will proceed from *Dao*, the very source of existence, and man will be one with the world. This is the solution Laozi brought to the problem of evil and unhappiness in man's life. It is a solution that depends ultimately upon achieving a unity with the great inner principle of reality, and is therefore, basically mystical.[3]

Many characterizations made by Koller are accurate. The centrality of the *Dao* in the *Laozi* is impossible to deny, and Koller is correct that the *Dao* transcends distinctions such as that between good and bad, for it is only "When the great way falls into disuse/ There are benevolence and rectitude."[4] Indeed, the *Dao* appears to be beyond all distinctions, "Only when it is cut are there names."[5] As such, it fits the classical description of a mystical unity that is at the same time the basis of all multiplicities. This type of mysticism was given influential formulation by Rudolf Otto in his 1932 *Mysticism East and West*:

> In relation to the many it becomes the subject in so far as it unifies, comprehends and bears the many. It is in fact its

essence, being, existence. Already at this point the One concentrates attention upon itself, draws the value of the many to itself, silently becoming that which is and remains the real value behind the many.[6]

Using such a definition, it is possible to portray the *Laozi*'s sage as seeking a unity with the *Dao*—the One that encompasses the Many—the quest that is the basis of mystical experience. In a similar way, scholars have been able to interpret the resemblances between the *Laozi* and archetypal examples of mysticism as indicative of an underlying identity, a unity of mystical experience.

On closer examination, however, it becomes evident that there are certain aspects of the *Dao* that serve to differentiate it from other "unities." In keeping with its meaning as "path" or "way," the *Dao* is followed (*cong* 從, chapter 21), held to (*zhi* 執, chapter 14), or possessed (*you* 有, chapter 24) but is not merged with. Although some have seen the *Dao* as "providential,"[7] it is certainly not an anthropomorphic "intelligence." The *Dao*'s relationship with the "One" (*yi* 一) is not necessarily one of identity, rather the *Dao* is anterior to it: "The *Dao* begets the One/ The One begets the Two . . ."[8] Do these points mean that the *Laozi* does not fit Otto's description? It was the consideration of characteristics peculiar to individual traditions such as these that led first to a concern with the varieties of mystical experience, and, more recently, to a questioning of the utility of comparisons of mysticism across different traditions.

While the assumption that there existed a mystical "perennial philosophy" that showed up in different guises in the religions of the world had been widely accepted until the last few decades, the recognition of differences such as those described above led in the 1960s to interest in the varieties of mystical experience. This produced the influential typologies of R. C. Zaehner in his *Mysticism, Sacred and Profane* (penenhenic, monistic, and theistic), and of W. T. Stace in his *Mysticism and Philosophy* (extrovertive and introvertive). Following the lead of Otto's comparison of Meister Eckhart and Shankaracharya, less theistic appeals to a reality outside the ordinary realms of experience were seen as a distinctively "Oriental" or "Eastern." Specifically, penenhenic and extrovertive mysticism were seen to lead to a sense of the oneness of all things through the transcendence of space or time in the case of the former category, and in the case of the latter an experience of unity wherein the subject does not look inward, but instead engages their senses.

Recent work has sought to locate the *Laozi* in a comparative mystical context using categories like these. Julia Ching, in "The Mirror Symbol Revisited: Confucian and Taoist Mysticism,"[9] classifies the text along with aspects of early Confucianism as instances of a more general mode of "Eastern mysticism." Ching sees early Daoism as a type of Nature mysticism, one that is characteristic of "Eastern" mysticisms in that it does not preserve the hierarchy between the subject and object inherent in Western forms.[10] The absence of a distinction between subject and object fits in with the taxonomies of Zaehner and Stace in the sense that these are characteristics of nontheistic and extrovertive types of mysticism.

Another author who groups the *Laozi* among uniquely "Eastern" styles of mysticism is Arthur C. Danto. He distinguishes between the two styles of mystical experience:

> The Western mystical literature is a literature of ecstasy and embrace. Santa Teresa is alone on her cloud, individuated at the moment of unity, when she is pierced by a golden arrow. Mrs. Moore's experience [in *A Passage to India*] is, instead, an Oriental blur and a profound spiritual dislocation rather than a fulfillment.[11]

Danto's explanation of the origins of the Oriental "spiritual dislocation" has to do with the underlying difference between the way distinctions are eliminated in the East and West.[12] The Eastern approach, according to Danto, is to seek to go beyond distinctions like good and evil and "become one with one's role." He uses the examples of Wheelwright Pian and Cook Ding from the *Zhuangzi* to illustrate this emphasis on practical knowledge at the expense of propositional knowledge. Danto sees the *Dao* of the *Laozi* as an illustration of this emphasis on practical knowledge, and characterizes the entire text as anti-intellectual in its "celebration of infants, children, and artisans."[13] Thus, for Danto, the *Laozi* is characteristic of an amoral strand of mysticism that stretches across Hinduism, Buddhism, and early Daoism.

Both Ching and Danto, then, attempt to locate the text within a subcategory of Eastern mysticism, although they do so in different ways. Their approaches may be seen to grow out of the work of Otto,

Zaehner, and Stace and reflect the essentialist assumptions inherent in their theoretical models. Problems arise from the fact that the *Laozi* fails to conform to the requirements of "Eastern" mysticism in several important ways. First of all, a very good case could be made that the text is *not* extrovertive in its orientation. The senses are not to be relied on (chapter 12), and instead one is to "Block the openings/ Shut the doors" (chapter 52 and 56). This state of turning inward is most often seen in the motif of regression to infancy: the sage values suckling the mother (chapter 20), and must emulate the infant's suppleness (chapter 10) and harmony (chapter 55). Further, if the *Dao* is the mother of this infant, then it is not the case that the subject/object distinction completely disappears, as Ching would have it. In a recent article on "Chinese Mysticism,"[14] Wu Kuang-ming rejects the notion that what he sees to be a uniquely Chinese style of mysticism eliminates the distinction between subject and object.[15]

Danto's picture of "Eastern" mysticism is different from other models already examined, but on closer inspection he also fails to adequately separate the *Laozi* from other "Eastern" texts. The critique of Daoism is almost entirely based on the *Zhuangzi*, and it is difficult to see *any* examples of Danto's "practical knowledge" in the *Laozi*.[16] The difference between the aims of these two texts is very great, a difference Livia Kohn has summed up in these terms:

> While the *Daode jing* wishes to remedy an unsatisfactory situation socially and through simplicity, the *Zhuangzi*, much more radically, encourages a thorough revolution of people's very minds.[17]

Throughout the *Laozi* the ruler and sage is the exemplary figure, as opposed to the skillful exemplars of the *Zhuangzi*. Although the intuitions the ruler is supposed to rely on may be characterized as "anti-intellectual," it is difficult to see how such a characterization could apply to "Eastern" thought in general. These observations suggest that there are significant problems with grouping the *Laozi* in a category of generic "Eastern mysticism" and point out some problems with the broad typologies that dominated the study of mysticism in the 1960s and 1970s.

That period's phenomenological approach assumed that, at least sometimes, local beliefs and attitudes mediated the core mystical experience, and this assumption set the stage for the current debate between the constructivists and their critics. Recent work on mysticism may be situated along a continuum between the position that each mystical experience is different since it is mediated by the tradition in which it occurs, and the position that a universal element of the experience of "pure consciousness" exists in mystical experience across traditions. The former position assumes that religious experience must pass through a series of cultural, doctrinal, and personal filters and is therefore constructed within a tradition. As championed in a pair of volumes edited by Stephen T. Katz beginning with *Mysticism and Philosophical Analysis* in 1978, the constructivist position assumes that "there are no pure (i.e., unmediated) experiences."[18] The latter position, developed to counter the constructivist position, is represented in a 1990 volume edited by Robert K. Forman called *The Problem of Pure Consciousness*. Forman argues that since mystical union is by definition a state that transcends ordinary consciousness to reach an undifferentiated unity, it is the single experience that might be considered unmediated by the filters emphasized by the constructivists.[19] In one sense, the debate between those such as Forman who argue that mystical experience is unmediated because it occurs on a level of pure consciousness and those such as Katz who see it is as socially constructed is a reflection of a broader debate about the nature of religious experience. In the latter context, Friedrich Schleiermacher's attempts to portray religious experience as intuitive may be seen as a move to avert a Kantian reading of it as constructed through practical reason.

The constructivist position is not one that sheds light on necessary conditions for applying the term mysticism to the *Laozi*, but instead calls into question the possibility of upholding a cross-cultural ideal of "mystical experience." On the other hand, the response to that position has served to illuminate the long implicit understanding of mysticism as experience that cannot be mediated. As such, the term mysticism has been increasingly applied to a level of experience that transcends the basic terms of a tradition, whatever that tradition may be.

We have seen how the text of the *Laozi* has provided problems for those who have tried to classify it using a criterion of mystical union, and those who would label it simply a form of characteristically Eastern mysticism. When one looks to the text for evidence of a level of experience so basic that it exists prior to any cultural mediation, it is no longer possible to bracket the fundamental distinction between text and practice. The issue of how exactly one infers experience from a text must be examined critically.[20]

Mystical Experience and Mystical Text

The gap between text and experience may not be as difficult to bridge for a text that purports to directly record experience, such as the *Castillo Interior* of Teresa of Avila, but the scope, ambiguity, and abstract nature of the *Laozi* makes any attempt to read it as a record or diary of mystical experience extremely problematical. There are records of unions with divinities in the early Chinese tradition, although these stylized poems, the *Chuci* 楚辭, have not been treated in discussions of mysticism.[21] By contrast, the *Laozi* is constituted of aphorisms and instructions that are often didactic rather than descriptive. A few isolated fragments (e.g., chapter 20) use first person pronouns, and the few dialogical passages (e.g., chapter 77) evidence little more than the addition of a rhetorical interlocutor. In other words, there are few explicit signs that mystical experience was connected to the text.

Nevertheless, two different approaches have been taken to infer that such experience guided the composition of the *Laozi*. One approach has been to isolate a technical vocabulary that demonstrates that the text is in some way the product of mystical experience. Marcel Granet was an early exponent of the view that early Daoist texts derived from religious practices. Writing in 1922, Granet proposed that the *Laozi*, along with two other early texts, "can be understood only by relating their ideas to the concrete religious practices to which they correspond."[22] More recently, Harold Roth has argued for the hypothesis that the *Laozi* contains "philosophies directly derived from the experience of practicing mystics."[23] References to the "bellows" (chapter 5), to "concentrating your breath" (chapter 10), and the previously mentioned imperative to "Block the openings/ Shut the doors" (chapters 52 and 56) have all been read as references to meditation techniques.[24] Recent archaeological evidence has been used to support the characterization of the *Laozi* as a record of experience or as a manual for specialized techniques.

Indeed, there is growing evidence that many medical and meditative strategies known to have been practiced in the late Han dynasty (c. 180 C.E.) onward existed in some form during the time that the *Laozi* was composed, raising the possibility that the text itself was based on early medical or meditative practice. A recent volume of essays in Chinese includes several attempts to link such practice to the *Laozi*. In it, Zhou Shirong 周世榮 has noted the similarity between the terminology of chapter 4 of the text and that used in traditional *qigong*. Zhou reads the chapter as a description of the location, method, and result of a type of breathing linked to longevity practice.[25] Wei Qipeng 魏啟鵬 has noted that the term *pu* 樸 "simplicity," used frequently in the *Laozi*, is also used in conjunction with certain medical regimens.[26] Whether or not statements as strong as Granet's and Roth's are true, it is difficult to avoid the conclusion that the *Laozi* incorporates the language of and perhaps even references to concrete medical or meditative practices of the period.

The similarity between the vocabulary of the *Laozi* and early medical or meditation texts, however, does not make the *Laozi* one of these texts. After all, the presence of the vocabulary of childrearing, farming, schooling, or moneylending does not make it a primer on any one of these subjects. The poetic form of the text is unsuited to be read as a manual for a specific practice. The presence of specialized vocabulary does provide proof that the accretion of text that became the *Laozi* took place against a background that included meditation practices. Yet there is nothing to show that the use of meditational vocabulary is anything but metaphorical. Even if it was not metaphorical, the analysis of Zhou and Wei suggests that the goal of meditation may have been more medical than experiential.

Another approach to linking the *Laozi* with mystical experience has been to link its use of paradox to the experience of the reader of the text. Benjamin Schwartz has singled out the use of paradox in the *Laozi* as a means of communicating the ineffability of the *Dao*, and identified this as a universal criterion for mystical *literature*:

The *Dao* in its aspect of the ineffable eternal is nondeterminate and nameless. It cannot be identified with anything nameable. . . . Here, as elsewhere, in all mystical literature, we find the constant paradoxical effort to speak the unspeakable.[27]

Schwartz makes a general claim about mystical texts, that they tend to use paradox to create a discourse capable of pointing to a type of truth that ordinary language cannot. When paradox is used in this way, it is an attempt to "point to" something that cannot be expressed using language. Michael A. Sells has compared the use of such apophatic language, speech that negates, in several mystical traditions, and argued that it functions within these traditions to eliminate distinctions between immanent and transcendent.[28] It has already been shown that various arguments that purport to demonstrate that the text arose as a record or commentary on mystical experience on the part of the author do not account for the form or much of the content of the *Laozi*. Schwartz's approach, however, focuses on the effect of the text on the *reader* of the text, so that the text becomes a member of Stanley Fish's category of "self-consuming artifacts."

This approach provides a criterion according to which the text might be connected to mystical practice without being a record of such practice. As a means of speaking about mystical literature separately from a specific basis in mystical experience, the existence of an apophatic discourse generated by the use of paradox is a useful criterion for determining whether or not the *Laozi* is a mystical text. Fortunately, the Chinese commentarial tradition allows us to examine the way the paradox in the *Laozi* has been read. Livia Kohn puts it this way:

> [The *Laozi*] conspicuously lacks concrete descriptions of mystical methods, physical or otherwise. Nor does it show the emphasis on the mind and on the development of the individual known from later mystical literature. In other words, the *Daode jing*, as it stands, is not obviously a mystical document. It could equally likely be read as a work on ideal government or on the moral and cultural decline of humanity. . . . On the other hand, by claims of the later tradition, the *Daode jing* is a mystical text of the first importance.[29]

If the *Laozi* fails to fit the definition of a mystical text based on direct testimony of mystical experience, the issue then becomes: has paradox been read so as to make the *Laozi* a "mystical text of the first importance"?

Apophatic Discourse in the *Laozi*

The language of the *Laozi* is rich in contradiction, a fact that has been pointed out by D. C. Lau.[30] Direct contradictions such as the linked imperatives of chapter 63: "Do that which is doing-less, attend to that which is attending-less, taste that which is tasting-less,"[31] are also common. Traditional strategies for interpreting the self-contradictory language of the *Laozi* have varied from seeing it as only an apparent contradiction to seeing it as apophasis that preserves its internal tension to destroy the assumptions that underlie ordinary discourse. Interestingly, it is the earlier commentaries that generally follow the first course, and it is in the Chan-influenced or post-Buddhist Confucian commentaries that the second course is used.

To explain these two strategies, that of "embracing" the contradiction in a text and that of "explaining" it, one might consider for a moment some possible responses a visitor to an art gallery might have when faced with the famous Magritte painting of a pipe that contradicts itself in its title "Ce n'est pas une pipe." One response would be to nod and accept the tension between the visual and linguistic cues as a means to liberate one's mind from limitations imposed by the hobgoblin of consistency. Magritte used the contradiction, perhaps as some try to use kōans, as a form of therapy that allows one to discard categories that block one's natural ability to engage the transcendent. A related response to the painting would be to focus instead on the assumption underlying any standard of consistency, whether it is a full-fledged concept of rationality, or simply a taste for titles that tell one what a painting is about. Once one has called into question such a standard, one must examine the grounds concerning the asking of questions, thereby translating the contradiction encountered in the gallery into a conundrum concerning how one knows what one thinks one knows. These two courses are similar in that the contradiction is accepted as an argument that leads to the reexamination of the viewer's assumptions, in the former case leading the viewer away from these assumptions, in the latter encouraging the viewer to pay more attention to them.

Alternately, the viewer might seek to resolve the contradiction so that such fundamental assumptions are not called into question.

Perhaps the painter sought to point to the difference between relying on what one sees with one's own eyes and what one reads.
Alternately, a claim might be being made about the difference between the general class represented by the word *pipe* and the very
specific pipe portrayed on the canvas. Finally, and perhaps most
literally, Magritte might simply be saying that a two-dimensional
representation of a pipe is different from a three-dimensional
wooden pipe. Among the visitors to the gallery who stop and look at
this work of art, most of these interpretations are probably represented each day.

These strategies of interpretation, as well as the general dis-
junction between approaches that "embrace" the contradiction and
those that "explain" the contradiction, have analogies in the history
of interpretation of the *Laozi*, and indeed represent only some of the
ways that its contradictory language has been read. While it would
be difficult to come up with criteria for arguing that one of these
strategies of interpretation is more "correct" than others, this
does not mean that there are no frames within which they may be
compared.

In examining the use of contradiction in the *Laozi*, a primary
goal will be to distinguish between the resolvable instances of contradiction and the ones that generate an irresolvable tension. Three
general categories of contradiction will be outlined: contradictions
arising out of incorrect perception, contradictions of action where
one thing leads to its opposite, and finally contradictions involving
things that are not themselves.

Contradictions of Perception and Reality

One of the most ubiquitous themes in the *Laozi* is that of incorrect
perceptions involving false semblances, as in phrases of the form
"(something) seems to be (the opposite of something)." The sage can
avoid this pitfall because he does not attempt to perceive the *Dao* in
an ordinary way:

> This is the reason that the sage does not move but
>   nevertheless knows,
> Does not look but nevertheless sees clearly,
> Does not act but nevertheless accomplishes.[32]

The mode of "seeing" in which the sage engages is not well-defined, but it appears that his stillness, sightlessness, and passivity guarantee a more reliable picture of the world than ordinary perception. This exceptional ability allows the sage to use intuition and inference to understand the *Dao*. There are many instances of false semblances in the text, such as "The clear *Dao* seems hidden."[33] However, the claim of semblance excludes the possibility of genuine contradiction between the two opposing elements. These dichotomies may be resolved rather effortlessly into those between "conventional" versus "true" sight, action, or knowledge.

Traditionally, such passages have usually not been read as any more than a claim about the difficulty of accurately perceiving the *Dao*. While the *Dao* exists in a prelinguistic realm that only the sage can intuitively observe, there are also distinct physical traces of it that the sage *can* directly observe. This is the dichotomy in chapter 1 between the "secrets" (*miao* 妙) of the *Dao* and the "manifestations" (*jiao* 徼) of the *Dao*. The earliest partial commentary on the *Laozi*, chapter 20 of the *Han Feizi*, comments on the description of the *Dao* as "a form without form, an image (*xiang* 象) without substance":

> People rarely see a living elephant (*xiang*) but when they come upon the bones of a dead elephant they imagine it alive on the basis of their structure. Therefore all instances of what people imagine by means of their traces are called images (*xiang*). Now, the Dao cannot be seen or heard, but the sage investigates its manifestations and uses them to determine its form.[34]

While the entire *Dao* is not directly perceptible, its form can be known through a kind of imaginative inference based on a skeleton provided by its trace image. This interpretation that it is possible to know of the *Dao*, but impossible to accurately represent it in the realm of the senses is shared by the later *Xiang'er* 想爾 commentary's explanation of the same passage:

> The most revered *Dao* is subtle and hidden without shape or structure. Although one may follow its admonitions, one cannot see or know it. Those who today through false arts point to the "name and form" of the *Dao*, imposing fancy clothes, a complete name, shape and size on it are all wrong. They are entirely pernicious and deceptive.[35]

This explanation of the phrase in chapter 14 of the *Laozi* sees the *Dao* as being impossible to perceive in its entirety, as some charlatans might claim, but its admonitions are something that may be followed. Again, the ineffability of the *Dao* is not a sign that *any* knowledge of the *Dao* is impossible to express, but instead that it may never be *entirely* expressed.

Another type of explanation of the statements in the *Laozi* that call into question the validity of the perceptions is one which stresses direct transmission of the *Dao*. This explanation posits the possibility of the transmission of the *Dao* from one person to another, but argues that, in the manner of Bodhidharma's robe, it must be passed directly from master to disciple. Closely tied to arguments centered on language skepticism of the sort that populate the *Zhuangzi*, such an explanation does not so much indict the senses, but instead conventional ways of using the senses. In the illustration of the opening lines of the first chapter of the *Laozi* in the Han Dynasty *Huainanzi*, the story of Wheelwright Pian from the *Zhuangzi* is invoked. In this story, Pian calls into question whether knowledge can be passed on through books.[36] The second chapter's admonition to wordless teaching is interpreted in the *Heshanggong* commentary to mean that the sage "teaches and leads them with his body."[37] In common with the above strategy of using "trace manifestations" this explanation resolves any apparent contradictions inherent in the paradox of false semblances, and explains them away.

Contradictions of Action and Effect

This sort of resolution is more difficult to reach with the second type of contradictory passage of the form "doing (something) leads to (the opposite of something)." This type of contradiction is usually a characteristic of the sage:

> Therefore the sage puts his person last and it comes first
> Treats his person as external and it is preserved
> Is it not because he has no self-interest
> That he is able to realize his self-interest?[38]

While it is quite possible that the sage only appears to be putting his person last, these passages carry with them no explicit indication that there is any difference between, for example, the "self-interest" the sage is without and the "self-interest" that he realizes. The question is whether these contradictions ought to be explained in the manner of "apparent" contradictions as with those above, or whether the contradiction expresses instead a deeper skepticism or criticism of the idea of self-interest, or perhaps even the idea of the sage.

Traditional commentators generally favor a resolution of such phrases, although the type of resolution varies. One strategy is to distinguish between long and short temporal horizons. Some of the earliest commentaries to the text favor this reading. The Western Han *Huainanzi* illustrates the phrase "the sage puts his person last and it comes first" with the following fish story:

> Gongyi Xiu 公儀休 was Chancellor of the state of Lu who had quite a taste for fish. A [delegation from another] country presented him with some fish, but Gongyi Xiu did not accept them.
> His disciples remonstrated with him: "Our master has a taste for fish but did not accept any. Why was this?"
> He answered: "Now, it was exactly because I have a taste for fish that I did not accept any. If I had accepted the fish but was dismissed from my post as Chancellor, then although I have a taste for fish I could not provide myself any. By not accepting any fish I will also not be dismissed from my post as Chancellor, and will be able to provide myself fish into perpetuity."
> This is an individual who understands how to act toward others and how to act toward himself.[39]

In this story, the correct self-interested action changes depending on the time frame being considered, and so the sage appears to have no short-term self-interest precisely because he has long-term self-interest. In two other early commentaries, the long-term benefits of longevity are seen to outweigh other short-term benefits. The *Heshanggong* commentary explains that "the sage puts his person last and it comes first" (chapter 7) means that "the people of the world revere him; 'comes first' means long life," while he "treats his person as external and it is preserved" means that

> the common people love him as if he were their father and mother, while the spirits and specters assist him as if he were their baby. Because of this his person will exist eternally.[40]

A similar understanding of the passage may be found in the *Xiang'er* commentary, where several "conventional" modes of putting oneself first are revealed to actually be ineffective means to that end:

> He who seeks long life does not belabor his essential thoughts with the pursuit of wealth to nourish himself. He does not, without achievements, coerce the ruler and receive a salary to glorify himself. He does not eat the five flavors to indulge himself. His clothes are inferior and his shoes have holes in them so as not to clash with those of regular people. All these are ways in which he "puts his person last." However, looking at it from the perspective of his gaining the long life of the immortals, reaping good fortune ahead of the regular people, these are how he "comes first."[41]

Putting oneself last and having oneself come first are not embraced as opposites in these readings, but rather as referring to fundamentally different types of action.

While such explanations of action and effect contradictions are the rule, the reading of Song commentator Ge Changgeng 葛長庚 provides a contrast. The Ge commentary provides the following perspective on "the sage puts his person last and it comes first": "I am Heaven and Earth, and Heaven and Earth are me."[42] This interpretation of the passage signals a style of interpretation that is fundamentally different from the earlier commentators, one in which the tension of the contradiction is used to eliminate distinctions between the individual and the natural. This is an interpretation that might well be categorized as evidence of an extrovertive mystical experience by Stace.

Self-Contradictions

The third and final form of self-contradiction is the general formula "(something) which is not (something)." In the *Laozi*, there are both indirect and direct instances of such formulas. The sage is the one who "dwells in doing-less affairs and practices not-saying teachings."[43] Earlier we saw that the way the sage goes about this is to *wei wuwei* 為無為 "do that which is doing-less" (chapter 63), a mode certainly related to the imperative *xue buxue* 學不學 "learn not to learn."[44] This approach is certainly appropriate to the object of these (non-) actions, since the *Dao* is *wuzhuang zhi zhuang* 無狀之狀 "the shape without a shape."[45] The direct symmetry of these phrases would seem to indicate that there is more to these passages than simply a condemnation of a "conventional" notion of action or learning.

Traditionally, however, this class of self-contradiction has also often been resolved using the interpretive strategy of explaining away the contradiction. For example, the *Heshanggong* commentary reads the character *xue* 學 in "learn not to learn" as "true learning" in the first case and as "conventional learning" in the second case. It reads:

> The sage studies what others cannot study.
> Others study wisdom and falsehood, the sage studies spontaneity.
> Others study governing the world, the sage studies governing himself.
> [So he] preserves the *Dao's* trueness.[46]

Governing oneself is simply another type of studying, and the apparent contradiction is explained away. In the same way, Wang Bi reads "taste that is tasting-less" as referring to actual substances that have no discernible taste.[47] These interpretations suggest that it is possible to explain away any of the contradictions in the text, even the most elemental ones, in terms of categories like those of "conventional" versus "exceptional."

Nevertheless, some traditional commentators have taken the contradictions in these passages as indicative of an irresolvable tension. This is the case for three such commentaries, the Tang or pre-Tang commentary attributed to Gu Huan 顧歡 (420–483 C.E.), and the eleventh-century Song commentaries of Ge Changgeng and Su Che 蘇徹 (c. 1100 C.E.). For Gu Huan, the apophatic discourse in the *Laozi* was intended to dissolve the distinctions between doing and not doing certain things. For example, he understands the statement "do that which is doing-less" to deny the difference between doing and not doing:

> Struggle to grasp the source of the mind, do not lose its true radiance. Once its radiance is emitted, doing is the same as the doing-less. This is what it means. So doing is doing-less and doing-less is doing.[48]

Gu affirms the destruction of the opposition in a similar way when the text speaks of learning "not to learn":

> Learning is not learning and not learning is learning. Not to engage in learning is different from not learning and is [also] different from learning. So the *Xishengjing* 西昇經 [*Scripture of Western Ascension*] says: "I learn without anything to learn and so can understand the natural."[49]

Here the commentary is explicitly challenging the identification of not learning with not engaging in learning, implying that there is a "not learning" that transcends the simple opposition of taking part in learning versus not engaging in learning. In this manner, the Gu Huan commentary attempts to point to something that surpasses learning and not learning, thereby embracing rather than explaining the contradiction in the original text.

The Song commentators are also interested in eliminating the distinction between a thing or action and its opposite, and in this way pointing to something that transcends such oppositions. Ge Changgeng uses the Buddhist metaphor of the "bright mirror hanging on the platform" from the *Liuzu tanjing* 六祖壇經 (*Platform Sutra of the Sixth Patriarch*) to explain how the sage "knows without moving" (chapter 47).[50] Su Che does not see the mind as what exists behind the distinctions, but rather the Neo-Confucian idea of principle (*li*). Su Che uses the same concept of transcendent principle to explain the chain of sentences in chapter 22 of the *Laozi* that begins "bowed then preserved":

> In moving, the sage must follow principle, where principle exists it may be straight or bowed. He simply must penetrate it. If he penetrates it then he will not be bogged down. If he is not bogged down then he will be preserved.[51]

The effort that the sage makes to penetrate principle is on a level different from physical attributes that are manifestations of substance (*qi* 氣). It is through this dichotomy that Su addresses the stark contradiction "learn not to learn":

> The sage . . . is not without learning. He learns and does not learn. So although he learns he nevertheless avoids doing harm to principle. Only then can inner and outer be vacuous

and clear. Solitarily acting-less, he can complement the spontaneity of the myriad things and rely on his own self-realization.[52]

In this interpretation, the sage is not "without learning," but instead combines the polar opposites of learning and not learning. By specifically affirming that the sage both learns and does not learn, Su embraces the tension that allows him to define a mode of action that resembles learning but is at the same time fundamentally different. As with the Ge commentary, the tension of the self-contradiction is preserved and the text is read apophatically.

While it is the case that commentators disagree over whether contradiction in the *Laozi* should be read as apophasis or not, there is an important conclusion here concerning traditional readings of the text. It is not the case that the history of the text's interpretation clearly supports a reading of the *Laozi* as a mystical text according to the criterion established by Schwartz. Even with the most stark contradictions, it is chiefly in the post-Chan Buddhist commentaries that the contradiction is embraced as apophatic language rather than explained away. Traditional commentators on the *Laozi* have not necessarily interpreted the text as containing apophatic language that preserves a tension pointing to ineffability.

Mystical Theory and Mystical Practice

It may seem surprising to try to deny the *Laozi* the therapeutic effect of apophasis, the one type of mystical experience that might be definitely connected with the text because it arises from the very act of reading it. Yet many traditional commentators sought to explain away the text's contradictions, calling into question even this link to experience. Thus, not only are explicit references to mystical experience lacking in the text, but it does not seem that the earliest commentators even read the text as an attempt to express knowledge implicitly gained through such experience. To the degree that mysticism has been fundamentally understood as a form of religious experience, then, it is not possible to state authoritatively that the *Laozi* is a "mystical" text.

This gap between text and experience is perhaps why it was possible to find flaws with the attempts to categorize the *Laozi* as mystical according to the use of the term by the successive generations of scholars during this century. Indeed, it might be argued that the compilation is pointedly abstract, with its systematic omission of proper names or dates and simple language. Herbert Giles's 1905 *Religions of Ancient China* makes a somewhat derisive reference to Laozi's doctrines along these lines: "Such a system was naturally far better fitted for the study, where in fact it has always remained, than for use in ordinary life."[53] Yet how can one speak of the possibility of having knowledge of a prelinguistic *Dao* without an attempt to tie it to experience? Returning for a moment to the mode of Magritte-style self-reference, this sort of theoretical discussion is not as foreign as it first seems—this article is doing precisely that.

Most scholarship in the history of religions, and in mysticism theory in particular, assumes that some commonality underlies the diverse traditions being examined, whether that commonality is supernatural or psychological. By placing the *Dao* prior to the formation of categories, the *Laozi* is performing much the same theoretical move we have already seen made by Forman in the discussion of mystical experience and Schleiermacher in the discussion of religious experience. Like these later theorists, the *Laozi* is trying to evoke an unmediated moment that is not reducible to ordinary modes of knowing. This is close to the way that Wayne Proudfoot understands the use of *Dao* in the *Laozi*:

> The term [*Dao*] acts as a formal operator, or placeholder, systematically excluding any differentiating description or predicates that might be proposed. The term functions in this way regardless of its meaning or connotations.[54]

Proudfoot goes on to draw the parallel between the use of placeholders like "*Dao*" in mystical texts and those like "numinous" in the literature of the history of religions.[55] In this sense, the *Laozi* has more in common with Rudolf Otto's discussion of Meister Eckhart than with Eckhart's writing itself. In this analysis, the text is less an expression of an experience of an ineffable *Dao* than a compilation of attempts to describe it.

Taking a step back, the question arises: what could the compiler of the *Laozi* have in common with a scholar such as Otto, so temporally and culturally distant? One answer might be that both are attempting to find a hidden thread that runs through a multiplicity of data. Early writers like Jia Yi 賈誼 (200–168 B.C.E.) state that the numinous thread of the *Dao* is what runs through the phenomenal world, and is the sum of the "techniques" (*shu* 術) that are used to act in that world.[56] The *Laozi* itself may best be understood as a composite text organized along thematic principles, centered on the various methods that people have evolved to speak about the *Dao*. The earliest classification of the *Laozi* in China, attributed to the late second-century B.C.E. historian and astrologer Sima Tan 司馬談, associates the text with a group intent on developing methods that drew on the expertise of each of the existing traditions.[57] The *Dao* was what united the approaches of these traditions, the common denominator that was behind "the great order of the yin-yang lineages," the "good points of the Confucian and Mohist lineages," the "essentials of the Nominalist and Legalist lineages," that the group selected out. The *Dao*, then, was also a way of speaking about a unitary phenomenon that appeared in different guises once it was constructed in different traditions.

To be sure, this does not rule out the possibility that one of the mediated manifestations of the *Dao* might be knowledge acquired via mystical union with ultimate reality. It is possible that the compiler of the *Laozi* was using the possibility of personal knowledge of such a mystical *Dao* to show the possibility of having similar knowledge in other spheres. Such a theory would provide a connection between philosophical aspects and the political and moral aspects of the *Laozi*. That there exists a transcendant *Dao* that undergirds reality provides a precedent for the sage ruler's ability to access political and moral knowledge directly—thereby undermining the ultimate authority of alternate traditions and texts devoted to rulership and ethics (e.g., Confucianism). The *Laozi* is then not an account of mystical experience, but an attempt to describe a "phenomenon" in the same way that scholars of mysticism do.

NOTES

The author would like to thank Philip J. Ivanhoe and Karl Plank for their comments on earlier drafts of this article.

1. James's requirements are that mystical experience "defies expression, that no adequate report of its contents can be given in words" and that such

experiences "are states of insight into depths of truth unplumbed by the discursive intellect..." *The Varieties of Religious Experience* (London: Collins, 1961), 300.

2. Chapter 22. D. C. Lau, trans., *Tao Te Ching* (Harmondsworth: Penguin, 1963), 79. For the use of this passage as evidence of mysticism, see Geoffrey Parrinder, *Mysticism in the World's Religions* (New York: Oxford University Press, 1976), 69.

3. John M. Koller, *Oriental Philosophies* (New York: Charles Scribner's Sons, 1970), 239. Koller is using a definition of mysticism similar to that of W. T. Stace, which assumes a unity "which the mystic believes to be in some sense ultimate and basic to the world..." Walter T. Stace, *Mysticism and Philosophy* (Philadelphia: Lippincott, 1960), 132.

4. Chapter 20. Lau, trans., *Tao Te Ching*, 74.

5. Chapter 32. Lau, trans., *Tao Te Ching*, 91. Note, however, the female/male and weak/strong distinctions appear to persist even in unity (see chapter 61, and also chapters 66 and 78).

6. Here, Otto is describing the second of three steps in "unifying vision" mysticism, that is, the mysticism of the "East." See Rudolf Otto, *Mysticism East and West* (New York: MacMillan, 1932), 68.

7. See, for example, Edward H. Parker's (1849–1926) translation of the first line of the *Laozi*: "The Providence which could be indicated by words would not be an all-embracing Providence," *China and Religion* (London: John Murray, 1905), 271.

8. Chapter 42. Lau, trans., *Tao Te Ching*, 103.

9. In *Mysticism and Religious Traditions*, ed. Steven T. Katz (Oxford: Oxford University Press, 1983): 226–246.

10. Ching's goal is to examine uses of the reflecting mirror as a metaphor for mystical union with the divine to confirm the distinction made by the German religious writer Friedrich Heiler (1892–1967) in his 1921 *Das Gebet* (*Prayer*) between "prophetic" religions grounded in divine revelation and "mysticisms" which do not rely on prophecy and instead are defined by their mystical traditions. The former religions, including Christianity, Judaism, and Islam, maintain a distance between the subject and object of mystical meditation, while the latter traditions, such as Hinduism, Buddhism, and Daoism, promote the elimination of the differences between the self and the divine. Ching contrasts the "Western" *attachment* of the subject and the mirror image with the "Eastern" *detachment* from the object reflected (242). For the purposes of understanding the *Laozi*, this analysis is generally inapplicable, since Ching's examples of mysticism are pre-Qin Confucianism and post-Han Daoism. Ching can replicate Heiler's results only through

this judicious choice of data. The application of the contrast between prophetic religions and mysticisms to Daoism and Christianity ignore the central nature of revelation in later Daoism and the influential nonprophetic traditions of early Christianity such as Gnosticism.

11. Arthur C. Danto, *Mysticism and Morality: Oriental Thought and Moral Philosophy* (New York: Basic Books, 1972), 56. Note that Danto's evidence for the nature of the "Eastern" mystical experience comes from the pen of E. M. Forster.

12. Danto, *Mysticism and Morality*, 55. According to Danto, in India the rejection of illusory distinctions was final and no attempt was made to account for their origins, as opposed to a situation where they are rejected but still have to be explained. This leads to the idea of "discipline of action" wherein one's actions "are, by the criterion of the *Gita* itself, beyond good and evil and, so, beyond moral appraisal, which is concerned with whether an act may be said to be good or evil" (95).

13. Danto, *Mysticism and Morality*, 111.

14. In Donald H. Bishop, ed., *Mysticism and the Mystical Experience: East and West* (Selinsgrove: Susquehanna University Press, 1995), 230–259.

15. Wu writes: "Nor does Chinese mysticism bring *down* the supreme deity, the exalted ancestor, the vital pervasive moral force, the Heaven. Instead, Chinese mysticism lets us realize that the world is up there without nullifying the distinction between the ultimate and the concrete; the distinction is reverently *accepted*" (Bishop, *Mysticism and the Mystical Experience*, 234).

16. For a good discussion of "skillfulness" in the *Zhuangzi* which could be used to engage Danto's critique on a number of points see Mark Berkson, "Language: The Guest of Reality: Zhuangzi and Derrida on Language, Reality, and Skillfulness," in *Essays on Skepticism, Relativism, and Ethics in the Zhuangzi*, ed. Paul Kjellberg and Philip J. Ivanhoe (Albany: State University of New York Press, 1996), 97–126.

17. Kohn, *Early Chinese Mysticism*, 58.

18. Stephen T. Katz, "Language, Epistemology, and Mysticism," in *Mysticism and Philosophical Analysis* (New York: Oxford University Press, 1978), 26.

19. Robert K. Forman, "Mysticism, Constructivism, and Forgetting," in *The Problem of Pure Consciousness* (New York: Oxford University Press, 1990).

20. Philip C. Almond notes that the gap between text and experience is sometimes finessed in Zaehner's discussion of Indian mysticism. See his

Mystical Experience and Religious Doctrine: An Investigation of the Study of Mysticism in World Religions (Berlin: de Gruyter, 1982), especially pp. 29–30.

21. Several parts of the *Chuci* have usually been classified as examples of shamanism, despite the fact that the "shamanistic" journey is rarely associated with the *wu* 巫, the term usually translated as "shaman." See David Hawkes, trans., *The Songs of the South* (Harmondsworth: Penguin, 1985), 42.

22. Marcel Granet, *The Religion of the Chinese People*, trans. Maurice Freedman (New York: Harper and Row, 1975), 121.

23. Harold D. Roth, "Some Issues in the Study of Chinese Mysticism: A Review Essay," *China Review International* 2, no. 1 (Spring 1995): 154–73.

24. See Donald Harper, "The Bellows Analogy in Laozi V and Warring States Macrobiotic Hygiene" *Early China* 20 (1995): 381–192, and Harold Roth's article "The *Laozi* in the Context of Early Daoist Mystical Practice," in this volume.

25. Zhou Shirong, "Cong Mawangdui chutu wenwu kan woguo daojia wenhua 從馬王堆出土文物看我國道家文化," in *Daojia wenhua yanjiu* 道家文化研究, v. 3, ed. Chen Guying 陳鼓應 (Shanghai: Guji, 1993), 395–407.

26. Wei Qipeng, "Mawangdui guyishude daojia yu yijia 馬王堆古逸書的道家與醫家," in *Daojia wenhua yanjiu*, v. 3, ed. Chen Guying, 360–377.

27. Benjamin Schwartz, *The World of Thought in Ancient China* (Cambridge: Bellknap Press, 1985), 197–198.

28. Michael A. Sells. *Mystical Languages of Unsaying* (Chicago: University of Chicago Press, 1994).

29. Livia Kohn, *Early Chinese Mysticism: Philosophy and Sotieriology in the Taoist Tradition* (Princeton: Princeton University Press, 1992), 40.

30. Lau, "The Treatment of Opposites in *Lao Tzu* 老子," *Bulletin of the School of Oriental and African Studies* 21 (1958): 344–360, 355. Lau examines previous theories about the superiority of the "female," paying particular attention to those of Feng Youlan 馮友蘭 and Yang Kuan 楊寬. Lau ultimately rejects both positions and argues that "The process of change is not necessarily circular. Decline, when a thing reaches the highest point, is inevitable, but development is not . . . [And] can be arrested. It is, therefore, both possible and useful to 'abide by the soft'" (354–355).

31. Compare Lau's translation: "Do that which consists in taking no action, pursue that which is not meddlesome; savour that which has no flavour" (Lau, trans., *Tao Te Ching*, 125).

32. Chapter 47, cf. Lau, trans., *Tao Te Ching*, 108. The Dao in particular should not be approached using the senses: "Go to meet it and you will not see its head . . ." (chapter 14, cf. Lau, trans., *Tao Te Ching*, 70).

33. Chapter 41, cf. Lau, trans., *Tao Te Ching*, 102. See other instances of such language in chapter 6 and chapter 45. Note that the certain dualisms created by human beings also tend to interfere with accurate perceptions (chapter 2).

34. *Han Feizi* 20, commenting on chapter 14. Chen Qiyou 陳奇猷, *Han Feizi jishi* 韓非子集釋 (Beijing: Zhonghua, 1962), 6:368.

35. Rao Zongyi 饒宗頤, *Laozi Xiang'er zhu jiaojian* 老子想爾注校箋 (Hong Kong: Tong Nam, 1956), 18.

36. *Huainanzi* 12, *Zhuzi jicheng* edition, 196. See also *Zhuangzi jishi* 莊子集釋 13, *Zhuzi jicheng* edition, 217–218 (cf. Burton Watson, trans., *The Complete Works of Chuang Tzu* [New York: Columbia University Press, 1968], 152–153). For a fuller treatment of language skepticism see Eric Schwitzgabel, "Zhuangzi's Attitude Toward Language and His Skepticism," in *Essays on Skepticism, Relativism, and Ethics in the Zhuangzi*, ed. Kjellberg and Ivanhoe, 68–96, and for the various types of skepticism in the *Zhuangzi* see Philip J. Ivanhoe, "Skepticism, Skill and the Ineffable *Dao*," *Journal of the American Academy of Religions* 61, no. 4 (Winter 1993): 101–116.

37. *Laozi Daodejing sijuan* 老子道德經四卷, *Sibu congkan* edition, 2a. As Qu Wanli 屈萬里 has pointed out, this explanation is elaborated in the commentary to chapter 34: "The sage teaches and leads with his body, unspeaking he transforms the myriad things and repairs the government" (*Zhongyang yanjiuyuan lishi yuyan yanjiusuo jikan* 中央研究院歷史語言研究所集刊 51, no. 4 (Dec. 1980): 749–796, 759.

38. Chapter 7, cf. Lau, trans., *Tao Te Ching*, 63. Some form of a contradiction of action is present in chapters 2, 4, 15, 22, 26, 27, 47, and 73.

39. *Huainanzi* 7, *Zhuzi jicheng* edition, 201. Note that Gongyi Xiu's taste for fish is paramount, and does not admit of competing goods. This is in contrast to Mencius's taste for fish, a metaphor for his desire for life, which must be balanced with his taste for bear paws, a metaphor for his desire to be righteous (*Mengzi* 孟子 6A10 in the traditional numbering, see D. C. Lau, trans., *Mencius* [Harmondsworth: Penguin, 1970], 166). Gongyi Xiu pointedly does not consider whether a Chancellor *should* accept fish, but only how to best satisfy his taste for fish.

40. *Laozi Daodejing sijuan*, 7:4a.

41. *Laozi Xiang'er zhu xiaojian*, 10.

42. *Daode baozhang* 道德寶章, *Wuqiu beizhai* edition, 4b.

43. Chapter 2, cf. Lau, trans., *Tao Te Ching*, 58. See chapter 43 for a similar phrase.

44. Chapter 64, cf. Lau, trans., *Tao Te Ching*, 126.

45. Chapter 14, cf. Lau, trans., *Tao Te Ching*, 70.

46. *Laozi Daodejing sijuan*, 14a. Cf. Chen Guying's 陳鼓應 modern rendering "those who possess the Dao study what others do not," *Laozi zhuyi ji pingjie* 老子註譯及評介 (Beijing: Zhonghua shuju, 1993), 310, n. 5.

47. *Wang Bi ji jiaoshi* 王弼集校釋 (Beijing: Zhonghua, 1980), 164.

48. *Daode zhenjing zhushu* 道德真經注疏, *Wuqiu beizhai* edition, 6.19a. "Radiance" here may be thought of as reflected light, and the mind's "doing" as consisting of passive reflection.

49. *Daode zhenjing zhushu*, 6.24b. For the *Scripture of Western Ascension*, see Livia Kohn, *Taoist Mystical Philosophy* (Albany: State University of New York Press, 1991).

50. *Daode baozhang*, 12b. Gu Huan uses a similar metaphor, but reads *buxing* 不行 to refer to the mind, making it an "unmoved mind" which reflects like a mindless mirror. See *Daode zhenjing zhushu*, 5.5b–6a. Ge, a Song Daoist writer and hermit, is quoting the late seventh-century monk Shenxiu 神秀. See Philip B. Yampolsky, *The Platform Sutra of the Sixth Patriarch* (New York: Columbia University Press, 1967), 130.

51. *Su Che Laozi Daodejing pingzhu* 蘇徹老子道德經評註, *Wuqiu beizhai* edition, 1:20b.

52. *Su Che Laozi Daodejing pingzhu*, 2:28b.

53. Herbert Giles, *Religions of Ancient China* (Singapore: Graham Brash, 1989), 41.

54. Wayne Proudfoot, *Religious Experience* (Berkeley: University of California Press, 1985), 127. Proudfoot is often grouped with Katz among the constructivists, but Proudfoot's position differs from Katz in ways that are important to this analysis (e.g., 244, n. 4).

55. Proudfoot, *Religious Experience*, 131.

56. The relationship of *Dao* to *shu* is explored in Mark Csikszentmihalyi, "Jia Yi's 'Techniques of the *Dao*' and the Han Confucian Appropriation of Technical Discourse," forthcoming in *Asia Major* 10 (1997).

57. Sima Qian, *Shiji* (Beijing: Zhonghua, 1959), 130:3289.

The *Laozi* in the Context of Early Daoist Mystical Praxis

Harold D. Roth

To know others is to be clever
To know oneself is to be clear . . . (*Laozi* 33)

Introduction

One of the few areas of agreement between sinologists and scholars of Comparative Religion is in regarding the *Laozi* as an important work of mysticism. Scholars from Wing-Tsit Chan to Benjamin Schwartz in the former group and from Walter Stace to Wayne Proudfoot in the latter group share this common understanding of the text as they make use of it in a wide variety of intellectual endeavors.[1] While this is by no means a unanimous view (see the contrary opinions of D. C. Lau and Chad Hansen), it is certainly held by a great many scholars.[2] Despite this surprising unanimity, when one examines the views of these scholars more closely, there is an equally surprising lack of a comprehensive discussion of why they regard the *Laozi* as a mystical text in the first place.

Some scholars simply use the term "mysticism" uncritically, as in Chan's accurate but overly general observation that the *Laozi* is a "combination of poetry, philosophical speculation, and mystical reflection."[3] Others use passages from the *Laozi* to illustrate their general theories about mysticism. For example, Stace uses chapters 4 and 14 in his discussion of the epistemology of mystical experience to illustrate an important characteristic of the "objective referent" of mystical experience, namely that it is paradoxically spoken of as a "vacuum-plenum."[4] Proudfoot uses chapter 1 of the *Laozi* to illustrate how the supposed ineffability of mystical experience is really a characteristic of grammatical rules embedded in religious doctrine.[5]

Two fuller approaches are found in the writings of Livia Kohn and Benjamin Schwartz. In her pioneering study of Daoist mysticism, Kohn correctly accepts the assumption that the mystical philosophy of the *Laozi* and *Zhuangzi* is derived directly from the experience of practicing mystics and she usefully defines such philosophy as ". . . the theoretical, conceptual description of the mystical worldview . . . the intellectual framework that provides an explanation and systematic interpretation of increasingly sophisticated spiritual experiences."[6] She founders, however, in a largely unsuccessful attempt to integrate several contradictory approaches in mysticism theory to forge her own definition. Furthermore, her discussion of the mysticism of the *Laozi* is simply an analysis of its philosophy with no specific attempt to demonstrate how this philosophy is mystical, according to her definitions.[7]

While hardly a thorough textual analysis, Schwartz provides a more sustained attempt to demonstrate the presence of mystical philosophy in the *Laozi*.[8] Arguing from a cross-cultural foundation that is rare among sinologists, Schwartz sees mystical philosophy in the *Laozi*'s cosmology of the paradoxically determinate and indeterminate *Dao*, the source of meaning for all human beings that can only be known through the "higher direct knowledge" of gnosis. However, in an effort to deflate arguments asserting the non-mystical nature of the *Laozi* based upon the absence of specific techniques for attaining mystical experience in the text, Schwartz downplays the importance of such techniques and emphasizes, instead, the vision of reality with which they are associated. In my opinion, he does not need to take such an approach.

What I will attempt to demonstrate in the following article is that mystical praxis is at the very heart of the *Laozi*. While, of course, it is not present in all its chapters, there is sufficient textual evidence for both mystical praxis and its resultant mystical experience in the work to provide a firm basis for any future scholars who wish to pursue the demonstration of how these two closely related aspects of mysticism are the foundations of the mystical philosophy of the text. Prior scholarship has not noted the extent of such textual evidence because the *Laozi* has been largely regarded as a work of philosophy produced by a school of philosophy. In order to counter this prevailing view, I will first summarize my recent research on the historical and religious context from which the *Laozi* emerged. I will next present the elements of mysticism theory that I have found most valuable in developing definitions of early Daoist mysticism. I will then proceed to a study of the passages on mystical praxis and mystical experience in the *Laozi* in which I will attempt to explain their meaning and significance by comparing them with parallel passages in a number of other important textual sources of early Daoist mysticism.

Historical Context

In contrast to the traditional view, I do not regard the *Laozi* and *Zhuangzi* as the sole foundational texts of Daoism. Nor do I think there was a "LaoZhuang" school of Daoist thought until its retrospective establishment by the Profound Learning (*xuanxue* 玄學) literati of the third century C.E. Indeed, I have grave doubts that any of Sima Tan's so-translated "schools of philosophy" were "schools," as we might think of today, with a clear self-identity and a well-defined organization and curriculum, much less schools whose principal *raison d'être* was philosophical speculation.[9]

Rather, my research has suggested that, particularly in the case of Daoism, the foundational texts of the tradition were produced within one or more closely related master-disciple lineages whose principal focus was on learning and practicing specific techniques (*shu*).[10] Indeed, these techniques are so central to the tradition that from a very early period, that of the "inner chapters" of the *Zhuangzi* (ca. 300 B.C.E.), they are referred to as the "techniques of the Way" (*Daoshu* 道術).[11] While these eventually came to include methods of political and social organization and a variety of investigations of the natural world (and their associated *yinyang* and Five Phase theories), the single most important technique was of guiding and refining the flow of vital energy or vital breath (*qi*) within the human organism.[12] This seems to have been accomplished in two possibly complementary ways, the first a kind of active or moving meditation whose postures resembled modern positions in *taiji* and *qigong,* and the second a kind of still, sitting meditation that involved regularized natural breathing.[13] It is this second form, which entails the apophatic practice of removing the normal contents of the mind to produce a profound tranquility with a decisively noetic character, that I have called "inner cultivation."[14]

According to this view, the texts we have come to regard as the foundations of Daoist philosophy are not filled with abstract metaphysical speculation that has no basis in nondiscursive experience, but are, rather, works written to elucidate the insight attained from inner cultivation practices and to discuss their practical benefits. This latter aspect would have been particularly critical in late Warring States China in order to persuade local kings of the value of adapting the teachings being advocated and thereby winning their favor and a position within the court from which to continue these pursuits. We have some historical certainty that such conditions did exist, for example, at such disparate courts as those of the states of Qi (ca. 320–260 B.C.E.), Qin (ca. 241 B.C.E.), and, later, the Han state of Huainan (ca. 150–122 B.C.E.). Each court produced a book containing collections of teachings from a variety of Daoist and not-Daoist lineages: the *Guanzi,* the *Lüshi chunqiu,* and the *Huainanzi,* respectively, which are all important sources for early Daoist thought.

Therefore, it is my contention that the *Laozi* can best be understood by placing it—as much as we possibly can, given the limits of the extant textual corpus—within its historical context. Perhaps the most ambitious attempt to do this until now is the work of Michael LaFargue in his innovatve application of the Biblical Studies methodologies of form and redaction criticism to the *Laozi.*[15] While LaFargue's work is not without its problems, it has developed some important hypotheses about the nature of the text and its origins. One of the most important (and one that I currently share) is that the *Laozi* is the product of a group or community whose foundation was first and foremost a shared practice of "self-cultivation." According to LaFargue, it is from this practice that many of the more "mystical" passages in the text arose, sayings that I shall be examining in the present essay.

The attempt to apply these "mystical" teachings to the problems of governing in late Warring States China constitutes an important element of the *Laozi.* The particular form of political thought it advocates helps to define one of the three principal phases of early

Daoism (the "Primitivist" as opposed to the "Individualist" and the "Syncretist") I have identified in previous publications.[16] However, in this essay I will focus not on the distinctive political philosophy of the *Laozi* but rather on the evidence it contains for this community's practice of inner cultivation and how it relates to similar evidence in the other early textual sources of Daoism. Most relevant among these sources is the essay entitled "Inward Training" ("Neiye") from the *Guanzi*. I will also place the *Laozi*'s evidence for inner cultivation in the context of evidence for analogous apophatic practices and results in the other early Daoist textual sources mentioned above.

Theoretical Context: Mysticism, Meditation, and the Laozi

Seeing the *Laozi* as the product of a lineage involved in apophatic practices of directed breathing meditation enables us to put the text directly into dialogue with similar practices in other cultures and traditions and with modern Western scholarship on the philosophical and psychological implications of such practices. In the following section I will define those elements of mysticism theory that I think are most relevant to the study of the *Laozi* and show how they are related to one another.[17]

The cross-cultural study of "mysticism" is very much a modern Western phenomenon that began with the publication of William James's *Varieties of Religious Experience* in 1902.[18] This work presents a phenomenology of religious experiences and identifies the subset of mystical experiences as being: 1. ineffable; 2. noetic; 3. transient; 4. passive; and 5. transformational.[19] Following the lead of James, scholars from Evelyn Underhill to Robert Forman have pursued the study of mysticism along the following two lines, clearly adumbrated by Peter Moore:

> The philosophical analysis of mysticism comprises two overlapping lines of inquiry: on the one hand the identification and classification of the phenomenological characteristics of mystical experience, and on the other the investigation of the epistemological and ontological status of this experience. The first line of inquiry is generally focused on the question whether the mystical experiences reported in different cultures and religious traditions are basically of the same type or whether there are significantly different types. The second line of inquiry

centres on the question whether mystical experiences are purely subjective phenomena or whether they have the kind of objective validity and metaphysical significance that mystics and others claim for them . . .[20]

In other words, the former line deals with the nature and characteristics of mystical experience and the latter deals with the various philosophical claims that are made on the basis of mystical experience. These overlapping lines of inquiry indicate that two fundamental aspects of mysticism are mystical experience and the mystical philosophy that is derived from it.

Walter Stace delineates two fundamental forms of mystical experience, "extrovertive" and "introvertive."[21] Extrovertive looks outward through the senses of the individual and sees a fundamental unity between this individual and the world. In this form there is a simultaneous perception of the one and the many, unity and multiplicity. Introvertive mystical experience looks inward and is exclusively an experience of unity, that is, an experience of unitive or what some scholars (Forman et al.) call "pure" or object-less consciousness.[22] I have found this basic differentiation to be extremely useful and see it in early Daoism in what I call the "bimodal" character of its mystical experience, a concept that I will explain further below.[23]

For Stace, mystical philosophy takes its most fundamental concepts from mystical experience. First and foremost are the varying notions of "the One" in different religious traditions that are ultimately derived from the introvertive mystical experience of complete union. Brahman for Hindu mystics, God for Christian mystics, the One for Plotinus, the *Dao* for the Daoists, the unconditioned for Hinayana Buddhists, these are all philosophical expressions of the "universal self" that is derived from this unitive experience.[24] While scholars may wish to debate whether these concepts are derivative of mystical union or cause this experience, the fact remains that there is a very intimate connection between these two aspects of mysticism.[25]

Peter Moore argues that a particularly crucial element of mysticism is the intimate connection between mystical experiences and what he calls "mystical techniques," the practices that are used to "induce" them.[26] He distinguishes between two primary techniques that represent the "immediate preconditions" for mystical experience, "meditation" and "contemplation." The former entails "the disciplined but creative application of the imagination and discursive thought to an often complex religious theme or subject-matter." The latter, a development of the former, entails the attempt "to transcend the activities of the imagination and intellect through an intuitive concentration on some simple object, image, or idea."[27] It seems to me that focusing on one's breathing in a systematic fashion would be an example of the latter. While this differentiation is instructive, because of the relatively poor state of our knowledge of the specifics of early Daoist mystical techniques—in particular how the imagination and intellect are used in them—and because of the use of the former term in common parlance, I have used—and will continue to use—"meditation" to refer broadly to both these techniques.

Mystical techniques are further clarified in the writings of Robert Forman and Donald Rothberg. Forman, following the phenomenological tradition of James and Stace, argues that the "Pure Consciousness Event (PCE)" (defined as a wakeful though contentless [nonintentional] consciousness)—his version of the latter's introvertive mystical experience—comes about through a systematic process of "forgetting."[28] This is elaborated upon by Rothberg:

> Robert Forman . . . has proposed a model of mystical development (in many traditions) as involving the "forgetting" (Meister Eckhardt's term) of the major cognitive and affective structures of experience. . . . In this process of "forgetting," there is an intentional dropping of desires, ideas, conceptual forms (including those of one's tradition), sensations, imagery, and so on. The end of this process is a contentless mystical experience in which the constructs of the tradition are transcended . . .[29]

Citing the twelve-year research project on meditative praxis in three Indo-Tibetan traditions by the psychologist Daniel Brown, Rothberg argues that the spiritual path involves, in many traditions, "a process of progressive deconstruction of the structures of experience."[30] These include, for Brown, attitudes and behavioral schemes, thinking, gross perception, self-system, and "time-space matrix."[31] This is not to argue that the spiritual path is the same in every tradition. Indeed, as Rothberg argues, "each path of decon-struction or deconditioning is itself constructed or conditioned in a certain way."[32] Nor do he and Forman argue that pure consciousness is the only goal of all mystic paths. Indeed, the entire Forman collection intentionally passes over the important extrovertive aspect of mystical experience, unfairly denigrated by Stace, and, I would argue, extremely important to the understanding of early Daoist mysticism.[33]

In a recent review essay I argued for the presence of a "bimodal" mystical experience in early Daoism, particularly evident in the "inner chapters" of the *Zhuangzi*.[34] The first mode is an introvertive unitive consciousness in which the adept achieves complete union with the *Dao*. This corresponds, in general, with Stace's "introver-tive mystical experience" and with Forman's "Pure Consciousness Event." The second is an extrovertive transformed consciousness in which the adept returns to the world and retains, amidst the flow of daily life, a profound sense of the unity previously experienced in the introvertive mode. This experience entails an ability to live in the world free from the limited and biased perspective of the indi-vidual ego. This second mode corresponds, in general, to Stace's "extrovertive mystical experience," although I would regard it as a quite profound subcategory of it.[35] This bimodal character of mysti-cal experience is, actually, quite prevalent in mystical experience across traditions, but it is often overlooked by scholars, who tend to focus on the introvertive mode exclusively.[36] While evidence for its presence is not as strong in the *Laozi* as in the *Zhuangzi*, it is, as we shall see, most certainly there.

Finally, in the philosophical analysis of mysticism there is also a great deal of attention paid to mystical language, and herein I will be concerned with one particular subset of it, the unique language that evolves within mystical praxis. Brown witnessed this in his study of Tibetan monastic communities where there was a body of teachings about the internal states attained through mysti-cal praxis to which an adept could compare his/her experience. He goes on:

> In such traditions, where meditation practice is socially orga-nized, a technical language for meditation experience evolved. This language was refined over generations. The technical terms do not have external referents, e.g., "house," but refer to replicable internal states which can be identified by anyone

doing the same practice, e.g., "energy currents," or "seed medi-
tations." Much like the specialized languages of math, chemis-
try, or physics, technical meditation language is usually
intelligible only to those specialized audiences of yogis familiar
with the experiences in question . . .[37]

LaFargue sees this kind of language present in the *Laozi*, and I
concur.[38] I would also extend this to the other textual sources of
early Daoism including, most importantly, "Inward Training." The
great challenge facing modern scholars who wish to study this
specialized mystical language is to make sense of what it really
meant to the people who used it. While this is not as much a problem
when technical terms are primarily descriptive, as for example, in
Zhuangzi's famous prescription for how to just "sit and forget," the
more metaphorical the language becomes (see later in the same
sentence, "I . . . merge with the universal thoroughfare") the more
challenging it is to interpret.[39] In the following article I will attempt
to explain the meaning of some of the important technical terms and
phrases of mystical praxis in the *Laozi* through extensive cross-
referencing to other early Daoist works and through cross-cultural
comparisons to mystical techniques in other traditions. I see this
attempt as a plausible reconstruction, but certainly not the only one
possible.

Using the above definitions of the various aspects of mysticism,
I will concentrate on presenting and analyzing the textual evidence
for mystical techniques and their resultant mystical experiences in
the *Laozi* under the general heading of "mystical praxis." In doing
this I will make extensive use of relevant passages from the other
important works that I have identified in my research on the historical context of early Daoism. Due to the practical limitations of the
present article, I will not make anything more than general assertions about the relationship of mystical experience to mystical philosophy in the *Laozi* and will leave a more detailed study for another
time.

Mystical Praxis in the *Laozi*

Mysticism and Meditation in Early Daoism

Perhaps the most direct passage on mystical praxis in the *Laozi* is
chapter 10:

Amidst the daily activity of the psyche, can you embrace
the One and not depart from it?
When concentrating your vital breath until it is at its
softest, can you be like a child?
Can you sweep clean your Profound Mirror so you are
able to have no flaws in it?
In loving the people and governing the state, can you do it
without using knowledge?
When the Gates of Heaven open and close, can you
become feminine?
In clarifying all within the four directions, can you do it
without using knowledge?[40]

Because this passage contains the kind of technical language
of meditation that Brown found in his Tibetan communities and
LaFargue sees in the *Laozi*, it has caused scholars great difficulty.
Lau sees "some sort of breathing exercise or perhaps even yogic
practice" here, but considers it an atypical passage that could have
come from a school interested in the prolongation of life, not the
avoidance of untimely death that characterizes the *Laozi*.[41] Chan
rejects the entire claim that breathing meditation is involved here:
"The concentration of *qi* (vital force, breath) is not yoga, as Waley
thinks it is. Yoga aims at transcending the self and the external
environment. Nothing of the sort is intended here."[42] Their failure to
understand the passage has a twofold origin: failure to understand
the larger context of early Daoist mystical praxis and the *Laozi*
passages that contain evidence of it and failure to understand the
nature of mysticism. After examining mystical praxis in the *Laozi* in
the light of these two critical understandings, I shall return to an
analysis of this passage.

A familiar place to begin discussing the greater context of early
Daoist mystical praxis is with the *Zhuangzi* passage on "sitting and
forgetting." Herein Confucius's favorite disciple Yan Hui ironically
"turns the tables" on his master by teaching *him* how to "sit and
forget" (*zuowang* 坐忘):

(Confucius:) What do you mean, just sit and forget?
(Yan Hui:) I let organs and members drop away, dismiss eyesight and hearing, part from the body and expel knowledge,
and merge with the universal thoroughfare. This is what I
mean by "just sit and forget."[43]

To let "organs and members drop away" (*duo zhi ti* 墮肢體) means to lose visceral awareness of the emotions and desires, which, for the early Daoists, have "physiological" bases in the various organs.[44] To "dismiss eyesight and hearing" (*chu cong ming* 黜聰明) means to deliberately cut off sense perception. To "part from the body and expel knowledge" (*lixing quzhi* 離形去知) means to lose bodily awareness and remove all thoughts from consciousness. To "merge with the universal thoroughfare" (*tong yu datong* 同於大通) seems to imply that, as a result of these practices, Yan Hui has become united with the *Dao*.[45]

The *locus classicus* for these apophatic practices is the "Inward Training" essay from the *Guanzi*, which I date to the second half of the fourth century B.C.E. Herein such practices are metaphorically referred to as "cleaning out the abode of the numinous mind" (*shen* 神). The numinous mind refers to an elusive and profound level of awareness that comes and goes within consciousness. It has its own unique physiological substrate, its "vital essence" (*jing* 精) and its presence confers a psychological clarity and centeredness.[46] Elsewhere in the text, these apophatic practices are linked to a guided breathing meditation that involves sitting with the body erect and the limbs squared and stable and refining the vital breath (*qi*).[47] It is through the refinement of the vital breath that emotions and desires are stilled, sense perception is restricted, the attention is unified and the mind is concentrated, and experiences of increased tranquility are produced through which one gradually reaches the deepest levels wherein the Way is attained.[48] This breathing practice is spoken of metaphorically in the following passage:

> For all to practice this Way:
> You must coil, you must contract,
> You must uncoil, you must expand,
> You must be firm, you must be regular in this practice.
> Maintain this excellent practice; do not let go of it.
> Chase away excessive perception;
> Abandon trivial thoughts.
> And when you reach the ultimate limit (*ji* 極)
> You will return to the Way and its Inner Power (*de*).[49]

In this passage, I interpret coiling/contracting to refer to the activity of exhalation in the breathing cycle and uncoiling/expanding to refer to the activity of inhalation. It is also important to note here the occurrence of the foundational pairing of the Way and its Inner Power (*Dao* and *de*). In this fourth-century B.C. text, its use predates all extant recensions of the *Laozi* and suggests that "Inward Training" may very well be closely connected to it. It also demonstrates a concrete link between the apophatic breathing practice of "Inward Training" and the attainment of a profound level of experience at which one is in touch with the Way and its Inner Power.

This general type of apophatic prescription and result is also found elsewhere in the "inner" *Zhuangzi*[50] and in other textual sources for early Daoism, including the Daoist essays of the *Lüshi chunqiu*, later chapters of the *Zhuangzi*, the inner cultivation essays of the *Guanzi*, and the *Huainanzi*, as I have discussed in a recent article (see the Appendix for a summary table).[51] Therein I identified a rhetorical structure of mystical praxis in early Daoism that has the following tripartite structure:

1. *Preamble* in which a variety of apophatic practices are listed that prepare the adept for the later stages of meditative experience. Typically, these feature various prescriptions for removing the normal contents of the mind: sense perception, desire, the emotions, knowledge and scheming, wisdom and precedent.

2. A *Sorites*-style argument (if x then y, if y, then z . . .) in which consecutive stages of meditative experience are presented. These include alignment of the body and breathing (*zheng* 正), tranquility (*jing* 靜), equanimity (*ping* 平 or *jun* 均), being unadorned (*su* 素), being concentrated or purified (*jing* 精), being clear or lucid (*ming* 明), having a numinous awareness (*shen* 神), and, finally, attaining the One or the empty Way, (*deyi* 得一, *de xu Dao* 得虛道) or becoming completely empty (*xu* 虛). These practices in the preamble and their results in the sorites section correspond, in general, with the basic deconstructive processes and results of mystical praxis that are enumerated by Brown.[52]

3. A *Dénouement* in which the practical benefits of the first two parts are enumerated. These include instantaneous accurate cognition (*jian zhi bu huo* 見知不惑), spontaneous responsiveness to things (*ying wu bianhua* 應物便化), being able to return to the Unhewn (*gui yu pu* 歸於樸), having perception in which nothing is unperceived (*shi wu bu jian* 視無不見), and taking no action and yet leaving nothing undone (*wuwei er wu buwei* 無為而無不為).

Examining this rhetorical structure from the standpoint of mysticism theory, we can see that the first part corresponds with the concept of mystical techniques, the second part with that of introvertive mystical experience, and the third part with that of extrovertive mystical experience, or, at least, with a discussion of the unique mode of cognition and action associated with it. I will make use of these three related categories to guide my analysis of mystical praxis in the *Laozi*.

Mystical Techniques in the *Laozi*

The discussion of mystical techniques in the *Laozi* should begin with the second line of chapter 10, which talks of refining the vital breath and parallels material in "Inward Training," but I will postpone analysis of this line until the end of the article when I can do a comprehensive analysis of the whole passage.

The first aspect of apophatic practice in early Daoism that is usually presented in our sources is to reduce to a minimum or entirely eliminate sense perception. We have evidence of such a practice and advice related to it in several passages in the *Laozi*. In chapter 52 we read:

> Block your openings
> Shut your doors,
> And to the end of your life you will not run dry.
> Unblock your openings,
> Increase your striving,
> And to the end of your life you will never get what you
>   seek . . .

This is echoed in chapter 56:

> Block your openings,
> Shut your doors.
> Blunt your sharpness,
> Untangle your knots.
> Blend into your brightness,
> Merge with your dust.
> This is called the "profound merging."

Therefore,
You can neither get close to it nor stay away from it.
You can neither help it nor harm it.
You can neither honor it nor debase it.
Therefore it is honored by all under Heaven.

The openings and doors refer to the sense apertures.[53] Both passages suggest the beneficial effects of the limitation or removal of sense perception.[54] Chapter 56 moves beyond sense perception and makes a broader reference to other aspects of apophatic practice. I take "blunting sharpness" to refer to setting aside clearcut perceptual and conceptual categories and "untangling knots" to refer to removing attachments to various aspects of the self. The next two lines speak metaphorically of merging with two contrasting qualities, darkness and light, which are perhaps symbolic of the emotional moods of the self.

Overall, this process is called "profound merging" (*xuantong* 玄同), another challenging technical metaphor used by the *Laozi* authors. The use of the term "profound," which is a characteristic of the Way in chapter 1, seems to suggest that this process leads to a merging or union with the Way itself, a foundational introvertive mystical experience that I will discuss further in the next section. This interpretation is further supported by the phrase "merge with the Universal Thoroughfare" (*tong yu datong*) from the sitting and forgetting passage in *Zhuangzi*. The conclusion to *Laozi* 56 provides more evidence for such an interpretation. It suggests "profound merging" is something that cannot be approached through dualistic categories or activities, but only through their removal. This is why it is valued by all under Heaven.

Chapter 12 also makes reference to limiting the sense desires and gives an explanation of why this is needed:

The five colors blind one's eyes;
The five notes deafen one's ears;
The five flavors damage the palate;
Galloping on horseback and hunting madden the mind;
Hard to obtain goods hinder one's progress.
For this reason, the sage is for the belly, not for the eye.
Therefore he discards that and takes up this.

The activities of the senses, riding and hunting, and the pursuit of material goods all seem to reinforce attachment to the individual self and also prevent it from being centered. They must be set aside if one is to make any kind of progress in inner cultivation. In this context, being "for the belly, not for the eye" would seem to refer to restricting sense perception by focusing on the regular circulation of the breath, which is centered in the belly. This is a well-known meditative technique in many traditions.[55] According to Brown, with "sense-withdrawl," the meditator "learns to disengage from external reality and the impact of sense objects so as to bring awareness carefully to bear on the stream of consciousness."[56] As a result, an increasing inner concentration develops. Furthermore, the belly is the location of the famous lower "cinnabar field" (*dantian* 丹田), so central in later Daoist meditation as the place where the One resides, the vital essence accumulates, and where the practitioner must focus attention in order to eliminate desires and emotions.[57] While anachronistic for our purposes, this theory could have emerged from such early breathing practices.

A further rationale for restricting sense perception comes from the theories of the inner cultivation tradition. As already mentioned, in these sources the vital essence (*jing*) is associated with tranquility and with the numinous mind as their "physiological" substrate. It is also a source of health and vitality in the human organism. It is therefore extremely important not to waste this vital essence. However, it is normally consumed during the everyday activities of sense perception, which are enhanced by its presence. As the *Huainanzi* says:

> When the vital essence flows into the eyes then vision is
>   clear.
> When it resides in the ears then hearing is acute.
> When it rests in the mouth then speech is appropriate.
> When it is collected in the mind then thinking comprehends.
> Therefore if you block these four gateways
> Then one's person will suffer no calamities.
> The hundred joints will not be sickly,
> Will not die, will not be born,
> Will not be empty, will not be full.
> We call (those who can do) this "the Genuine" (*zhenren*
>   真人).[58]

If one can retain the vital essence, one can also retain the inner tranquility and numinous mind with which it occurs. This is a further reason to restrict sense perception.

To this point we have seen references to the removal of sense perceptions, desires, emotions, attachment to selfish concerns, and conceptual categories in the *Laozi*. There are further references to the removal of various aspects of thought. First, we have the famous prescription in chapter 19: "Eliminate sageliness, discard knowledge, and the people will benefit a hundred fold." This is similar to such phrases as to "cast off wisdom and precedent" (*qu zhi yu gu* 去智與故), which is commonly found in inner cultivation sources.[59] This chapter ends in the three appended statements:

> Manifest the Unadorned and embrace the Unhewn.
> Reduce self-interest and lessen desires.
> Eliminate learning and have no worries.[60]

This passage restates the need to move past self-interest, desire, and learning, which, as we have seen above, is inherent to early Daoist apophatic practice. The latter connects with the famous passage in chapter 48 about losing accumulated learning in order to cultivate the Way. We also find here two technical terms, the "Unadorned" (*su*) and the "Unhewn" (*pu*), which seem to refer to states of mind that would have been well understood in the community of inner cultivation practitioners that produced the *Laozi*. Our analysis of these terms takes us into the next section on mystical praxis in the *Laozi*.

Introvertive Mystical Experience in the Laozi: The Profound Merging

In the context of mystical praxis that I have been developing, I would argue that both the Unadorned and the Unhewn refer to states of mind that arise from apophatic practice. In *Laozi* 19, the Unadorned is associated with selflessness. In the "*HuangLao boshu* 黃老帛書" it refers to a meditative state that arises after tranquility and equanimity and precedes the refined state of inner concentration that is linked to the vital essence (see Appendix). In

Laozi 19, the Unhewn is linked with having few desires. In chapter 28 the Unhewn appears as an undifferentiated state attained through being like a valley and developing constant Inner Power (*de*). In chapter 37 it is referred to as "nameless" and free from desire, and it is said that this desireless state is brought about through tranquility. As technical terms of meditation, it is difficult to know for certain what their meanings are. However, what we can say is that both arise from the cultivation of tranquility and stand in the spectrum of stages of introvertive meditation bounded by two other important technical terms in the *Laozi*, tranquility (*jing*) and emptiness (*xu*). Chapter 16 presents them both:

> Complete emptiness is the ultimate limit (*ji*).
> Maintaining tranquility is the central (practice).
>
> The myriad things arise side-by-side
> And by this I contemplate their return.
> Heaven makes things in great numbers.
> Each one returns to its root.
> This is called "tranquility."
> Tranquility: this means returning to the inevitable
>   (*ming* 命).
> To return to the inevitable is a constant.
> To know this constant is to be lucid.
> Not to know this constant is to be confused.
> If you are confused you will create misfortune.
>
> To know this constant is to be detached.
> To be detached is to be impartial.
> To be impartial is to be kingly.
> To be kingly is to be with Heaven.
> To be with Heaven is to be with the Way.
> If you are with the Way, to the end of your days you will
>   suffer no peril.[61]

The statement that "complete emptiness is the ultimate limit" fits well with the fact that emptiness appears as the penultimate meditative state in several of our early Daoist sources, as can be seen in the Appendix. So, too, does the emphasis on maintaining tranquility, which develops directly from apophatic practice at an earlier level, just following the alignment of the body and breathing.

These two terms frame a series of meditative stages in early Daoist praxis that include the Unadorned and the Unhewn. Given its nameless, desireless, and undifferentiated characteristics (all adjectives applied also to the Way), the latter term seems to refer to the unitive consciousness attained by merging with the Way.

As for the remainder of this chapter, whereas many commentators—starting with Wang Bi—see this as referring to the production of the things of the phenomenal world, in the context of the opening lines on emptiness and tranquility, I would argue that it is a phenomenological description of how one observes the arising and passing away of the contents of consciousness during guided breathing meditation. Accordingly, the myriad thoughts, emotions, and perceptions are metaphorically spoken of as the things that Heaven makes. Just as inevitably as these things arise while one is sitting in meditation, they pass away and out of consciousness. As one deepens this practice, when all these contents disappear and no longer recur, one returns to a condition of tranquility. This proceeds through a series of stages of increasing profundity until one reaches an ultimate level at which one is utterly empty.

If one knows about this inevitable process, one will realize that the variegated contents of the stream of consciousness are transient, and one can become detached from them. This lack of attachment confers the ability to be impartial in everyday interactions, as even the opinions and preferences of the individual self are also seen to be transient. This impartiality is the human counterpart of the dispassionate objectivity of Heaven, which "treats the myriad things as straw dogs" (chapter 5), and an important aspect of the desireless Way (chapter 37). It is a quality of mind the *Laozi* authors see as critical to cultivate in the ruler and I will have more to say about it in the following section on extrovertive mystical experience. Following the apophatic practice of the *Laozi* authors will produce it.

Chapter 16 also appears to be connected to the coiling and uncoiling passage from "Inward Training" through the concepts of reaching the ultimate limit (*ji*) of apophatic practice and returning to the Way found in both. The coiling and uncoiling of breathing meditation yield a profound tranquility which, at its ultimate level, results in complete emptiness. In complete emptiness, one returns to the Way. Moreover, as we have seen, the attainment of, first, tranquility, and then emptiness through apophatic practice is found in the *Lüshi chunqiu* 25, *Zhuangzi* 23, and *Guanzi* "Techniques of the Mind I" ("*Xinshu, shang*" 心術上) meditation passages summarized in the table in the Appendix. Indeed, in the last passage, the ultimate result is "to attain the empty Way" (*de xu Dao*). Finally, in *Zhuangzi's* "fasting of the mind" passage, the attainment of emptiness through apophatic practice leads directly to merging with the Way: "It is only that the Way coalesces in emptiness. Emptiness is the fasting of the mind."[62] All these passages provide a fuller context from which to interpret *Laozi* 16.

The cultivation of this state of emptiness is highly prized by the authors of the *Laozi*. This valuation results in some of the most famous images of the text: the nothingness at the hub of the wheel, inside the clay vessel, and within the empty room in chapter 11; the empty Way that use cannot drain in chapter 4 (*chong* 沖; not *xu* 虛 repeated in chapter 35, where its emptiness is implied by the recurrence of this non-draining metaphor and in chapter 45 where the Way is implied by the emptiness and non-draining metaphor from chapter 4); the empty space between Heaven and Earth that is never exhausted in chapter 5; the spirit of the empty valley that use will never drain in chapter 6, the empty ravine and valley in chapter 28 and the expansive valley in chapter 15; and, the blank mind of the fool in chapter 20.

Furthermore, tranquility, the "central practice" and the root to which all things inevitably return from chapter 16, is repeatedly emphasized in the text. The prescription to hold fast to the center (*shouzhong* 守中) in chapter 5 seems to refer to this "central practice" (*zhong* 中) of tranquility (chapter 16). In chapter 37 we read that "if one ceases to desire by being tranquil, all under Heaven will settle of its own accord." Chapter 45 states that "if one is clear and tranquil, one can set all under Heaven aright." Chapter 61 states that the feminine overcomes the masculine through tranquility. Both emptiness and tranquility are central to the metaphorical description of the ancient skilled practitioners of the Way in chapter 15:

The ancients who excelled at manifesting the Way:
Were subtle and marvelous, profound and penetrating,
So deep they could not be conceived of.
It is only because they could not be conceived of that if I
were forced to describe them I would say they were:

> Tentative, as if fording a stream in winter.
> Hesitant, as if in fear of being surrounded.
> Solemn, as if someone's guest.
> Melting, like thawing ice.
> Undifferentiated, like the Unhewn.
> Murky, like muddy water.
> Vast, like a valley.
>
> When muddy water is made tranquil, it gradually becomes
>   clear.
> When the calm is made active, it gradually springs to life.
> Those who maintain this Way do not wish to become full.
> It is only because they do not wish to become full that they
>   can wear out yet be complete.[63]

The apophatic practice of breathing meditation is the process through which the normal contents of the self become emptied out and the murky consciousness gradually becomes clear. Tranquility, the Unadorned, emptiness, the Unhewn, and the "profound merging," all discussed above, are technical terms that refer to various stages in the process of introvertive meditation leading to the experience of union with the Way. The attainment of the state in which all normal conscious contents are emptied out would certainly qualify as an "introvertive mystical experience" for Stace and a "Pure Consciousness Event" for Forman. Yet, for the *Laozi* authors, as we begin to see in chapter 15, when completely calm, one can still return to activity. The sages who do so maintain a clear and empty mind and detachment from the self that present few clearly defined characteristics to others. Hence they can only be described metaphorically. This, then, leads us to our third and final category of mystical praxis in the *Laozi*.

Extrovertive Mystical Experience in the Laozi:
Holding Fast to the One

This detachment from self spoken of in chapter 15 is also mentioned in chapter 7, where the sage's lack of self-interest (*wusi* 無私) parallels that of Heaven and Earth and confers longevity, and in chapter

19, where lack of self-interest is called "manifesting the Unadorned" (*xiansu* 見素). It is an integral part of the *Laozi's* unique expression of extrovertive mystical experience that places a strong emphasis not on some unitive conscious experience, but on the mode of cognition and being in the world that it confers. An excellent place to begin examining it is chapter 48:

> Those who cultivate learning gain something every day.
> Those who cultivate the Way lose something every day.
> They lose and further lose until they arrive at the point of
>   taking no deliberate action.
> They take no deliberate action and yet nothing is left
>   undone . . .

This saying is a succinct summary of apophatic practice, which can be thought of as the systematic loss of thoughts, feelings, perceptions, and eventually, the self. Deliberate action comes from the biased perspective of the individual self. When this perspective is eliminated through apophatic practice, one still acts, but from a different center. While there are no passages that explicitly identify this new center for nondeliberate action, we can identify it through the famous phrase *wuwei er wu buwei*. For not only is this a mode of acting that develops as the result of apophatic practice, it is the mode of acting of the Way. Chapter 37 begins with the sentence: "The Way constantly takes no deliberate action and yet nothing is left undone." Thus the sage, when completely empty, acts precisely as the Way acts. This suggests that the sage has become one with the Way and gives further support for our interpretation of the "profound merging" in chapter 56.

The table of early Daoist meditative stages in the Appendix shows a similar pattern to *Laozi* 48. The *wuwei* phrase—or some variation on it—is the result of apophatic practice in each of the six passages summarized therein. I would argue that this table indicates the presence of the two basic modes of mystical experience, introvertive and extrovertive. The final stage of the introvertive mode is spoken of as becoming empty, but also as both "attaining the One" in *Lüshi chunqiu* "Assessing Others" and "attaining the empty Way" in *Guanzi's* "Techniques of the Mind I." The former suggests the attainment of a unitive consciousness, in other words, Stace's introvertive mystical experience and Forman's "Pure Consciousness Event." The latter suggests that the "object" of this unitive consciousness is the Way, and seems to confirm LaFargue's theory that the concept of the Way developed as the hypostatization of "the quality of mind one is cultivating internally" in the *Laozi*.[64]

The extrovertive mode of mystical experience occurs in the Table as the result of the introvertive. The variations on *wuwei* are modes of selfless experience, experience that is extremely efficacious precisely because it is selfless. It comes from the Way and not the individual self. If this is true, we would expect that there would be some evidence in the *Laozi* of the retaining of some sense of the empty Way experienced at the pinnacle of introvertive mystical experience when one returns to the phenomenal world. I would assert that such evidence is found in the closely related concepts of holding on to (*zhi* 執), maintaining (*bao* 保) or holding fast to (*shou* 守) the Way, and embracing (*bao* 抱) the One.[65]

There are several important prescriptions to "hold on to" or "maintain the Way" in the *Laozi*. In chapter 14 we have the saying:

> Hold on to the Way of the present
> In order to manage the things of the present.
> And to know the ancient beginning.
> This is called the thread running through the Way.[66]

Chapter 15 talks of one who "maintains the Way" being first tranquil and clear, then calm and active. In chapter 32, "holding fast to the Way" results in all things spontaneously submitting to one's rule. In chapter 52, we read of the Way as mother of all things (as in chapters 1 and 25):

> All under Heaven had a beginning
> And we take this to be the mother of all under Heaven.
> If you attain the mother, you will know the children.
> If you know the children, return to hold fast to the mother,
> And to the end of your life you will never see danger.

As in chapter 14, holding fast to the Way (the mother) enables one to know intimately all things that are generated because of it (its children) because the Way continues to be their basis, as well as one's own. Other benefits of being in touch with the Way come about because of the transformed consciousness this confers. Because of it one is able to be selfless and desireless and to take no deliberate action and yet accomplish everything one undertakes.

Further related aspects of these benefits are explored in the other early sources of Daoist inner cultivation theory. Some examples are given in the table. According to the *HuangLao boshu* essay "Assessing," "seeing and knowing are never deluded." In the "Assessing Others" essay of the *Lüshi chunqiu*, after attaining the One, one can "respond to the alterations and transformations of things and return to the Unhewn." In the "Numinous Essence" essay of the *Huainanzi*, "in seeing, nothing is left unseen, in hearing nothing is left unheard, in acting, nothing is left undone." All of these are possible because after the "profound merging" with the Way at the pinnacle of introvertive mystical experience, one retains a sense of this unitive power when one returns to the world of the myriad things. Retaining this experience of unity upon this return is further presented in the "embracing the One" passages in the *Laozi*.

In chapter 22, after a description of the sage as being "bowed down then preserved" that contains further metaphors of self-yielding as opposed to self-asserting, we read:

> Therefore the Sage embraces the One and is a model for
>   all under Heaven.
> He does not show himself, and so is conspicuous.
> He does not consider himself right, and so is illustrious.
> He does not brag and so has merit.
> He does not boast and so endures . . . [67]

This means that sages can be selfless because of being able to embrace the One. Why? Because by retaining a sense of this unitive ground amidst daily life they have an unbiased source for their actions that is not the individual self. For *Zhuangzi* in the "Essay on Seeing Things as Equal" (*Qiwu lun* 齊物論), this non-self-based orientation leads to a complete freedom from attachment to basic conceptual categories, as in the famous "three every morning" story in which the monkey keeper spontaneously adapts his feeding plan to that of the monkeys.[68] For *Zhuangzi*, to "see all things as equal" means to regard them from this unbiased perspective of the One. Therefore, "holding fast to the One" (and its many variants) can justifiably be seen as the central descriptive metaphor in the *Laozi* for its understanding of what, in mysticism theory, is called the extrovertive mystical experience.

Laozi 10 as a Summary of Mystical Praxis

With this understanding of mystical praxis in the *Laozi* we can now return to analyze the critical chapter 10 that discusses "embracing the One" and links it with guided breathing meditation and other aspects of inner cultivation and its application to daily life:

> Amidst the daily activity of the psyche,[69] can you embrace
>   the One and not depart from it?
> When concentrating your vital breath until it is at its
>   softest, can you be like a child?
> Can you sweep clean your Profound Mirror so you are
>   able to have no flaws in it?
> In loving the people and governing the state, can you do it
>   without using knowledge?
> When the Gates of Heaven open and close, can you
>   become feminine?
> In clarifying all within the four directions, can you do it
>   without using knowledge?

This passage is probably the most important evidence for guided breathing meditation in the *Laozi* and it contains three close parallels to "Inward Training." In the first line "embracing the One" is seen as something one adheres to amidst everyday psychological activities. I take this to be talking about retaining the sense of the unitive consciousness experienced in introvertive mystical experience when one returns to the phenomenal world. It is paralleled in "Inward Training" by the concepts of "holding on to the One" (*zhiyi* 執一) amidst the daily transformations of things and the daily alterations of events, thus enabling the sage to "master the myriad things,"[70] and of "holding fast to the One" (*shouyi* 守一) in the following passage:

> When you broaden your mind and relax it,
> Expand your vital breath and extend it,

> And when your physical form is calm and unmoving:
> You can hold fast to the One and discard the myriad
>   vexations.
> You will not be lured by profit,
> Nor will you be frightened by harm.
> Relaxed and unwound, yet acutely sensitive,
> In solitude you delight in your own person.
> This is called "revolving the vital breath:"
> Your thoughts and deeds resemble Heaven's.[71]

This passage implies that "holding fast to the One" is accomplished through guided breathing meditation. It confers a selflessness that prevents being lured by profit or frightened by harm, results similar to those in *Laozi* 22 for the sage who "embraces the One." "Inward Training" contains the *locus classicus* for this concept of *shouyi*, a central tenet of the early inner cultivation tradition that became extremely important in the practice of meditation in later Daoist religion. There it sometimes refers to what I have called the extrovertive mystical experience of seeing unity amidst the multiplicity of the phenomenal world and sometimes refers to a specific meditative technique for focusing on the One, both in sitting in silence and in the affairs of daily life.[72]

"Concentrating the vital breath" is a second important tenet in the inner cultivation tradition of early Daoism. It seems to refer to developing a refined and subtle level of breathing in introvertive meditation. Once again, its *locus classicus* in the extant literature is in "Inward Training":

> By concentrating your vital breath as if numinous,
> The myriad things will all be contained within you.
> Can you concentrate? Can you unify?
> Can you not resort to divination yet know bad and good
>   fortune?
> Can you stop? Can you halt?
> Can you not seek it in others,
> But attain it within yourself?
> You think and think and think further about this.
> You think, yet still do not penetrate it.

> The daemonic and numinous in you will penetrate it.
> It is not due to the inherent power of the daemonic and
>   numinous.
> But rather to the utmost refinement of your essential vital
>   breath.
> When the four limbs are set squarely
> And the blood and vital breath are tranquil:
> Unify your awareness, concentrate your mind.
> Then your eyes and ears will not be overstimulated.
> Then even the far-off will seem close at hand.[73]

When one sits in a stable posture and practices a form of guided breathing meditation, one becomes increasingly tranquil and the breathing becomes concentrated and subtle. This leads to a well-focused mind, minimal perception of the external world, and a numinous awareness in which "the myriad things will all be contained within you." This sounds very much like the attainment of a unitive consciousness. Retaining it when one returns to interact with the phenomenal world results in the lack of self-consciousness possessed by the child in the second line of *Laozi* 10.

In the third line of this chapter, we encounter the phrase "sweep clean your Profound Mirror" (*ti chu xuan jian* 滌除玄鑒), an abstruse meditational metaphor which Lau interprets as cleaning out the mind.[74] This phrase is extremely close in meaning to one of the most important metaphors for apophatic practice in the inner cultivation tradition, which is first found in "Inward Training":

> There is a numinous awareness that naturally lies within.
> One moment it goes, the next it comes,
> And no one is able to conceive of it.
> If you lose it you are inevitably disordered;
> If you attain it you are inevitably well-ordered.
> Reverently clean out its abode (the mind)
> And its vital essence will come on its own.
> Still your attempts to imagine and conceive of it.
> Relax your efforts to reflect on and control it.
> Be serious and reverent and its vital essence will naturally
>   settle.
> Grasp it and don't let go,
> Then the eyes and ears will not be overstimulated,

And the mind will have no other focus.
When a properly aligned mind lies within your center,
The myriad things will be seen in their proper context.[75]

To "reverently clean out the abode" of the numinous awareness shares the syntax and key verb (*chu* 除) of *Laozi* 10's "sweep clean your Profound Mirror." The metaphor is repeated in the related *Guanzi* essay "Techniques of the Mind I," where emptying the mind of desires is synonymous with "sweeping clean" (*saochu* 掃除) the abode of the numinous awareness.[76] The "Inward Training" verse seems to imply that the cleaning process involves setting aside the attempt to conceive of or control the numinous awareness. Then the mind will be ordered and concentrated on an inner meditation that allows the "myriad things to be seen in their proper context," a rather vague phrase that perhaps parallels the "myriad things will all be contained within you" from the previous passage.

The presence of all three parallels between *Laozi* 10 and "Inward Training" provide further evidence that the two works are closely related. I would hypothesize that the lineages of practitioners that produced each work shared a common apophatic meditative practice but, due to perhaps regional traditions and to the particular experiences of individual teachers, developed somewhat different metaphors for conceiving of their practice and its results.

Conclusion

When taken together, these passages provide important testimony to the presence of mystical praxis in the *Laozi*. They further indicate that the *Laozi* is not an isolated product but was part of a greater tradition of lineages that shared a common meditative practice as their basis. Furthermore, this practice, as much as we can tell from the surviving textual evidence, is similar to apophatic meditative practice in many other cultural and religious traditions. This practice also yields both introvertive and extrovertive mystical experiences that seem to be similar to those in other traditions; I have made no attempt here to claim that these experiences are identical. What I have claimed is that these experiences are the likely basis of the distinctive cosmology and political theory of sage rulership for which the *Laozi* is renowned.

APPENDIX:
Comparative Table of Early Daoist Meditative Stages

TEXT	HUANGLAO BOSHU, "NORMATIVE STANDARDS" 6: "ASSESSING"	LÜSHI CHUNQIU 3.4: "ASSESSING OTHERS"	LÜSHI CHUNQIU 25.3: "HAVING LIMITS"	ZHUANGZI 23: "GENGSANG CHU"	GUANZI 13.2B: "TECHNIQUES OF THE MIND, I"	HUAINANZI 7: "THE NUMINOUS ESSENCE"
Preparatory stages	[Knowledge of preservation and loss] generates wisdom. Wisdom generates alignment.	Relax hearing and seeing; limit lusts and desires; let go of wisdom and scheming; cast off cleverness and precedent . . .	Break through perturbations of the will; Release the fetters of the mind; Cast off the constraints to Inner Power; Break through blockages of the Way.	Penetrate perturbations of the will; Release the fetters of the mind; Cast off the constraints to Inner Power; Pass through blockages of the Way.	Clean out the abode; cast off desires; direct inner concentration.	Concentrate blood and breath; fill chest and belly; eliminate lusts and desires; purify seeing and hearing; conquer perturbations of the will . . .

Consecutive stages of

meditation	aligned	nothing injures the heavenly	aligned	aligned	aligned	patterned
	tranquil equanimous serene unadorned concentrated numinous	concentrated numinous attain the One	tranquil clear and lucid empty	tranquil lucid empty	tranquil concentrated solitary lucid numinous attain the empty Way	balanced absorbed numinous
Benefits	perfectly numinous; then seeing and knowing are never deluded ...	respond to alterations and transformations of things; be grand and deep; be unfathomable ... return to the Unhewn (*pu*)	take no action and yet nothing is left undone	take no action and yet nothing is left undone		seeing: nothing is unseen; hearing: nothing is unheard; acting: nothing is unaccomplished.

────────────── *NOTES* ──────────────

1. Wing-Tsit Chan, *A Sourcebook in Chinese Philosophy* (Princeton: Princeton University Press, 1963); Benjamin Schwartz, *The World of Thought in Ancient China* (Cambridge: Belknap Press, 1985); Walter Stace, *Mysticism and Philosophy* (London: Macmillan Press, 1960; reprint Los Angeles: Jeremy P. Tarcher, 1987); Wayne Proudfoot, *Religious Experience* (Berkeley: University of California Press, 1985). Specific references will be given as the ideas in these works are discussed below.

2. D. C. Lau, trans., *Chinese Classics: Tao Te Ching* (Hong Kong: Chinese University Press, 1982), xxv–xxvii; Chad Hansen, "Linguistic Skepticism in the *Lao Tzu*," *Philosophy East and West* 31, no. 3 (July 1981): 321–336.

3. Chan, *Sourcebook*, 137.

4. Stace, *Mysticism*, 168, 255.

5. Proudfoot, *Religious Experience*, 126–129.

6. Livia Kohn, *Early Chinese Mysticism: Philosophy and Soteriology in the Taoist Tradition* (Princeton: Princeton University Press, 1992), 34.

7. Kohn, *Early Chinese Mysticism*, 45–52. For a critical assessment of this work, see my review article, "Some Issues in the Study of Chinese Mysticism: A Review Essay," *China Review International* 2, no. 1 (Spring 1995): 154–173.

8. Schwartz, *World of Thought*, 192–201.

9. Harold D. Roth, "Psychology and Self-Cultivation in Early Taoistic Thought," *Harvard Journal of Asiatic Studies* 51, no. 2 (1991): 599–650; and "Who Compiled the Chuang Tzu?" in *Chinese Texts and Philosophical Contexts: Essays Dedicated to Angus C. Graham*, ed. Henry Rosemont Jr. (LaSalle, Ill.: Open Court, 1991), 79–128.

10. Harold D. Roth, "Redaction Criticism and the Early History of Taoism," *Early China* 19 (1994): 1–46.

11. See the first traditional occurrence of this term in *Zhuangzi*, 6/73. *Zhuangzi yinde* 莊子引得. Harvard-Yenching Institute Sinological Index Series no. 20 (Peking, 1947). All references to the *Zhuangzi* are from this edition. In this passage, a dialogue between Confucius and Zigong in which the former explains to the latter how the Daoist sage Sanghu and his friends "are at the stage of being fellow men with the maker of things, and go roaming in the single breath that breathes through heaven and earth,"

we read that it is through the techniques of the Way that such men can forget themselves. A. C. Graham, *Chuang Tzu: The Inner Chapters* (London: Allen and Unwin, 1981), 89–90. The only other use of this term in the *Zhuangzi* is also significant. It occurs in the thirty-third and final chapter, "Below in the Empire" (*Tianxia* 天下), in which the comprehensive Way of Heaven and Earth advocated by the Syncretist author is contrasted with the "techniques of one-corner" (*fangshu* 方術) found in other, less complete teachings, such as those of Zhuang Zhou himself (*Zhuangzi* 33/1 ff.; Graham, *Chuang Tzu*, 274 ff.) These two occurrences, separated by a century and one-half and found in both "Individualist" and "Syncretist" sections, serve like bookends to indicate an important continuity in this tradition's self-understanding and demonstrate how the "techniques of the Way" developed beyond breathing methods to include methods of political and social organization.

12. My hypothesis on the origins of Daoism is that it began as a lineage of masters and disciples that practiced and transmitted a unique form of guided breathing meditation involving this regular circulation of vital breath. Political and social concerns and naturalist techniques and philosophy represented later developments. One of the strongest pieces of evidence for this is presented in my article, "Redaction Criticism and the Early History of Daoism," in which I demonstrate that "Inward Training," a collection of verses on this practice of guiding the vital breath that dates from the origins of Daoism, was deliberately summarized and restated in the much later work, "Techniques of the Mind II." This deliberate abridgment and restatement was done for the purposes of commending this practice of inner cultivation to rulers as one of the principal arcana of governing.

13. For the former, see Catherine Despeux, "Gymnastics: The Ancient Tradition," in *Taoist Meditation and Longevity Techniques*, ed. Livia Kohn, vol. 61, Michigan Monographs in Chinese Studies (Ann Arbor: University of Michigan Center for Chinese Studies, 1989), 225–262. The precise relationships between these two techniques and their practitioners is still unclear. However, by the time of *Zhuangzi* 15, which criticizes the practitioners of "gymnastic" exercises, the groups who advocated these two techniques seem to be clearly differentiated (*Zhuangzi yinde* 15/5–6).

14. I use the term "apophatic" in its more general and original sense of "(of knowledge of God) obtained by negation," *Concise Oxford Dictionary Sixth Edition*, (Oxford: Oxford University Press, 1976). It has come to be associated with a particular mode of approach to the nature of God in the writings of Christian mystics, the so-called "*via negativa*," in which God is described using negative language. I consider this a subset of "apophasis" and I wish to clarify that I use the term more broadly to indicate a method

of negating the self in order to facilitate an experience of the Absolute, however that is conceived. While more culturally specific than my own use, A. H. Armstrong argues for this kind of more general meaning of apophasis in *Plotinian and Christian Studies* (London: Variorum, 1979), especially in essays XXIV and XXIII. I wish to thank Janet Williams of the University of Bath for this reference.

"Inner cultivation" (*neixiu* 內修) refers to the apophatic methods of emptying the mind practiced by the various master-disciple lineages of early Daoism. Its *locus classicus* is in the "Inward Training" text of the *Guanzi*, which will be discussed below. "Self-cultivation" (*zixiu* 自修) is a more general term that I take to refer to all methods of practical discipline aimed at improving oneself and realizing one's innate nature and potential to the fullest. Self-cultivation was practiced by Confucians and Yangists as well as Daoists. Daoist self-cultivation is what I call inner cultivation.

15. Michael LaFargue, *The Tao of the Tao Te Ching* (Albany: State University of New York Press, 1992); *Tao and Method: A Reasoned Approach to the Tao Te Ching* (Albany: State University of New York Press, 1994). The former book is an abbreviated version of the latter. Both contain the same translation of the *Laozi*.

16. The Individualist aspect is the earliest. It advocates a cosmology of the Way and the inner cultivation practices that I will be adumbrating in the present essay. Its representative extant texts are *Guanzi*'s "Inward Training" and the "inner chapters" of the *Zhuangzi*. The Primitivist contains the same cosmology of the Way and inner cultivation practices as the former but to these adds a political philosophy that rejects social conventions (especially Confucian and Mohist) and recommends returning to a political and social organization based on small agrarian communities. Its representative works are the *Laozi* and chapters 8–11 (1–57) and 16 of the *Zhuangzi*. The Syncretist embraces the same cosmology and inner cultivation practices as the other two aspects but in its political thought conceives of a complex hierarchically organized society whose customs and laws are modelled on the overarching patterns of heaven and earth and which freely uses relevant techniques and ideas from other intellectual lineages. Representative texts include the "HuangLao silk manuscripts" from Mawangdui, chapters 12–15 and 33 of the *Zhuangzi* and the *Huainanzi*. For further details, see my "Psychology and Self-Cultivation," especially 599–608; "Who Compiled the Chuang Tzu?" especially 80–88 and 95–113. See also A. C. Graham, "How Much of Chuang Tzu Did Chuang Tzu Write?" in *Studies in Chinese Philosophy and Philosophical Literature* (Albany: State University of New York Press, 1990), 283–321 and Liu Xiaogan, *Zhuangzi zhexue ji qi yanbian* 莊子哲學及其演變 (Peking: Chinese Social Sciences Press, 1987).

17. This presentation is not intended to be comprehensive but will deal principally with the theoretical role of mystical praxis and its relationship to mystical experience. I differ from Kohn by focusing more on the phenomenological and typological studies of William James and Walter Stace and "anti-constructivists" such as Donald Rothberg, which seriously entertain the possible veridicality of the epistemological claims of the mystics, rather than on the "constructivist" theories of Steven Katz, Wayne Proudfoot et al., which reject the veridicality of such claims. For details, see my "Some Issues," 161–168.

18. William James, *The Varieties of Religious Experience* (1902; reprint, New York: Penguin Books, 1982), 380–381.

19. This fifth characteristic is implicit. James uses the transforming influence of mystical experience as a means of clarifying where they differ from religious experiences in general but he does not include it in his list of characteristics. See 381–382, 400–401, 413–415.

20. Peter Moore, "Mystical Experience, Mystical Doctrine, Mystical Technique," in *Mysticism and Philosophical Analysis*, ed. Steven Katz (London: Oxford University Press, 1978), 101.

21. Stace, *Mysticism*, 67–87.

22. See Robert K. C. Forman, ed., *The Problem of Pure Consciousness, Mysticism and Philosophy* (New York: Oxford University Press, 1990).

23. The two modes correspond well with Stace's introvertive and extrovertive mystical experiences. Where I would differ from him is in his devaluing the latter (Stace, *Mysticism*, 132); I see no evidence of this in early Daoist sources. See "Some Issues," 160–162.

24. These concepts are discussed throughout Stace's third chapter, "The Problem of Objective Reference."

25. The foremost champion of the latter position is Steven Katz. See his "Language, Epistemology, and Mysticism," in Steven Katz, ed., *Mysticism and Philosophical Analysis* (Oxford: Oxford University Press, 1978), 22–74, especially 26.

26. Moore, "Mystical Experience," 113.

27. Moore, "Mystical Experience," 113.

28. Robert Forman, "Mysticism, Constructivism, and Forgetting," in Forman, *Problem*, 3–49, especially 3–9, and 30–43.

29. Donald Rothberg, "Contemporary Epistemology and the Study of Mysticism," in Forman, *Problem*, 184.

30. Rothberg, "Contemporary," 186.

31. Daniel Brown, "The Stages of Meditation in Cross-Cultural Perspective," in *Transformations of Consciousness and Contemplative Perspectives on Development*, ed. Ken Wilber, Jack Engler, and Daniel Brown (Boston: Shambala, 1986), 263–264. In his analysis of the results of this study, Brown states that he has discovered "a clear underlying structure to meditation stages, a structure highly consistent across traditions . . . " which, despite the "vastly different ways they are conceptualized", "is believed to represent natural human development available to anyone who practices" (223).

32. Rothberg, "Contemporary," 186.

33. Forman, *Problem*, 8. This is a deliberate strategy on the part of Forman, who recognizes that this extrovertive form can be a more permanent mystical state that is typically thought of as a more advanced stage in the mystical journey. He omits it, not out of disregard, but in order to limit the focus of his collection of essays.

34. Roth, "Some Issues."

35. Roth, "Some Issues," 159–161. See also n. 14, which calls for further research to clarify various types in a continuum of extrovertive mystical experience.

36. Roth, "Some Issues," 167–168.

37. Brown, "Stages of Meditation," 221–222.

38. LaFargue, *The Dao*, 61.

39. *Zhuangzi yinde*, 6/92–93.

40. In this article, I will most often use the text of the received recension of the *Laozi* as found in the edition of D. C. Lau, *Tao Te Ching*. However, whenever I find their readings preferable, I will also make use of the Mawangdui manuscript redactions as found in the edition of Robert Henricks, *Lao-Tzu Te-Dao Ching* (New York: Ballantine Books, 1989). Translations are my own unless otherwise noted. I will explain the unique elements of it when I fully analyze this passage below.

41. Lau, *Tao Te Ching*, xxxvii.

42. Chan, *Sourcebook*, 144.

43. *Zhuangzi yinde*, 6/92–93; Graham, *Chuang Tzu*, 92. I deviate only in translating *tong* 同 as "merge" instead of "go along."

44. I follow Graham in understanding *zhiti* as the four limbs or members and the five orbs or visceral organs that are the physical manifesta-

tions of the five basic systems of vital energy in the human body. This is preferable to the alternative "drop off limbs and body" because two lines later the text refers to parting from the body (*lixing*), which would be redundant if the second interpretation were taken. For the associations of the emotions with the various internal organs or "orbs" see Manfred Porkert, *The Theoretical Foundations of Chinese Medicine* (Cambridge: MIT Press, 1974), 115–146.

45. On the imagery of the character "Dao" in *Zhuangzi* see A. C. Graham, *Disputers of the Dao* (LaSalle, Ill.: Open Court Press, 1989), 188: "Chuang-tzu . . . sees man as coinciding with the Way by ceasing to draw distinctions. To be on the unformulable path is to merge into the unnameable whole, so that what we are trying to pin down by the name 'Way' is revealed as nothing less than the universe flowing from its ultimate source . . ."

46. For the link between psychological states and physiological substrates, see Roth, "Psychology and Self-Cultivation," 599–603.

47. *Guanzi, Sibu congkan* edition, 16.2a5, 2b6, 3b6. All textual citations for the *Guanzi* are to this edition. For translations, see Roth, "The Inner Cultivation Tradition of Early Daoism," 131–132.

48. *Guanzi*, 16.5a4, 5a5, 1b10 and 4a2. For translations, see Roth, "Inner Cultivation," 133–134, 130, and 133.

49. *Guanzi*, 16.3b6.

50. See, for example, the other famous passage on meditation, the "fasting of the mind" dialogue, also between Confucius and Yan Hui (wherein Confucius is now the teacher): *Zhuangzi yinde*, 4/24–34: Graham, *Chuang Tzu*, 68–69.

51. Harold D. Roth, "Evidence for Stages of Meditation in Early Daoism" *Bulletin of the School of Oriental and African Studies* 60.2 (1997): 295–314. These important sources for early Daoist mystical praxis include the "HuangLao boshu," chapters 3, 5, 17, and 25 of the *Lüshi chunqiu*, chapters 15 and 23 of the *Zhuangzi*, and the "Inward Training" and two "Techniques of the Mind" works from the *Guanzi*.

52. Brown, "Stages of Meditation," 230–245 and 272–276.

53. Lau, *Tao Te Ching*, 77.

54. The restriction of the senses through focusing on the breathing is discussed in Brown, "Stages of Meditation," 232–24. As a result, the meditator becomes "less sensitized to external events and more to internal events" (233).

55. Brown, "Stages of Meditation," 232–233.

56. Brown, "Stages of Meditation," 233.

57. According to the *Baopuzi* 抱朴子 (ca. 300 C.E.), the "lower cinnabar field" is located 2.4 inches below the navel. It is one of the major locations of the One in the human being. In the later *Huangtingjing* 黃廷經, the Daoist adept makes the vital breath circulate through the lower cinnabar field where it helps to nourish and retain the vital essence. In the Tang dynasty meditation texts of Sima Chengzhen 司馬承禎, fixing the attention on the lower cinnabar field is a technique used to control the desires and emotions. See Livia Kohn, "Guarding the One: Concentrative Meditation in Taoism," and "Taoist Insight Meditation: The Tang Practice of *Neiguan*," in *Taoist Meditation and Longevity Techniques*, ed. Livia Kohn, 135 and 194–195, respectively; and Henri Maspero, "An Essay on Taoism in the First Centuries A.D.," in Henri Maspero, *Daoism and Chinese Religion*, trans. Frank Kierman (Amherst: University of Massachusetts Press, 1981), 339–345.

58. *Huainanzi, Sibu congkan* edition, 8.8a1–3. All references to the text of the *Huainanzi* are to this edition.

59. Roth, "Who Compiled," 96, finds this phrase in "Techniques of the Mind I," chapters 13 and 15 of the *Zhuangzi*, and chapters 1, 6, and 7 of the *Huainanzi*. I can add *Lüshi chunqiu* 3.4 to this list (see "Evidence for Stages of Meditation in Early Taoism," 302).

60. I follow Henricks, 234, in moving the first line of chapter 20 to the last line of chapter 19, where it constitutes the third of the three statements indicated above in the text of chapter 19.

61. Here I follow the Mawangdui B manuscript reading from Henricks, 219: *zhi xu ji ye; shou jing du ye* 至虛極也守靜督也.

62. *Zhuangzi yinde*, 4/28.

63. I follow Lau in emending the negative *bu* 不 ("not") to *erh* 而 ("and"), based on semantic considerations. Lau, *Tao te Ching*, 23.

64. LaFargue, *The Dao*, 245.

65. For the purposes of this article, I have taken the concept of the One to be the functional equivalent of the Way as it is manifested within the phenomenal world. This certainly seems to be the implication of chapter 39 in which the most important phenomena (Heaven, Earth, numen, the valley, the myriad things, sage-rulers) each attain their essential defining characteristics as the result of the One. Chapter 42, in which we read that the "Way generated the One," indicates that there is some difference be-

tween them. This could simply mean that there is a certain aspect of the Way that transcends its manifestation as the solitary unifying power within the phenomenal world. For a fuller discussion of the polysemy of the concept of the One in the Daoist tradition, see Livia Kohn, "Guarding," 127–137.

66. Here I follow the Mawangdui variant *jinzhi Dao* 今之道 (not *guzhi Dao* 古之道; Henricks, 215), because it better fits the phenomenological interpretation I have been developing in this article. The Way, as both the source merged with in introvertive mystical experience and the constant source of the universe from before its beginnings, is directly experienced in the present (not past, as in the received versions). Because it has existed from antiquity, if one knows it in the present, one can know it in the past and, through it, "know the ancient beginnings."

67. Lau, *Tao te Ching*, 33–34.

68. *Zhuangzi yinde*, 2/38–40.

69. The phrase *dai ying po* 戴營魄 is extremely problematic and has puzzled commentators since *Heshanggong*. The *po* is the "bodily soul," associated with *yin*, and the counterpart of the "spiritual soul" (*hun* 魂) associated with *yang*. The former governs the body; the latter governs the mind. They work harmoniously together during life, but separate after death, the *po* returning to Earth and the *hun* to Heaven. According to Yü Ying-shih, the former concept developed first; there are a few references in the oracle bones. The concept of *hun* seems to have been derived from it and intended to represent the locus of daily conscious activities, somewhat akin to our modern notion of the conscious mind, in my interpretation. Along these lines, I would suggest that we might think of the *po* as rather like our modern notion of the unconscious mind. That is, the mental phenomena we now associate with the conscious and unconscious minds were explained in early China by the concepts of the *hun* and *po*. Eduard Erkes follows the *Heshanggong* commentary by taking the term *ying* as the functional equivalant of *hun*; he suggests it was a variant of *ling* 靈 in Chu dialect. Thus, a literal translation of this phrase would be "to sustain the conscious and unconscious souls." I have rendered it more freely because the constant activity of these two aspects of the mind does constitute "the daily activity of the psyche." For more information see Yü Ying-shih, 'O Soul, Come Back!' A Study of the Changing Conceptions of the Soul and Afterlife in Pre-Buddhist China," *Harvard Journal of Asiatic Studies* 47, no. 2 (December 1987): 363–395; and Eduard Erkes, trans., *Ho-Shang-Kung's Commentary on Lao-Tse* (Ascona: Artibus Asiae, 1950), 141–142.

70. *Guanzi*, 16.2b1–3. Translated in Roth, "Inner Cultivation," 133.

71. *Guanzi*, 16.5a2–4.

72. Kohn, "Guarding," especially 154–156.

73. *Guanzi*, 16.4a2–7. Close parallels of this passage are found in "Techniques of the Mind II" from *Guanzi* (13.5a2) and in the "Gengsang Chu" chapter of *Zhuangzi* (*Zhuangzi yinde*, 23/34–35).

74. Lau, *Tao Te Ching*, 15. The mirror is one of the most important metaphors in Chinese religious thought. The mirror is often seen to symbolize the clarified mind of the sage, which reflects things exactly as they are without even an iota of personal bias. For further details, see the pioneering study by Paul Demieville, "Le miroir spirituel," *Sinologica* 1, no. 2 (1948): 112–137.

75. *Guanzi*, 16.2b9–3a1.

76. *Guanzi*, 13.1a11.

Qian Zhongshu on Philosophical and Mystical Paradoxes in the *Laozi*

Zhang Longxi

As an honorary member of the Modern Language Association of America, Qian Zhongshu 錢鍾書 is certainly known to many Western scholars, especially sinologists, but compared with the other scholars honored with this prestigious membership in the same year (1985)—Jacques Derrida, Umberto Eco, Gérard Genette, Wolfgang Iser, and Robert Weimann—Qian's rich and important scholarly works are still largely unknown in the West.[1] Perhaps this is due not only to the content of Qian's writings, which comment on ancient Chinese texts in an extremely dense intertextuality of both Chinese and Western writings, many of which are works little known outside the small circle of specialists, but also due to the form of his writings, because they are not systematic treatises but fragments of insight, written in the elegant but difficult language of classical Chinese. The commentary form of Qian Zhongshu's *Tan yi lu* 談藝錄 [*Discourses on Art*] and *Guan zhui bian* 管錐編 [*The Tube and Awl Chapters*] is surely traditional, but it is also deeply personal and related to his deep suspicion of systems and systematic argument. All philosophical systems will collapse in time, Qian argues, and when they do, they will lose all their impressive structural complexity and organization, but bits and pieces of their original ideas may retain their value and validity, just as bricks and timbers may still be of use when huge buildings crumble to dust. "Remnant ideas that are dislodged from systems and nascent ideas that are not yet assembled into systems are all fragmented," says Qian. "It is therefore a shallow and vulgar view— if not an excuse for laziness and coarseness—to take notice only of big volumes and long treatises but look down upon terse expressions and pithy phrases, or to be so intoxicated by quantity as to discard a gram of seemingly insignificant words in favor of a ton of nonsense."[2] Thus, in writing his commentaries, Qian is not systematically explicating the philosophical, literary, or some other aspect of ancient Chinese books, but discussing specific points in reading particular words and phrases, and putting together valuable ideas from a great many sources. His commentaries are short entries ranging from a few lines to a few pages, with no apparent connections among them, and they always begin with textual details and then proceed to develop freely, touching on any number of diverse realms of knowledge, such as philosophy, history, literature, psychology, philology, and so on. He always cites a wealth of materials in classical Chinese and several Western languages, weaving a rich tapestry of quotations that bear on one another in unexpected ways, but he never follows the protocols or the predictable route of a disciplinary argument.

All these features make Qian Zhongshu's writings rather difficult to classify and extremely hard to translate, and to readers with a habitual urge for the logical connections and clear boundaries of scholarly "fields" or academic "disciplines," they may appear overwhelmingly rich and waywardly exuberant. But once we surrender our usual expectation of a linear argument and let ourselves be guided by the seemingly erratic turns of a great mind, Qian's erudition, the dazzling brilliance of his insights, the apposite quotations, the revelation of deep affinities and connection of ideas in a wealth of texts, and the knowledge and wisdom released from ancient works through his commentaries will reward us with a special kind of pleasure, a deep sense of intellectual gratification. Therefore, the lack of any English translation and analysis of Qian's major scholarly works is unfortunate, because his works represent the very best of Chinese scholarship in our time, which would immensely improve our understanding of Chinese culture and let readers appreciate the rich legacy of that culture not as something alien, exotic, and mysterious, but fully accessible in a rational discourse and the mutual illumination of the East and the West.

The present essay is an attempt to substantiate the claims made above by looking at Qian Zhongshu's commentaries on the *Laozi* as an example of his scholarly writings. I shall quote and translate from the second volume of *Guan zhui bian*, in which Qian has nineteen entries on the *Laozi* that provide a cornucopia of ideas, insights, wit, and elegance, which make that ancient book truly alive. Qian begins by commenting on the different editions of the *Laozi* and justifies his preference for Wang Bi's 王弼 (226–249) annotated text over other versions, especially the one inscribed on a stone tablet in the Daoist temple called Longxing Guan 龍興觀 in Yizhou 易州 in the year of 708, which Qing scholars Qian Daxin 錢大昕 (1728–1804) and Yan Kejun 嚴可均 (1762–1843) promoted as the most authentic text of all. According to Qian Daxin, the Longxing Guan text is authentic because its characters "follow the ancient form," but Qian Zhongshu argues that "the ancient form of its scripts shows precisely that its text is not genuinely ancient."[3] The archaic form of characters is a conscious and artificial attempt to make the text *look* old. Perhaps those Daoist priests thought that they could present their text as truly ancient by inscribing each character in the archaic form, deleting all function words they deemed superfluous, and confusing obscurity with profundity. The result is an absurdly elliptical text that sometimes does not make sense.

In debunking the claim to authenticity of the Yizhou stone inscription, Qian Zhongshu borrows a line from the Qing scholar Feng Jing 馮景 (1652–1715) to describe his own reading experience. Feng Jing once wrote to a friend: "The beginning section of the *Analects* has thirty characters. Once a merchant said that he had seen an ignorant scholar overseas (*haiwai mangru* 海外盲儒) suddenly gone mad and cutting out sixteen characters—all function words—and thus reading the text to his students: 'Learn time practice, pleasure. Friend far come, joy. Not know, not angry, gentleman.' That is surely concise, but does it make good sense at all?" By drawing an analogy between the Daoist priests and this fictitious mad scholar in Feng's account, Qian Zhongshu ridicules the absurdity of mutilating a classical text and mistaking function words for useless characters. While brevity may be a sign of antiquity, obscurity as a result of textual mutilation is not. "When I read the text of the Yizhou stone inscription of the *Daodejing*," says Qian, "I often feel like seeing the ignorant scholar overseas tightening up the

Analects, or a stingy miser sending out a telegram" (402–403). Given the great antiquity of the *Laozi*, we may never know for certain what its original text looks like, but what matters is not how the characters are written, but whether the text makes good sense. Qian prefers the Wang Bi text for the obvious reason that Wang Bi, perhaps more than any other traditional commentator, understood the fundamental ideas of Laozi's philosophy and often brought out the meaning of that philosophy in his concise but illuminating annotations. Comparing the Wang Bi text with the oldest known version to date—the Mawangdui text—we find only minor differences except for the chapter order, and it is interesting to note that the Mawangdui text contains some function words that are omitted in later versions.[4]

The most important aspect of the *Laozi* is of course its mixture of philosophy and mysticism, both of which are intimately related to its form of presentation or language. This is what the opening verses of the *Laozi* indicate in setting up the paradox of *Dao* and name, thinking and speaking: "The *Dao* that can be spoken of is not the constant *Dao*. The name that can be named is not the constant name." To this Wang Bi provides a brief note: "The sayable *Dao* and the nameable name point to things and define their shapes, but they do not capture their constant nature; therefore [the constant *Dao*] cannot be spoken and cannot be named." Qian Zhongshu points out that Wang Bi's idea was already adumbrated in pre-Qin philosophy:

> In explicating these first two verses, the "Explaining the *Laozi*" (*JieLao*) chapter of the *Han Feizi* already says in effect that all that is present or absent, lives or dies, flourishes or perishes, "cannot be said to be constant," and whatever is constant "has no duration or change, follows no fixed rules, and therefore cannot be spoken." Wang's note means to say the same, but it does not give a word-by-word exegesis. (403)

The question of speaking and naming, or the relationship between thinking and language, is thus the first question presented at the beginning of the *Laozi*. It is a philosophical question, not a philological one. Some Qing scholars who are great philologists, however, tend to substitute philology for philosophy and create ancient thinkers in their own images. By quoting a long passage from Yu Zhengxie's (1775–1840) *Guiyi cun gao* 癸巳存稿, in which Yu cites various sources to support his claim that in the *Laozi*, "*Dao* refers to speech, and 'name' refers to written words," Qian Zhongshu exposes the textual scholar's complacency and shows how Yu missed the crucial point in seeing the problem of *Dao* and name in purely philological terms. Commenting on ancient texts by way of commenting on earlier commentaries is one of the important features of Qian's writing, and it is often in dismantling some revered but erroneous past authorities that his work breaks new ground in understanding the rich textual tradition of China. In criticizing Yu as overreaching himself in making philology the sole concern of textual criticism, Qian's commentary opens the text of the *Laozi* to much deeper probing of its metaphysical and dialectical dimensions without neglecting the textual details. Given Laozi's own distrust of words, his radical linguistic skepticism already apparent in the opening verses, it is especially appropriate to emphasize the philosophical aspect of the *Laozi* beyond the mere explication of single words.

In refuting Yu's assertion that "the ancients called words 'names,'" Qian Zhongshu carefully differentiates naming as the act of signification from words as signifiers. Insofar as a word has meaning, it can serve its purpose, but that has nothing to do with how the word is used, or whether the meaning of words accords with substance or reality, which, Qian argues, is the concern of naming or signification. Proper naming aims to be truthful, and the rectification of names becomes necessary precisely because words may not mean what they are supposed to signify, but can be abused, corrupted into empty talk, and formed into a deceptive, devious, and evil facade. The difference here is one between semantics and epistemology, between meaning in a lexicon and meaning in real communication. "How can one take words and names as the same thing," asks Qian, "since their functions and purposes differ so much from one another?"

In *juan* 173 of the *Taiping guangji* 太平廣記, Dongfang Shuo 東方朔 is recorded as saying, "What is called a horse when grown up is called a colt when it is little; what is called a hen is called a chick when small; the big cow is a calf when it is young; a human being is a baby at birth and grows to be an old person. How can one have a fixed name?" This is also what Han Fei in "Explaining the *Laozi*" means when he speaks of the "initial growth and the subsequent decline" of things. The initial or old name will not fit the subsequent or new substance, and so one changes the word and renames it. This is what it means to say that "the name that can be named is not the constant name." (405)

What Laozi indicates in the opening verses is thus the essential problem of language: the inadequacy of all verbal expressions, either spoken or written. Not only do things change and require that names must change to suit the occasion, but there are many things, conditions, qualities, and sensibilities that cannot be appropriately named or put in words. Speech and writing are absolutely necessary in our daily communication, but because we use language so much and have such high expectations of its efficacy, we often find it less than perfect and complain about its many defects. "Authors often blame it for falling short of what exactly they would have desired it to be in expressing emotions, in argumentation, description, or narration," says Qian. "Desiring to touch the finest, they hate it for being so coarse and clumsy; intending to reach the deepest, they dislike it for being so superficial; some accuse it of wooden ineptitude, while others blame its ambiguity and opacity" (406). As the central notion of Laozi's philosophy, *Dao* is thus inexpressible in language, but Qian shows that the inadequacy of language is a basic problem not just for conveying philosophical ideas. From a couplet by the Tang poet Liu Yuxi 劉禹錫 (772–842), "How often I regret that words are too shallow/Ever to reach the depth of human feelings!" to Confucius's famous proclamation that "I will not speak" (*Analects*, xvii.19), various complaints about the failings of language indicate that this is a problem recognized by poets as well as philosophers.

What makes Qian Zhongshu's commentaries unique in all Chinese scholarship on ancient classics, however, is the incredibly rich source of materials at his disposal, a virtual treasure of texts not just within but also beyond the Chinese tradition. By putting many pieces of writing and fragments of ideas together from different traditions, he not only helps illuminate the meaning of a difficult text like the *Laozi*, but also relates Laozi to many other thinkers and writers, and reveals the deep affinities of the human mind, despite the cultural differences and the linguistic, geographical, and temporal boundaries.

Extensive textual evidence cited in Qian's commentaries make a compelling case that the perceived inadequacy is indeed a basic problem of language that philosophers, poets, and mystics in the East and the West all recognize and reflect on. "Some say that the language philosophers attempt to use originated in the cries of monkeys and dogs (*le cri perfectionné des singes et des chiens*); and some claim that it is as sly as a snake (*der Schlangenbetrug der Sprache*), against which scholars are always on the alert"[5] (406–407). Hegel charges that language expresses the inner "both too much and too little" (*daß diese Äußerungen das Innere zu sehr, als daß sie es zu wenig ausdrücken*); Nietzsche despises language as something vulgar and "vulgarizing," designed only for the ordinary and the mediocre (*Die Sprache ist nur für Durchschnittliches, Mittleres, Mitteilsames erfunden. Mit der Sprache vulgarisiert bereits der Sprechende*);[6] the "Xiao qu" 小取 [Minor Illustrations] chapter of the *Mozi* warns us that "language has many tricks," that "it changes at every turn, it moves afar and gets lost, and flows away and becomes detached from its origin"; and the "Cha chuan" 察傳 [Investigating Hearsay] section of the *Lüshi chunqiu* states that "words cannot but be investigated," because "they often seem wrong but are right, and often seem right but are wrong" (407). Further examples include similar doubts and cautions articulated by Spinoza, Hobbes, and Jeremy Bentham. Then we hear from poets and writers, who often blame language for failing to express what they have conceived in their mind, even though they specialize in the art of language, which makes them what they are. For Chinese examples, Qian quotes Lu Ji 陸機, Tao Qian 陶潛, Liu Xie 劉勰, and Huang Tingjian 黃庭堅, while Favorinus, Dante, and Goethe provide corroborating Western examples.

The last group Qian cites are the mystics, who outdo all others in condemning language, and among whom Qian places Laozi and his ideas. The mystics maintain that the supreme truth, intense religious experience, and the subtle *Dao* are all beyond language. "What in the 'Autumn Floods' chapter of the *Zhuangzi* is described as 'impossible to discuss in words or to intend in the mind,'" according to Qian, "is also what Buddha means in the second *gatha* he utters in the "Fangbian pin" 方便品 [Tactfulness] chapter of the *Miaofa lianhua jing* 妙法蓮華經 [*Saddharma puṇḍarīka sūtra* or *Lotus sutra*] when he says, 'Stop! stop, no need to speak! My law is wonderful and beyond thinking.' This is also what the wise one calls 'the world of the unthinkable' in *juan* 5 of the *Mohe zhi guan* 摩訶止觀 [*Great Meditation and Great Wisdom*]" (408). In both Buddhist and Western mystic writings, the sacred or the saint is often described as "silent".[7] And that, Qian observes, is precisely what Laozi tries to say in the opening verses.

The paradox of the *Dao* and name is, then, the difficulty of speaking of something that cannot be spoken. Qian Zhongshu gives his own reading of the first verse and points out Laozi's ingenious play on the meanings of *Dao* as thinking and as speaking:

> "The *Dao* that can be spoken of (*dao*) is not the constant *Dao*"; here the first and the third character *dao* 道 is the *dao* as in *dao li* 道理 [reason], and the second *dao* is the *dao* as in *dao bai* 道白 [speech], or as in the line "*buke dao ye* 不可道也 [cannot be told]" in the poem "Qiang you ci" 牆有茨 ["There is Thistle on the Wall"] in the *Book of Poetry*, that is, words and speech. We may compare this with the ancient Greek word *logos*, which means both "reason" (*ratio*) and "speech" (*oratio*); in more recent times, some have argued that the proverbial statement that "man is the animal of reason" originally meant that "man is the animal that speaks."[8] (408)

The intimate relationship between thinking and speaking or reason and language is thus preserved in one and the same word: *Dao* in Chinese or *logos* in Greek. It may be a mere coincidence that both Chinese and Greek have a word that possesses this significant duality of meaning and allows the problem of language to be formulated in language itself, but the coincidence also suggests that the problem—or the dialectics—of thinking and speaking is common to the East and the West, even though its manifestation necessarily takes different forms.

Qian Zhongshu further explains the meaning of *Dao* by relating it to the problem of naming and by drawing on internal evidences from the *Laozi*. "What one looks for but cannot see is called the colorless," says Laozi. "What one listens to but cannot hear is called inaudible; what one tries to touch but cannot reach is called the infinitesimal" (chapter 14). "I would constrainedly name it 'Great.' Being great, it is said to vanish. Vanishing, it is said to move far away. Being far away, it is said to return" (chapter 25). All these different ways of saying or naming the *Dao*, says Qian, indicate its constantly changing nature and hence the impossibility of giving it a constant name. No word or name can signify the totality of *Dao*: "the various analogies and metaphors can only describe its rough outline and sketchy resemblance, but are never sufficient to be its definite name," because "what is definite is finite (*le défini est le fini*)"[9] (409–410). The limitation of names is again something we find not just in China, but also in the West. "No intelligent man will ever be so bold as to put into language those things which his reason has contemplated, especially into a form that is unalterable," says Plato in one of his philosophical epistles. "Names, I maintain, are in no case stable."[10] This readily reminds us of what Han Fei says, in explicating the *Laozi*, about the "initial growth and the subsequent decline" of things and hence the inadequacy of names. Whatever differences may exist between the Greek and the Chinese traditions, linguistic skepticism is thus common to philosophers in both traditions. "This passage," says Qian of Plato's philosophical letter, "may almost be translated to annotate the *Laozi*" (410).

The inadequacy of language and speaking is the idea behind one of Laozi's famous antimetaboles: "The one who knows does not speak; the one who speaks does not know" (chapter 56). The same sentence also appears in the *"Tian dao"* 天道 [The *Dao* of Heaven] and the *"Zhi beiyou"* 知北遊 [Knowledge Journeys North] chapters of the *Zhuangzi*. In the latter chapter, the idea is carried further when Zhuangzi declares that "to argue is not as effective as to keep silent, for *Dao* cannot be heard, . . . *Dao* cannot be seen, what is seen is not *Dao*; *Dao* cannot be spoken, what is spoken is not *Dao*." Qian Zhongshu compares this with similar expressions in Buddhist writings, such as the *Weimojie suoshuo jing* 維摩詰所説經 [*Vimalakīrti nirdeśa sūtra*], *Zhong lun* 中論 [*Mādhyamikakārikā*], *Da zhidu lun* 大智度論 [*Mahāprajñāpāramitā-śāstra*], and others. Of these perhaps two examples are most memorable: one is a brief exchange between a Chan master and his disciple in *juan* 16 of *Wu deng hui yuan* 五燈會元 [*The Perfect Union of Five Lanterns*]: "A monk asks: 'How is it that one knows it is there, but cannot say it?' The master replies, 'A dumb one tasting honey.'" The other is a line from one of Friedrich Schiller's philosophical epigrams: "The soul speaks, but it is no longer the soul speaking" (*Spricht die Seele, so spricht, ach! die Seele nicht mehr*).[11] The paradox of knowing and speaking often takes dramatic forms in both Daoist and Buddhist writings, in which the mute and deaf often become metaphors for possessing true knowledge. Again, Qian Zhongshu points out analogies in the West: Giordano Bruno also makes the blind and dumb the model of knowing so as to show that perception is deceptive and that speech is corrupt (*per tema che difetto di sguardo o di parola non lo avvilisca*).[12] "The blind, the deaf, and the dumb," says Qian in conclusion, "are indeed the fit images of the Darkness of Unknowing" (455). As Qian observes, "Positive words appear to be negative" (*zhengyan ruo fan* 正言若反) (chapter 78), is "Laozi's way of expression that is ubiquitous in his five-thousand-word book, and it is indeed the mystics' favorite form of expression, what in rhetoric is known as paradox and oxymoron"[13] (463). Evidently, many of the interesting paradoxes and extraordinary images in mystic writings arise from the very dilemma of writing, the perceived difficulty of conveying what is believed to be ineffable and beyond language. By acknowledging the difficulty of speaking and writing, however, mystics call our attention to the very paradoxical nature of language and representation, and by typically putting their ideas in a negative way of expression, they indirectly point at that which cannot be positively stated. The negative or suggestive way of expression, the many metaphors, images, parables, and allegories often make mystic writings symbolic and poetic. Thus, the language of the *Laozi*, and especially that of the *Zhuangzi*, becomes in itself highly literary; that is to say, it calls attention to itself by foregrounding the problem of all language and expression.

The impossibility of naming or speaking, however, is just one side of the coin. The other side, which constitutes what I have called an "ironic pattern,"[14] is the overuse of language to counter its alleged inadequacy. The difficulty of speaking often presents a challenge that does not impede but rather incites speech. "If *Dao* cannot be spoken or named, one must hold one's tongue and shut one's mouth, and never put down a word," says Qian, "but instead it gives rise to all sorts of talk and a myriad of names. Even though one knows that full expression is impossible, one still hopes to hit the mark by chance, or that each expression has at least something appropriate in it" (410). Various efforts to capture an intense aesthetic experience or to describe the impression of a poetic style, like Sikong Tu's 司空圖 (837–908) famous *Shi pin* 詩品 [*Moods of Poetry*], exemplify the dauntless human will to speak in spite of the inadequacy of language. Like "circling around the inexpressible (*ein Herumgehen um das Unaussprechliche*),"[15] such attempts at speaking and naming recall Laozi's confession that, even though he does not really know its name, he would still "call it *Dao*, and constrainedly name it 'Great'" (chapter 25). Thus the mystics condemn language only to circle around the ineffable in an ironic pattern, speaking not less but more, of that which cannot be spoken.

A typical way for the mystics to get out of this dilemma is to erase the difference between speaking and not speaking, language and silence. Zhuangzi's notion of "speaking in non-words" (*yan wuyan* 言無言) offers an intriguing example. In the "Yuyan" 寓言 [Words with Hidden Meanings] chapter of the *Zhuangzi*, we read that "Hence it is called non-words. Speaking in non-words, even if you speak all your life, you would not have spoken; otherwise, even if you have never spoken in all your life, you would still have not kept silent." In the "Xu Wugui" 徐無鬼 chapter, Confucius is described as saying, "I have heard the words of non-words"; and in the "Ze Yang" 則陽 chapter, the Daoist sage is represented as speaking in a language of non-words: "though his mouth utters words, his heart has not spoken." In the "Zhongni" 仲尼 [Confucius] chapter of another Daoist book, the *Liezi*, it is said of Nanguozi 南郭子 that "there is nothing he does not say and nothing he does not know; and yet he says nothing and knows nothing." Qian Zhongshu further cites Buddhist instances that likewise eliminate the distinction between speaking and not speaking, the positive and the negative. One interesting example is a Chan master's remark to his pupils in *juan* 15 of the *Wu deng hui yuan*: "In the case of an enlightened one, he can speak of fire without burning his mouth. He can talk about things all day and yet has nothing hanging on his lips or teeth and has never uttered a word. He puts on clothes and eats his meal everyday, but he never touches a single grain of rice or wears a single thread of silk." As Qian Zhongshu observes, this indicates a common but intriguing mystical method of dealing with the problem of language, that is, "to get rid of words with words in a constant process of constructing and deconstructing" (457). The most interesting example is a passage from the Daoist book, the *Guanyinzi* 關尹子, in which the mutual cancellation of words is vividly symbolized by three creatures that were believed to prey on one another:

The cricket preys on the snake, the snake preys on the frog, and the frog preys on the cricket: one preying on the next. So do the words of the sages: they speak of the imperfection of being

and nonbeing, then they speak of the imperfection of the negation of being and nonbeing, and then they speak of the imperfection of the negation of that negation. They are, so to speak,
sawing up words; only the good ones will leave no word behind.
(457)

Although language may appear inadequate, no other alternative
is available for our attempt at perfect communication, and complaints about linguistic inadequacy in mystic writings are often
exaggerated. Qian Zhongshu considers the statement in the "Appended Words" of the *Yi* 易 [*The Book of Changes*]—"Writing cannot
fully convey the speech, and speech cannot fully convey the meaning"—most closely accordant with the reality of things, while the
mystics far exceed what is reasonable in their condemnation of
language. "Because writing and speech cannot fully convey meaning," says Qian, "the Daoists and the Buddhists would abandon
writing and speech altogether, as if they would cure headache
by cutting off the head" (458). This is in fact a metaphor used in
the Buddhist work the *Yuanjue jing* 圓覺經 [*Mahāvaipulya
pūrṇabuddha sūtra*]: "Both light and awakening are obstacles.
. . . The light and the lighted perish simultaneously, like a person
cutting off his own head. Once the head is cut off, no one can cut it
off any longer." Those bragging mystics, Qian comments, "gladly
congratulate themselves for taking the worst possible plan for the
best shortcut" (458–459). Likewise in Laozi's remarks on language,
speaking, and silence, we can find such mystic exaggerations along
with philosophical insights.

From the move to eliminate the difference between speaking
and silence, Laozi goes further to erase differences between any two
opposite categories. "The world knows beauty as beauty, and that is
ugliness," he claims. "It knows the good as the good, and that is the
not-good. Thus being and non-being give rise to one another; the
difficult and the easy complement each other; the long and the short
measure each other; the high and the low aspire after each other;
sound and note harmonize with each other; the front and the back
follow each other" (chapter 2). Here Wang Bi's note reads: "Joy and
anger have the same roots, right and wrong belong to the same
category; therefore one cannot just list one without the other." These
few words, says Qian, "sum up both the insights and the foibles of
mystics Chinese and foreign, for all mystics, as Saint-Martin re-

marks, are compatriots and share the same language"[16] (411). In seeing the dialectical interaction of opposites, mystics obtain some philosophical insight into the nature of things, but in erasing all differences between the opposites, they also risk lapsing into facile solutions to their dilemma and, in some degenerate cases, making a cheap excuse for their lack of criteria and their indulgence in doing what they are not supposed to do. When Laozi says that the knowledge of beauty already implies that of ugliness, and the knowledge of good already implies that of evil, he means something like Spinoza's famous proposition that *"Determinatio est negatio."*[17] But in arguing that the great *Dao* eliminates all opposition and all differences, he makes a far more extreme claim that when the world knows beauty as beauty, "that *is* ugliness," and when it knows the good as good, "that *is* the not-good." The erasure of differences, Qian remarks, is a commonplace in mysticism, and in expounding the meaning of *Dao*, Laozi tries to emphasize the "eventual return to quiet unity after the splitting of the *Dao* and the shattering of the uncarved block" (412). A fundamental idea in Laozi's philosophy is thus the levelling of all things under heaven, a concept of universal nondifferentiation.

The "Gui gong" 貴公 [Valuing Fairness] section of the *Lüshi chunqiu* has an interesting parable that exemplifies the kind of radical erasure of the difference between things and human beings in Laozi's philosophy: "A man from Jing lost his bow but would not try to find it, saying, 'A man from Jing lost his bow, and people from Jing will get it. Why bother to search for it!' When Confucius heard this, he said, 'It will do if we remove Jing.' But when Laozi heard this, he said, 'It will do if we remove people.'" The point is clear: the man who lost the bow shows his spirit of magnanimity in thinking of his loss as the gain of people from his own area. For Confucius, however, magnanimity means to think of people everywhere, not just from one's home town. Laozi goes further and suggests that true fairness means to think of everything under heaven, not just human beings. For him, to make distinctions between humans and things is to run against the great *Dao* that treats all things equally and always turns back toward the primordial, undifferentiated condition of things. This may indeed be a profound idea of true magnanimity, but as Qian Zhongshu points out, the total erasure of difference between human beings and inanimate things is hard to practice in reality, and even Laozi himself could not always avoid making distinctions. Laozi has said that "the sage is for the belly, not for the eye, and thus he abandons the one and takes the other" (chapter 12); also that "a great man resides in the thick, and does not dwell in the thin; he resides in the fruit, and does not dwell in the flower, so he abandons the one and takes the other" (chapter 38). Isn't it true, then, asks Qian, that in all these cases Laozi does "'know beauty' and 'know the good,' and categorically makes choices and decisions?" (413). In *juan* 92 of *Chengzhai ji* 誠齋集, Yang Wanli 楊萬里 (1127–1206) criticized Laozi for "removing people" in the parable quoted above. Laozi's suggestion may appear profound for its radical challenge to our commonsense distinctions, but, says Yang from a human-centered Confucian perspective, it hardly sounds reasonable. "Moreover, the bow exists for a useful purpose. If we 'remove people,' who will get the bow? And once found, who will use it?" The poet Bo Juyi 白居易 also faults Laozi for contradicting himself in writing a book of some five thousand words about what he believes to be beyond language and cannot be talked about. Indeed, one can find many statements in the *Laozi* that are inconsistent and very difficult, if not utterly impossible, to put in practice.

Such self-contradictions and inconsistencies, Qian Zhongshu observes, are not accidental but ineluctable in all philosophy and mysticism. "Philosophers may leave their audience in wonderment with high-sounding and obscure theories and endless tall talk," says Qian, "but they can hardly take one step in putting these into practice, and consequently they speak of what they cannot do, and do what they do not permit in their speech" (436). Laozi declares in chapter 13 that "When I do not have a body, what do I have to worry about?" The human body, he maintains, is the source of all our troubles, and once we do away with it, we would have no trouble. And yet, he also says that the sage "takes his body as something extraneous, and it is preserved" (chapter 7). He asks, "Name and body, which is dearer?" (chapter 44) and he also admonishes us with, "Do not leave your body to peril" (chapter 52). To preserve one's own body and to speak of what one knows, Qian argues, are fundamental needs and desires in real life, while the elimination of one's body and language is just a metaphysical idea or wish that can be fulfilled only in imagination. Like everyone else, the mystics are subject to the needs and desires of real life, but they also want to hold on to their metaphysical ideas and mystical fantasies, and as a result they cannot but fall into the quandary of self-contradiction. This is why, Qian suggests, Laozi's philosophy becomes the source of very different theories once it enters real life, the realms of action and politics:

> As words are empty in themselves, when they are attached to events by force, they become sophistical and evasive. As deeds are common in life, when they are embellished with words, they become false and obstinate. "No words" thus leads to quoted authoritative words, words with hidden meanings, words responding to occasions, and words that are fanciful and absurd; "no body" thus turns to justify oily manners and slick acquiescence in order to save one's skin and to obtain longevity; "no action" thus comes to legitimize any action, action with no scruples or constraints. When manifest in practice and deeds, the HuangLao philosophy of purity and quietude thus becomes the secretive but firm and stern action advocated by Shen Buhai 申不害 and Han Fei. (413–414)

What in Wang Bi's note is called the "six categories"—being and non-being, the difficult and the easy, the long and the short, the high and the low, sound and note, the front and the back—like the ten binary oppositions in Pythagoras,[18] forms a dialectical relationship of theses and antitheses that give rise to each other. To recognize the mutual production of opposite categories is an important philosophical insight, but the mystics want to transcend the differentiation of categories by simply denying their difference and levelling the thesis with the antithesis. Commenting on Laozi's mystic erasure of difference, Yan Fu 嚴復 (1853–1921) remarks that "When cornered in hot pursuit, the African ostrich would bury its head in sand, believing that seeing no danger is out of danger. What difference is there between that and Laozi's way of 'eliminating learning'?" Qian Zhongshu quotes this with approval and adds a similar sarcastic comment, borrowed from Hegel's remarks on Schelling, that such obscure undifferentiation is "as dark as night, wherein all cows are black (*sein Absolutes für die Nacht ausgeben, worin alle Kühe schwarz sind*)"[19] (414).

Standing at the opposite end from such Daoist ideas, the Confucians seem to have a more balanced view. Zhu Xi 朱熹 (1130–1200) is recorded as saying in *Zhuzi yulei* 朱子語類 [*The Classified Conversations of Master Zhu*]: "Though good and evil are opposite to one another, we must differentiate the main from the minor; though heaven's laws and human desires are equally distributed, we must understand which is near kin and which is not." He clearly indicates that things in binary opposition are not exactly equal. Dong Zhongshu 董仲舒 (179–104 B.C.E.), among others, also remarks in the "*Jiyi*" 基義 [Basic Meaning] chapter of the *Chunqiu fanlu* 春秋繁露 that "Nothing will not come to unity, but each unity has both the *yin* and the *yang*," and that "the *yin* cannot go on its path alone." In other words, though the *yin* and the *yang* form a pair of opposites that eventually harmonize with each other, the *yin* is subject to the rule of *yang*. The universe the Confucians conceived of is thus clearly differentiated into a moral and political hierarchy, in which human agents are invested with knowledge, judgment, choices, and responsibilities. The Buddhists, as Qian goes on to show, also try to avoid the either/or dilemma by proposing a theory of the middle path (*zhongdao* 中道) or *madhyama pratipad*, which navigates between the conflicting demands of a binary opposition.

"Heaven and earth are not benevolent and treat all things as straw dogs," says Laozi; "the sage is not benevolent and treats all people as straw dogs" (chapter 5). As Wang Bi notes, in treating people as "straw dogs," that is, insignificant creatures, the sage is following heaven and earth. Qian's commentary makes two important points here. First, "not benevolent" (*bu ren* 不仁) in this context does not mean "cruel" or "ruthless," but "numb" or "unconcerned" in the sense of being destitute of human emotions and feelings. Heaven and earth, or Nature and all the things in it, exist in and of themselves; they are not there to benefit human beings. They are "not benevolent" or "numb" because they have neither love for humans nor ire against them, "just as the wreck of a floating boat or the fall of a loose tile, which may leave you drowning or break your head, but is nonetheless completely unplanned and coming out of no one's intent" (418). Laozi's notion of the cosmos is thus resolutely antiteleological, and Qian compares it with similar views expressed by Lucretius, Francis Bacon, Spinoza, Voltaire, Heinrich Heine, and some other Western writers. On the Chinese side, there are also many echoes of the same idea. Du Fu's 杜甫 (712–770) lines in "*Xin'an li*" 新安吏 [The Official at Xin'an]—"Withered eyes will appear so bony, /Heaven and earth have no feelings, after all"—can be taken, says Qian, as "a ready-made interpretation of Laozi" (419). Xunzi 荀子, Wang Chong 王充, and Han Yu 韓愈 all provide apposite quotations to illustrate the point. So do many Western thinkers and writers, among whom John Stuart Mill's *Three Essays on Religion* is especially helpful in pointing out Nature's "most supercilious disregard both of mercy and of justice"[20] (420). To say that heaven and earth are "not benevolent," however, already describes the universe as if it were endowed with a will and intention, thus making a sort of personification allegory.

The second point in Qian's commentary deals with the sage's indifference, in his effort to imitate heaven and earth, toward the average person. But if heaven and earth are "not benevolent," it is only because they are not human and have no heart or human feelings. The same is not true of the sage, however. "Though the sage (*sheng ren* 聖人) is 'saintly' (*sheng* 聖)," says Qian, "he is also 'human' (*ren* 人). Being human, he has a heart, and it is only by turning callous, and more likely out of cruelty and sadistic pleasure, that he can become 'not benevolent'" (420). The desire to become such callous and unfeeling saints and sages, Qian continues, is not that uncommon in different philosophical and religious traditions. "The 'apathy' of the Stoics and the 'saintly indifference' of the Christian mystics all dwell in the same area as Laozi's idea that 'the sage is not benevolent'" (420). In following the nonhuman heaven and earth, the sage thus goes against his own nature and may become completely inhuman. Here again, Qian points out the possible connection between Laozi's Daoist philosophy and the high-handed political theory of the pre-Qin Legalists:

> Trying to conform to the "virtue" (*de*) of heaven and earth in being "unbenevolent" and to make it their principle in life, the rough and rowdy ones necessarily become cruel and pitiless, while the soft and submissive ones necessarily become oily and shamelessly conniving. Once materialized in the real world, the HuangLao *Dao* and *de* turn into the harshness and cruelty of Han Fei's Legalism; and when put to practical use, Christian mysticism becomes Père Joseph's cunning and conspiracy.[21] Can we say that all these are only degenerate epigones' corruption of the origin, their loss of primary source? Or shall we say that these are indeed marks and traces without which the origin will not be able to manifest itself? The biography of Han Fei in *Shiji* [*Records of the Grand Historian*] already notes that "all his harsh and merciless ideas originate in the

meanings of *Dao* and *de*"; and the biography of Zhong Hui 鐘會
in *Wei shu* 魏書 [*The Book of Wei*] of the *San guo zhi* 三國志
[*Chronicles of the Three Kingdoms*] also records that "twenty
books were found in Hui's home, which carry the title of *Dao
lun* 道論 [*Treatise on the Dao*], but in fact they are works of
the Legalist school." These can all be seen as illuminating
evidences. (421–422)

Refusing to grant any special privilege or status to sages or
saints, Qian Zhongshu's commentaries are radically iconoclastic.
Laozi states that in following heaven and earth, "the sage puts his
body last, and it comes out first; he takes his body as something
extraneous, and it is preserved" (chapter 7). Qian points out that
though the sage claims to imitate heaven and earth in putting his
body last and taking it to be extraneous, he is motivated to do so in
order precisely to let his body come out first and have it preserved.
The sage, in other words, is not at all eliminating his own body to
become completely selfless as he claims, but turns out to be more
selfish than the ordinary person. "I have great worries only because
I have a body," says Laozi. "When I do not have a body, what do I
have to worry about?" (chapter 13). Qian again discusses how these
words adumbrate or provide an excuse for later occult practices in
Daoism as a popular religion to search for the magic panacea of
longevity and immortality. The fundamental desire here is to have
a body but not the bodily pain or the thousand natural shocks that
flesh is heir to. Qian quotes many occult Daoist books to show how
they willfully misquote or misinterpret Laozi to endorse their absurd projects of magic and occultism. They all borrow Laozi's authority to legitimize their strange practices, as if "selling cheap
horsemeat under a signboard of sheep's head, and the other uses of
charms, magic words, secret recipes, and delirious talk all attempt
at having a body but no worries, and having life but no old age, no
disease, no death" (428). The mystics are thus exposed to be not
superhuman, but human, all too human, despite their effort to
conceal that fact in deliberately obscure and arcane language.

The second offshoot of Laozi's statement is not occultism but
asceticism. Mystics often look upon their body and bodily needs as
great impediments to their ultimate goal, and so they advocate
"diminishing one's body and reducing it to almost nothing so that
one would have no worry or nothing to worry about" (428). Qian
quotes a phrase that appears in the *Wenzi*, *Lüshi chunqiu* and

Huainanzi: "not to let internal desires go out is called to bolt the door from outside, and not to let external desires come in is called to shut the door from inside." Thus, the first target for the ascetic to attack and control is basic human desires and sensibilities. Zhuangzi describes the way to "long life" as "seeing nothing in the eye, hearing nothing in the ear, knowing nothing at heart . . . be cautious of what is inside and closed to what is outside." Laozi admonishes that "not to let people see what is desirable will keep their minds from being confused" (chapter 3); he also warns that "five colors blind people's eyes, five notes make their ears go deaf, and five flavors make their palates lose the sense of taste" (chapter 12). There are many other examples, and Qian mentions some Buddhist formulations in particular. We find this typical dialogue in *Da zhidu lun* or *Mahāprajñāpāramitā-śāstra*: "Question: 'Why do you ask whether I have less trouble and less illness? . . . Why don't you ask whether I have no trouble and no illness? . . .' Answer: 'If you have a body, then you have misery, . . . the body is the source of miseries, and at no time is it free from illness.'" A more graphic example appears in both *Fenbie gongde lun* 分別功德論 [*Gunanirdēsa-śāstra*] and *Piyu jing* 譬喻經 [*Avadāna sūtra*], which describes a man's soul whipping his dead body and crying, "This is the corpse that imprisoned me," and "This is my former body that did evil things." Calling the body a corpse is common enough in mystic writings, and many ascetics practiced self-mortification. The philosopher Democritus blinded himself because he held that physical sight is the impediment to truth, while blindness will let him see internally (*oculorum impedimentis liberasset*).[22] Both the *Sishi er zhang jing* 四十二章經 [*Forty-Two Chapter sutra*] and *Faju piyu jing* 法句譬喻經 [*Dharmapadāvadāna sūtra*] mention a man who wants to castrate himself in order to put an end to his sexual desires, and Buddha admonishes him first to "put an end to his mind." In Western literature, Qian quotes the words of Jesus that there are true believers "which have made themselves eunuchs for the kingdom of heaven's sake" (Matt. 19:12). Some Christian writers claim that "The Lord himself opens the kingdom of the heavens to the eunuchs."[23] Qian also mentions Origen's self-castration as a prominent example.

The last of Qian's examples in this section is taken not from history, but from fiction: the great novel *Honglou meng* 紅樓夢 [*The Dream of the Red Chamber*]. In chapter 21, having read the "Quqie" 胠篋 [Prying Coffers] chapter of the *Zhuangzi* and goaded by the idea of eliminating all sensual pleasures, a tipsy Bao Yu took up his writing-brush and put down the thoughts that came to his mind, declaring that he would sever his emotional attachment to all the women in his life, that he would "burn Aroma and scatter Musk," "discard Bao Chai and destroy Dai Yu," so that "female beauty and ugliness will become alike," and that he would "no longer have a heart of tender love." As Qian Zhongshu observes, internal desires and external things are closely related, "to shut the door to the inside is meant to cut off the outside, and cutting off the outside gradually leads to a misanthropic attitude, and thus the hatred of one's own body becomes hatred of all others" (430). After reading Bao Yu's ludicrous misogynistic harangue, Dai Yu, who is always superior in intelligence, wrote a quatrain to ridicule him, in which she says of Bao Yu, "Not feeling sorry for his own ignorance,/He turns to vilify others with ugly words." Ignorance, says Qian Zhongshu, is indeed the fault of all those self-loathing and misanthropic ascetics, because they do not seem to understand that "the heart is necessarily connected with the body, and the soul is necessarily linked with one's physical form (*Leib bin ich und Seele; und Seele ist nur ein Wort für ein Etwas am Leibe*)"[24] (430).

The third offshoot of Laozi's idea of the body and its relationship with the outside world is the most dubious, because it argues that the body, being extraneous and inessential, does not affect the inner course of the mind or spirit, and consequently it does not matter what one does with the body. Thus, the *Weimojie suoshuo jing* or *Vimalakīrti nirdeśa sūtra* declares that "you need not break away from lust, anger, or foolishness, nor go along with them"; and that "to walk in the devious way is meant to reach Buddha's way." The "Yang Zhu" 楊朱 chapter of the *Liezi* calls two men addicted to alcohol and sex enlightened "true men" (*zhen ren* 真人), because "those who are good at managing the inside will not necessarily cause disorder in things outside, but will feel comfortable with them in their own nature." This may of course easily become a pretext for self-indulgence, and indeed there are numerous phrases that make excuses for debauchery or gluttony, such as "a prostitute in the eye but no prostitute at heart," and "Buddha stays in my heart while wine and meat pass through my stomach" (431). Qian also cites Western examples of the separation of the body and the mind, the idea that sin is mental rather than physical (*Mentem peccare, non corpus*), and that chastity in the mind is not affected by physical blemish (*Si autem animi bonum est [pudicitia], etiam oppresso corpore non amittitur*).[25] In literary works, says Qian, such arguments are often used either for expediting seduction or for offering consolation.

It is not just to the problematic side of the *Laozi*, however, that Qian Zhongshu's commentaries call our attention, for he has reserved some of his highest praise for Laozi's important philosophical insights. For example, Laozi says that "Turning back (*fan* 反) is the way the *Dao* moves" (chapter 40). Wang Bi provides this brief note: "The high has its base in the low, the noble has its roots in the humble, and having has its function in non-having; this is the 'turning back.'" According to Qian Zhongshu, however, Wang Bi's annotations to the many passages in which the word *fan* appears "are all superficial and fail to unfold the subtleties," because Laozi uses the word *fan* to mean two opposite things at the same time, the way Hegel uses the word *aufheben*. "The word *fan* has two meanings," says Qian. "The first is the *fan* as in *zhengfan* 正反 (positive and negative), that is, negation; the second is the *fan* as in *wangfan* 往反 (going out and coming back), that is, return" (445). The best description of the way the *Dao* moves is in Laozi's remarks in chapter 25: "I would constrainedly name it 'Great'. Being great, it is said to vanish. Vanishing, it is said to move far away. Being far away, it is said to return." Qian Zhongshu compares this with the syllogistic movement of opposites in the Hegelian dialectics:

> "Great" is the positive (*zheng*); to "vanish" is to depart from it, to run counter to Great in self-alienation, and that is the negation. "To move far away" is the end result of departure, the extreme of negation, and it is said to "return" because moving far away will reverse the course, that is, the negation of the negation (*dé-négation*), and the "ultimate conformity" (*zhishun* 至順) will "harmonize" (*he* 合) with the positive. Therefore, the word *fan* means both countering (*weifan* 違反) in its negative sense, and return (*huifan* 回反) in its positive sense. What Hegel calls "the negation of the negation" (*Das zweite Negative, das Negative des Negation, ist jenes Aufheben des Widerspruchs*)[26] characterizes the same principle. (446)

Hegel had declared the Chinese language unfit for philosophizing, which Qian Zhongshu refuted most effectively by pointing out

the use of terms like *Dao*, *fan*, and *yi* 易 in Chinese that contain two
opposite meanings simultaneously, just like Hegel's favorite term,
the much-vaunted *Aufhebung*, which presumably exemplifies the
dialectical nature of the German language. Laozi's insight into the
dialectic movement of things thus adumbrated what in Hegel was to
develop into a ponderous system:

> The word *fan* in *fan zhe dao zhi dong* 反者道之動 ("Turning back
> is the way the *Dao* moves") thus means both "negation" and
> "return" or "the negation of negation," and the phrase contains
> both sides of the movement: to move against the positive, and
> also to move against negation and harmonize with the positive.
> It is my humble opinion that among all our ancient writings,
> these five characters from the *Laozi* epitomizes the principles
> of dialectics, while the seven characters from the "Jinxin" 盡心
> chapter of *Mencius*, "*Wu chi zhi chi, wu chi yi*" 無恥之恥無恥矣
> ("The shame of having no sense of shame is truly shameless")
> provides an example of dialectics; both phrases are concise and
> profound. . . . Hegel remarks that contradiction is the root of
> all movement and liveliness (*die Wurzel aller Bewugung und
> Lebendigkeit*), that dialectics can be conceived of as a circle
> that winds up in itself (*als einen in sich geschlungen Kreis*),
> that its moving forward (*ein Vorwärts*) is also moving
> backward (*ein Rückwärts*), and that the true (*das Wahre*)
> manifests itself in an opposite doubling (*die entgegensetzende
> Verdopplung*); he also describes the process of thinking as a
> circle that turns back to itself (*ein Kreis, der in sich
> zurückgeht*).[27] All his hundreds of words are nothing but the
> unfolding and expansion of what is meant by the one phrase in
> the *Laozi*. (446)

By citing from many different sources, Qian Zhongshu shows
that Hegel's and Laozi's insights into the dialectical relationships of
things find many different expressions in other writers in the East
and the West. In the Chinese tradition, the idea that *wu ji bi
fan* 物極必反 ("When things reach their extreme, they will necessarily take the course of a reversal") is a commonplace and is articulated
in such diverse work as the *Yi, Shiji, Wenzi, Liezi, Zhuangzi, Xunzi,
Lüshi chunqiu, Huainanzi*, as well as Buddhist writings. Closely
related to this idea is Laozi's claim that "The further one goes out,
the less one knows" (chapter 47). Qian points out that here Laozi is

not speaking of knowledge of the usual kind, but the search for the knowledge of *Dao* that is not to be found out there in the external world. The external (going out) and the internal (knowledge) forms another pair of dialectical opposites, and the one who searches for such knowledge will eventually find it, having gone to the extreme of distance, not outside but inside, at the end point which turns out to be the initial point of departure. As the "Daoyuan" 道原 [On the *Dao*] chapter of the *Wenzi* has it, "Flat is the thoroughfare that lays not far outside, but the one who searches far and wide will go and then come back." The Daoist book the *Guanyinzi* offers an interesting bodily metaphor: "The contemplation of *Dao* is like contemplating water. A man feels that looking at a pond is not enough, so he goes to a river, a big river, and then the sea, saying, 'This is the extreme of waters!' And yet he does not know that our saliva, bodily fluid, spittle, and tears are all water as well." This is not just a Daoist metaphor, but also found in Buddhist and other mystic writings. The parable of a poor son who forsakes his father only to come back home and find his father's house filled with treasure, as told in the fourth chapter, "Xinjie pin" 信解品 [Faith-discernment], of the *Lotus sutra*, symbolizes the same idea. Qian Zhongshu then cites three examples from the West: Plotinus (*Ennéades*, I.vi.8; V.ix.1), Augustine (*Confessions*, X.27), and a German mystic poet who writes, "Heaven is in you/What are you looking for by another door?" (*Der Himmel ist in dir/Was suchst du ihn dann bei einer andern Tür?*).[28] He goes on to show that "these are not just words of Buddhists, Daoists, and those who have forsaken the mundane world, for the Confucians, in speaking of their teachings, happen to reach the same point" (451–452).

From the Confucian *Analects*, Qian quotes the Master saying, "Is benevolence far away?" (vii.30), implying that this supreme virtue is to be sought inside, near at hand. The *Mencius* offers more examples: in the "*Li lou*" 離婁 chapter, Mencius criticizes those who do not start with themselves in their search for *Dao*: "the *Dao* is nearby but one seeks it far off, and a thing is easy but one tries to do it as something difficult" (4A11); he also says that when the gentleman finds *Dao* "in himself," he will be able to "find its source wherever he turns" (4B14). In the "Gaozi" 告子 chapter, Mencius again emphasizes the idea that *Dao* is to be found inside, not outside: "the *Dao* is like the thoroughfare, how can it be difficult to know? The only worry is that people will not seek it. If you go home and seek it, you will find more than enough teachers" (6B2); and in the "Jinxin" 盡心 chapter, we find one of the most well-known of Mencius's propositions: "All the ten thousand things are present within me. I turn to myself and be true, . . . there is no way nearer than this in seeking benevolence" (7A4). What Laozi means by *Dao* of course differs from Mencius's *Dao*, but here Qian Zhongshu is concerned with the way in which the search for *Dao* is expressed as a dialectic reversal, the idea that what one looks for outside turns out to be present inside, but only to be discovered after a long detour of seeking externally, in all the wrong places. In that sense, then, the thing looked for may be anything one wishes for, and the expression of a reversal is found not only in philosophy but also in literature.

An interesting example is a poem written by a nun, recorded in *juan* 18 of *Helin yulu* 鶴林玉露: "All day long I sought for but couldn't find spring,/My straw sandals were all worn in treading clouds in the fields;/Returning home, I culled a bundle of plum blossoms and smelled,/There it was, spring in full bloom on top of every branch." Another example, quoted from the "Shen si" 神思 [Miraculous ideas] chapter of Liu Xie's *Wenxin diaolong* 文心雕龍 [*The Literary Mind or the Carving of Dragons*], describes the difficult search for the perfect literary expression: "Sometimes the idea resides in the mind and at heart, but one seeks it on the surface of the earth; and sometimes the meaning is near at hand, but one's thinking seems blocked from it by mountains and rivers." The Goncourt brothers provide a similar description of the search for literary originality as a process of going out and then coming back: "In literature, one starts searching for originality in others, far from oneself, and finally finds it naturally in oneself, and very close to oneself" (*En littérature, on commence à chercher l'originalité laborieusement chez les autres, et très loin de soi, . . . plus tard on la trouve naturellement en soi . . . et tout près de soi*).[29] All these examples bear upon one another and illuminate the compact phrase in the *Laozi* about the movement of things in a process of gradual reversal, the return of what moves forward in the shape of a circle, in which the end meets with the initial point of departure. All these expressions of a dialectical reversal, as Qian Zhongshu remarks, "are testimonies of human experiences in life, not to be monopolized by the mystics and their esoteric words" (453). This remark can of course be taken as disclosing Qian Zhongshu's method and his major contribution in *Guan zhui bian*, because to bring the esoteric words or ideas of a difficult work to the testimonies of human experience is precisely what Qian has accomplished in his commentaries. By making connections between the text of an ancient work with what we can understand from our own experiences in life, he is able to render what is esoteric fully accessible, and elucidate its meaning with a wealth of examples.

That may explain why reading Qian's *Tan yi lu* or *Guan zhui bian* is not just to find out what a particular passage from an ancient book means, but to discover a whole world of meaning that relates not only to books, but to life and our experiences in life, life of the body and of the mind, life as living as well as feeling and contemplating. That may also explain why Qian Zhongshu's commentaries are always intertextual and, some may even say, digressional. While traditional commentaries mostly limit themselves to the explication of single words or lines and rarely go beyond to illuminate the original with much else, Qian's elucidation not only makes the text clear but unfolds its many aspects by comparing it with many other texts, texts of different genres, languages, and traditions. The numerous quotations in Qian's commentaries thus expand the meaning of a particular text and fully develop its ramifications, and often put it in comparison with Western texts and ideas. The point of having quotations from Western sources is not just to add more examples to illustrate or decorate what is already clear in the Chinese context, but to reveal the wide scope and deep affinities of the human mind across linguistic and cultural boundaries. As Qian Zhongshu puts it himself, "By the sea in the East and the West, the mind and reason are the same, though at distant places; in the learning of the northern and the southern schools, the moral teaching and scholarship are not divided."[30] Those who want to see precisely the division and separateness of the human mind may harbor a deep suspicion of any East-West comparison, but they can hardly answer the challenge of Qian Zhongshu's scholarship.[31] Since differences are everywhere on the surface, and those between China and the West are glaringly obvious, it takes a great deal of knowledge, insight, and critical thinking to discern the underlying connections, analogies, and affinities in unexpected locations. In Qian Zhongshu's writings, those connections, analogies, and affinities are never simply assumed or stated, but always come out in detailed contexts as concrete words and phrases, as textual evidence in the form of copious quotations. And that, one must admit, is impressive erudition and scholarship.

It would be misleading, however, to think of *Guan zhui bian* as concerned only with the search for similarities. In fact, important distinctions are often made at the appropriate points. For example, the Daoists and the Buddhists all advocate a mystic teaching of silent intuition, and Confucius also claims that "I will not speak" (*The Analects*, xvii.19). Some have argued that Confucius's desire to keep silent is similar to the silence of the Buddhist Vimalakīrti, but Qian Zhongshu maintains that "to inject Confucianism into Buddhism is like mixing water with oil, and that is very different from mixing Buddhism with Daoism, which is like blending water and milk." He goes on to quote one of Lu Jiuyuan's 陸九淵 remarks (*Yulu* 語錄) in *juan* 34 of *Xiangshan quanji* 象山全集 that "if Confucius said, 'I will not speak,' he had already spoken." What Lu meant to do here, says Qian, is "to differentiate Confucius from Vimalakīrti" (459). Some of the basic terms are shared by different schools of thinking, but the meanings of such terms differ significantly, and where similar language is used, the relationship between different authors may not be a direct influence. Qian Zhongshu says:

Some teachings and theories may agree with others, but are not derived from them, as in the case of LaoZhuang and the Buddhists; and some may threaten to attack others but surreptitiously follow them, as in the case of the pseudo-Daoist classics after Wang Fu 王浮 with regard to the Buddhist sutras. If one claims to find a relationship of source and derivation when there is occasional convergence of purpose or interest, one would fall into the same category as Shizu's 世祖 edict as recorded in *Shi Lao zhi* 釋老志 [Records of Buddhism and Daoism] of the *Weishu*, or the epilogue in the biography of Li Wei 李蔚 in the *XinTangshu* 新唐書 [*The New Chronicles of Tang*], which declare that all Buddhist sutras were nothing but expansion on what they had stolen from Laozi and Zhuangzi; or one would resemble those Qing scholars who asserted that Western religion and sciences were all based on the *Mozi*, and that Western political writings and social institutions all derived from the *Zhou guan* 周官. If at the glimpse of some similarities in appearance, one would rush to the arbitrary judgment of family relations, then, how does that differ from taking the cat for the tiger's uncle, the elephant for the hog's nephew, and the ostrich for the camel's kin? (440)

Difference and similarity, like determination and negation, are mutually defined and mutually implicated, so it would be pointless to emphasize one at the expense of the other in the abstract. When we tell the difference between two things, we have already assumed their comparability and put them in a larger context within which it would make sense to compare them as two items of a more general category. Otherwise, it would be pointless and indeed impossible to say that they are different. To understand Laozi in the context of Eastern and Western philosophy and mysticism, says Qian, is "not to reconcile differences, nor to claim false kinship relations," because all mystics share important ideas and terminology, "like old friends or close neighbors, though separate at the ends of the world, and they do not need anyone to put them into a forced marriage in the first place" (465). And yet, it takes a great deal of knowledge and thinking to recognize the connections and similar ways of expressing ideas in the various philosophical and mystic writings. Once Qian Zhongshu has disclosed those connections and similarities, we can read the *Laozi* as we have never read it before, and understand its many ideas as meaningful and significant to us in our own time, capable of enriching our own experience, far beyond the confines of a mysterious and arcane Daoism. It is hard to imagine a better way to introduce us to that little ancient book.

——————————— *NOTES* ———————————

1. Born in 1910, Qian Zhongshu began to publish his important works in the 1940s: *Xie zai rensheng bianshang* 寫在人生邊上 [*Written on the Margins of Life*, 1941], *Ren shou gui* 人獸鬼 [*Humans, Beasts, and Ghosts*, 1946], *Wei cheng* 圍城 [*Fortress Besieged*, 1947], and *Tan yi lu* 談藝錄 [*Discourses on Art*, 1948]. From the fifties till the late seventies, however, the political situation in China made it impossible for him to produce much, and he kept an extremely low profile. With the end of the Cultural Revolution and the publication of his major work *Guan zhui bian* 管錐編 [*The Tube and Awl Chapters*] in 1979, Qian Zhongshu was rediscovered by Chinese readers, and both his literary and scholarly works have since been in great demand. The title *Guan zhui bian* is excessively modest, as it alludes to a famous phrase in the "Qiushui" 秋水 [Autumn Flood] chapter of the *Zhuangzi* "to peep at the sky through a tube and to point at the earth with an awl," which of course produces a very limited and inadequate view. In reality, however, this immense work of commentaries on ancient Chinese classics is widely admired as representative of the very best of Chinese scholarship in modern times. Qian's novel, *Wei cheng*, was made into a hit television series in 1990,

and the study of Qian Zhongshu has become one of the most lively events on the Chinese cultural scene.

In the early seventies, C. T. Hsia was among the first to introduce Qian Zhongshu as a writer to Western readers in *A History of Modern Chinese Fiction* (New Haven: Yale University Press, 1971). Qian's novel, *Wei cheng*, appeared in an English translation as *Fortress Besieged* in the late seventies (Jeanne Kelly and Nathan Mao, trans. [Bloomington: Indiana University Press, 1979]). There are some critical comments on Qian's literary creations, but except for a few of Qian's essays in *Renditions*, a translation journal published by the Chinese University of Hong Kong, there is no English translation of Qian's major scholarly works. Theodore Huters's valuable critical biographical study, *Qian Zhongshu* (Boston: Twayne Publishers, 1982), remains the only work of its kind in English; it mentions but does not discuss Qian's magnum opus, the multi-volume *Guan zhui bian* or what Huters calls *Pipe-Awl Chapters* (Beijing: Zhonghua shuju, 4 vols. 1979); second ed., 5 vols., 1986. The situation seems better in France. Simon Leys (Pierre Ryckmans) calls Qian "un écrivain de génie," and highly praises his erudition and critical insight. "Sa connaissance de la littérature chinoise, du patrimoine occidental, de la littérature universelle," writes Simon Leys in *Le Monde* (June 10, 1983), "est prodigieuse. Qian Zhongshu n'a pas son pareil aujourd'hui en Chine et même dans le monde." There is a French translation of five of Qian's critical essays, but so far no English version of Qian's major scholarly works is available. I have heard that Professor Ronald Egan of the University of California at Santa Barbara is preparing an English translation of some selected passages from *Guan zhui bian*, which will no doubt be an important contribution and will make Qian's commentaries on Chinese classics more widely appreciated in the West.

2. Qian Zhongshu, "Du La'aokong 讀拉奧孔" [Reading *Laokoon*], *Qi zhui ji* 七綴集 [*Collection of Seven Essays*] (Shanghai: Shanghai guji, 1985), 30. For a discussion of Qian's suspicion of systems and its relation with his form of writing, see Zhang Longxi 張隆溪, *"Zi cheng yijia fenggu: tan Qian Zhongshu zhuzuo de tedian jian lun xitong yu pianduan sixiang de jiazhi* 自成一家風骨：談錢鍾書著作的特點兼論系統與片斷思想的價值" [On the Features of Qian Zhongshu's Writing and the Values of Systems and Fragmented Ideas] in *Dushu* 讀書 [*Reading Monthly*] (Oct. 1992): 89–96.

3. Qian Zhongshu, *Guan zhui bian*, 2 ed. (Beijing: Zhonghna shuju, 1986), vol. 2, 402. Further quotations from *Guan zhui bian* will be included in the main text with reference to page numbers only.

4. For a comparison of the differences between the Wang Bi text and the Mawangdui text, see Appendix III in Paul J. Lin, *A Translation of Lao Tzu's*

Tao Te Ching and Wang Pi's Commentary (Ann Arbor: Center for Chinese Studies, The University of Michigan, 1977), 157–176.

5. [Qian's note] A. France, *Le Jardin d'Epicure, Oeuvres complètes*, Calmann-Lévy, IX 430–431. Hamann, quoted in F. Mauthner, *Kritik der Sprache*, 3 Aufl., I, 355; II, 718.

6. [Qian's note] Hegel, *Phänomenologie des Geistes*, Berlin: Akademie Verlag, 229. Nietzsche, *Götzendämmerang*, "*Streifzüges eines Unzeitgemässen*," § 26, *Werke*, hrsg. K. Schlechta, II, 1005.

7. [Qian's note] Mauthner, op. cit., I, 81–82, 117–120 (*das heilige Schweigen*), III, 617–618 (*die Stummen des Himmels*); M. Scheler, *Die Wissensformen und die Gesellschaft*, 63 (*sanctum silentium*).

8. [Qian's note] S. Ullmann, *Semantics*, 173. Cf. Hobbes, *Leviathan*, Routledge, p. 18. Heidegger, *Sein und Zeit*, Ite Hälfte, 3. Aufl., 165 (*der Mensch als Seiendes, das redet*).

9. [Qian's note] Plotin, *Ennéades*, V.3.13: "C'est pourquoi, en vérité, il est inéffable; quoi que vous diriez, vous direz *quelque chose*: or ce qui est audelà de toutes choses, . . . n'a pas de nom; car ce nom serait autre chose que lui"; 14: "Nous pouvons parler de lui, mais non pas l'exprimer luimême . . . il est trop haut et trop grand pour être appelé l'être . . . supérieur au verbe" (tr. É. Bréhier, V, 67, 68).

10. [Qian's note] *Thirteen Epistles*, Letter VII, tr. L. A. Post, 96–97. Cf. E. Cassirer, *Die Philosophie des symbolischen Formen*, I. 63–65.

11. [Qian's note] Schiller, "Sprache," *Werke*, hrsg. L. Bellermann, 2. Aufl., I, 184.

12. [Qian's note] Bruno, *Degli eroici furori*, II, Dial. iv, *Opere di Bruno e di Campanella*, Ricciardi, 648.

13. [Qian's note] Jonas Cohn, *Theorie der Dialektik*, 219: "Die beliebteste Ausdruckform dieser Geisteshaltung, die man 'intuitionistisch' nennen kann, ist das Oxymoron"; cf. 110.

14. See Zhang Longxi, *The Tao and the Logos: Literary Hermeneutics, East and West* (Durham: Duke University Press, 1992), 37–43.

15. [Qian's note] B. Croce, *La Poesia*, 5th ed., 131 (W. Humboldt).

16. [Qian's note] Evelyn Underhill, *Mysticism*, 12th ed., 80.

17. [Qian's note] *Correspondence*, Letter L (to Jarig Jelles), tr. A. Wolf, 270. Cf. *Ethica*, I, Prop. viii, Schol. 1, "Classiques Garnier", I, 30.

18. [Qian's note] Aristotle, *Metaphysics*, I. 5, 985 b 23.

19. [Qian's note] *Phänomenologie des Geistes*, op. cit., 19.

20. [Qian's note], J. S. Mill, *Three Essays on Religion*, Longmans, p. 29.

21. [Qian's note] A. Huxley, *Grey Eminence*, 137–138, 186.

22. [Qian's note] Aulus Gellins, X. xvii, "Loeb", II, 260. Cf. Descartes, *Méditations métaphysiques* III: "Je fermerai maintenant les yeux, je boucherai mes oreilles, je détournerai tous mes sens" etc.

23. [Qian's note] E. Westermarck, *Early Beliefs and their Social Influence*, 122–123.

24. [Qian's note] Nietzsche, *Also sprach Zarathustra*, "Von den Verächten des Leibes", *Werke*, hrsg. K Schlechta, II, 300.

25. [Qian's note] Livy, I. 1.viii.9 (Collatinus et al to Lucretia), "Loeb", I, 202; St. Augustine, *The City of God*, I.xviii, "Loeb", Vol. I, p. 80; cf. VIV.iii: "*anima peccatrix fecit esse corruptibilem carnem.*"

26. [Qian's note] *Wissenschaft der Logik*, op. cit., III, 365.

27. [Qian's note] Ib., II, 80; III, 373, 375; *Aesthetik*, Aufbau, 69; *Phänomenologie des Geistes*, op. cit., 20; *Geschichte der Philosophie*, Felix Meiner, I, 118, cf. 109.

28. [Qian's note] Angelus Silesius, *Der Cherubinische Wandersmann*, F. J. Warnke, *European Metaphysical Poetry*, 192.

29. [Qian's note] *Journals des Goncourt*, 5 Avril 1864, Éd. définitive, II, 149.

30. Qian Zhongshu, Preface to *Tan yi lu* (Beijing: Zhonghua shuju, 1984), 1.

31. François Jullien, for example, advocates a "comparatisme de la différence," and he dismisses *Guan zhui bian* as engaging in a pointless comparison in which "tout est toujours *plus ou moins* pareil" (Jullien, *La valeur allusive: Des catégories originales de l'interprétation poétique dans la tradition chinoise* [*Contribution à une réflexion sur l'altérité interculturelle*] [Paris: École française d'Extrême-Orient, 1985], 126, n. 1). However, Jullien offers nothing remotely like Qian Zhongshu's rich textual evidence to persuade us of the importance of his search for "l'altérité interculturelle," as if the mere assertion of the difference between the East and the West, that "tout est toujours *plus ou moins* différent," would count as serious scholarship.

The Diverse Interpretations of the Laozi

Isabelle Robinet

The *Laozi* is a short work, concise and full of metaphors that are often obscure. It is poetic in form and has inherited the tendency toward multiple voices that characterizes that genre. Consequently, the door is open wider than usual to multiple interpretations, which may all be held to be legitimate, according to A. C. Graham.[1]

Recently, Western scholars have provided a perfect illustration of this aspect of the text by proposing interpretations that are not only different from one another, but sometimes mutually contradictory. Three principal issues are brought out in these works: (1) Is the *Dao* ineffable? (2) What is the *Laozi*'s view on language? and (3) What is the connection between *wu* 無 (Nonexistence), the absence of any determinate thing, and *you* 有, the presence of some things? For the sake of brevity, I will set aside the political aspects of the thought of the *Laozi* and will limit myself to a precise treatment of a certain number of issues that surround the concept of *Dao*.

Contemporary Exegetes

The interpretation of Benjamin Schwartz[2] is the most traditional of those I will be examining, but highlights several interesting issues. The *Laozi*, in his estimate, is above all a work that gives an account of mystical experience and comes up against the universal difficulties encountered in this domain, the difficulty of explaining the experience coupled with the temptation to do so. Schwartz then reaches a reflection on language, which he says is only capable of giving an account of the natural order that is limited and impermanent. The text represents a mystical attitude, according to Schwartz, concerned with a vision of the attainment of ultimate reality, and not with the techniques that may lead there. But the name *Dao*, which is given to this ultimate reality, is paradoxical because it evokes an order both all-inclusive and dynamic, a principle of organization that actually indicates the means by which order is established, and yet which is unknowable. The *Dao* is *wu* (which he translates as "nonbeing"), a new understanding opposed to the sense given to the word *Dao* before *Laozi*. Earlier, *Dao* had referred to the cosmos—*wu* in the sense of a reality that corresponds to no determinate entity, finite and changing (*you*), yet a reality that mystical experience allows one to know. The specific character of Daoism, says Schwartz, consists of attempting to find the mysterious place where *wu* and *you* meet. Additionally, he detects immanentist and pantheistic implications in the text of the *Laozi*, where opposites are treated in pairs of often, but not always, equal value.

A. C. Graham[3] takes a position opposed to that of Schwartz. The *Laozi* does not deal with the ineffability of the *Dao*, he says, but with the inadequacy of words. He stresses the inherent limits of all acts of naming, naming cannot name that which names, moreover it establishes divisions in what is unitary. The *Dao* is an unbreakable and nameless block; two reasons why language fails to name it. This name given to the *Dao* results from the Chinese mentality that does not seek to know what a thing is in itself, but rather asks how to name it. *Dao* signifies "Way" and answers the question: how do we live life based on a "unity"? That is why the *Laozi* does not advocate the reversal of established values, but always promotes "holding the two extremes": turning toward A without abandoning B, and acquiring a multidimensional consciousness.

Chad Hansen[4] agrees with Graham in not regarding the *Dao* of the *Laozi* as a metaphysical entity. The *Laozi*'s goal concerns the demystification of language, which is nothing more than an instrument of social control that must be discarded. The content of different discourses, *dao*s, or guides for behavior, are multiple and do not reside in any constant "*Dao*"; they are unable to furnish a norm for their referents across changing circumstances. It is therefore necessary to reject all names, to "forget" them since they lead to the molding of the human spirit in the interests of society. Nevertheless (and here too Hansen agrees with Graham), the *Laozi* doesn't teach the adoption of values contrary to those of the society. The text is satisfied with showing that naming starts from an act of distinguishing which generates two opposites from a single movement, and that this obliges one to make a choice. The arbitrary nature of this choice leaves open a skepticism that tends toward the identity of opposites. As a result, the text advocates no single *Dao*, nor an anti-*Dao*, and falls back on a tendency to anarchy, opposed to all forms of social authority. This is what leads him to exalt the silence that permits the escape from the vehicle of this authority—language.

The approach of Michael LaFargue[5] is different still. Trying to place the *Laozi* in its strictest possible historical context and thereby recover its spirit without being influenced by the different interpretations that have followed, he sees it as a manual of conduct in the art of governing and in prolonging lifespan (which comes close to what resulted in the HuangLao movement). It is the kind of work appropriate to a small circle of initiate "Laoists" (he brings into play the notion of "competence") and expresses a personal form of real-life experience. He protests against those who, like Schwartz, see a metaphysical truth in the *Laozi*. The supreme good which the author of the work praises comes from the "organic harmony" (LaFargue follows Needham), which carries a surplus of meanings and which is discovered and tested by their self-cultivation. This supreme good brings with it a reversal of values and participates in a reality greater than society, with the *Dao* as its organic center. It is not transcendent, except as a norm outside human existence, since it can exist nowhere else. An object of experience, it is hypostasized, lived as an intimate and cosmic presence but not a metaphysical one.

The Laozi

Let us examine how, relying strictly on the *Laozi*, it is possible to characterize the notion of the *Dao*.[6] We notice first that the *Laozi* places the *Dao* above Heaven (chapter 16, chapter 25), at a time in the history of China when Heaven was looked at as the supreme power. It then offers a superior and new meaning, the *Dao* that is the productive force (chapter 4), the source of life and all things (chapter 4, chapter 25). It is primary (we know not who is its progenitor, chapter 4) and, pre-cosmic, it exists before Heaven and Earth (chapter 25). Everything returns to it; it is then the ultimate origin and ending. It is the sacred place for beings (chapter 62).[7] It is empty (chapter 4) while containing something (chapter 25). It begets the One, that which makes each thing what it is (chapter 39), which gives birth to the Two, then the Three, then the multiplicity (chapter 42). Although it produces and sustains beings (chapter 34, chapter 51), it does not make them dependent upon it (chapter 34). It acts universally without intervening (chapter 37), through spontaneous action (chapter 25), preferring neither the left nor the right (chapter 34). It moves cyclically, universally and endlessly[8] (chapter 25, chapter 40), returning upon itself, at times close and at times distant (chapter 25). Its appearance, like those who follow it, is contrary to what it is (chapter 41). In contrast to what our modern exegetes have observed, it is ineffable, capable of being apprehended by neither the senses nor language (chapter 14), indistinct (chapter 14, chapter 21), empty (chapter 4), eternal without beginning or end (chapter 4, chapter 14), alone and unequal (chapter 25). It cannot be named (chapter 1, chapter 25, chapter 32), although its name might be "constant" from yesterday to today (chapter 21).

Starting from some of the main points that have been raised and will be filled in and discussed below, we may say that, metaphysical or not (this word has several different senses that are not distinguished by our exegetes, so it would be better to avoid using it), it is the fundamental origin, the "absolute" in the sense of a "first term which is conceived from itself, and ultimate principle from which everything that may be conceived is conceived," and a "primary, self-sufficient term"[9] (alone and without equal), singular and eminent, that grounds the world in a unity. It seems that the *Laozi* alludes to a quest for the *Dao* (chapter 14: one looks, listens, touches, and moves to discover and pursue it; chapter 20: one may be nourished by it), even if the quest has no tangible or conveyable outcome: this is the sign of the inaccessibility of the absolute. Likewise, this *Dao* admits of a character that is paradoxical, where opposites fuse or are not distinguished from one another, which is almost the same thing.

The term *Dao* also has the sense of a "guide for behavior." The *Laozi* gives instructions for the making of a saint who is as imperceptible and inaccessible as the *Dao*, which is nevertheless advanced as a model. In the human realm, even in politics, the ultimate principle of *Dao* must be taken as a model. Here, its primary characteristic is *fan* "reversal," its movement (chapter 40) comparable to the cyclical movement that the *Laozi* attributes to a *Dao* that departs in order later to return (chapter 25). Those who are close to the *Dao*, in contrast to what is commonly done in the world, adopt a low profile (chapter 8), do not display knowledge (chapter 48), withdraw (themselves) and avoid all displays of or any resort to force or prestige (chapter 30, chapter 31), all desire for accumulation, riches, and power (chapter 9, chapter 15). The *Laozi* appeals to remote antiquity, perhaps as a metaphor for the origin of the world, when people spontaneously followed the Way. By moving away from this origin, human beings departed from the *Dao* and thereby lost its spirit (chapter 18, chapter 21, chapter 23, chapter 38). Its rediscovery will be a means to know how to manage the present and to assure themselves long life.

The Chinese Commentators

Let us now move to review the major works that characterize how the Chinese of various ages have understood the *Laozi*, or those they have placed the most value upon. We will only refer to Daoist and Confucian commentaries.

A first examination leads us to say that on the whole these commentators understood the *Laozi* in a similar way, or at least that one does not find the same degree of divergence as with the modern exegetes already surveyed. These commentators were not as influenced by modern preoccupations, be they linguistic or historical. On the other hand, it is clear that their interpretations, instead of seeking to reconstruct the thought in a strict manner, are strongly colored by those developments in Chinese thought that followed the *Laozi*. This happens even when, as sometimes turns out to be the case, they attempt to be accurate to the *Laozi* and to distinguish it from the work of other thinkers.[10] Nevertheless, in general, all of what is said by one would be accepted by the others. The differences reside in the orientation of their interpretations, whether they are more philosophical, more cosmological, more political, or more mystical. It should then be clearly understood that the citation of specific commentators will be, except where duly noted, done for the purpose of illustration, and not to explain a specific difference of opinion between one commentator and others.

The Productive Dao

The term *Dao* has been glossed by a homophone or by a synonym: either *dao* 導 (to guide, open a road, communicate), or *dao* 蹈 (to walk, cf. Du Daojian 3.1b),[11] or even as *lu* 路 (road, cf. Wu Cheng 1.1a). It is then a guide for behavior to be followed.

But when commentators go on to explain the term further, the accent is placed on the *actions* of the *Dao*, the *Dao* exists *because* it produces—as Wing-tsit Chan remarked, "There is no depreciation of phenomena."[12] One might say that in Western terms, the "evidence" of the existence of the *Dao* is in the world. This is its tangible characteristic, and the reason that it is sometimes identified with the primordial breath and its cosmic aspect is often emphasized. The *Dao*, says Zhao Bingwen (1.25a), who quotes many other commentators whose remarks are similar to his own, is "that from which beings arise." Heshanggong expressly says that it is named *Dao* because the ten thousand beings are produced by it (chapter 25). Du Guangting (21.4b) and Sima Chengzhen define the *Dao* by saying that "it is the universal life."[13] These all signify that regarding the *Dao*, insofar as it is knowable and known, its *esse objectivum* is its production, its totality of phenomena.

The *Dao* exists before Heaven and Earth, it takes it bearings from "another time" that is not opposed to "today." From this comes the idea of the slow gestation of the universe from the "Mother" *Dao*, and of a cosmology most often presented in a genealogical mode. Many commentators have had recourse to descriptions of successive genesis that start with *Dao* or with the void, and through slow progression produce a state of chaotic fusion and the One before giving way to the universe. Such accounts may be found in two Han Dynasty apocryphal works and in the first chapter of the *Liezi*[14] (e.g., Shi Yong 1.1.15a; Shao Ruoyu, preface 4b; Niu Miaozhuan 724.3.23b; Cheng Taizhi 724.2.26a; etc.).

The *Dao* is the cause of causes: all causes, all the *suoyi* 所以 "that by which," have an original cause ("whereby it emerges," or "from which it emerges,"[15] says Wang Bi, chapter 51, who is thus making a distinction between immediate and more distant causes). The *Dao* is the foundation of the world, a point upon which the commentaries are unanimous, and it concerns the metaphysical in the sense of being "primary philosophy," speculation about nonmaterial nature (according to one of the senses given the term in the *Encyclopédie philosophique universelle*).[16]

The Unknowable Dao

The term *Dao* does not connote any single thing precisely, but since it connotes the production of things, it connotes things other than itself. *Dao* is an extrinsic name that does not designate more than its visible and intelligible aspects, its universal and pervasive power (*tong* 通), its *de* (virtue), or its grandeur (chapter 34). But it is also more than this power.

In effect, this universal production, this creative power, does not define it, "does not exhaust it," according to the Chinese, because the *Dao* also presents an ineffable aspect, indistinct and transitory, which is the foundation of what it produces, a "that by which," which cannot be known (except in its effects). In other words, there are two questions: "Does the *Dao* exist?" and "What is the *Dao*?" The answer to the question of whether the *Dao* exists (*you*) is that it both does (as evidenced by its activity and the world itself) and is nothing determinate, it does not distinguish itself from anything (since it is unique and is the total Unity) at the same time. The second question, "What is it?" concerns its essence. Now, the name one gives it only reaches to its existence, it does not reach to its nonexistence, nor does it reach to the "that by which" of that existence, nor yet does it distinguish itself from anything since it does not distinguish itself from nothing. So it has no possible definition, and that which it signifies surpasses any intelligence one may have of it.

In Chinese terms, the *Dao* comprises two aspects: the *Dao* in terms of its *ti* 體 "foundation," immobile, silent, unknown and unknowable, and the productive *Dao*, which is its appearance in action, *yong* 用 "function," at times identified as virtue, *de* (cf. Lu Xisheng,

3.17a–b), at times as what comes *houtiandi* 後天地 "after Heaven and Earth," as opposed to what came before, which is the foundation. Some commentators place this function and the foundation on which it depends on the same level (e.g., Wang Bi);[17] for others there is an asymmetry: the function depends on the foundation, but the latter does not fundamentally presuppose any function (Lu Xisheng, 1.1a); this is the logic whereby the foundation is "anterior."

Although one may say that the *Dao* exists because the world exists and life exists, one cannot reverse this proposition: the *Dao* precedes the world, as the *Laozi* stipulates. It comes first logically and, by metaphor, chronologically. This is why it is "nonexistent," "ancient," it is the "beginning" (Lu Xisheng, 1.13b). There are therefore two correlates, A and B, on the one hand the unnameable "thing," indeterminate, anterior to the world, and on the other hand the nameable *Dao*, determinate insofar as it is at the same time producer and its production, present in the world of today. Both issued from a common source (chapter 1), from a "root" which is another metaphor for the *Dao*. This origin is indeterminate such that it is beyond the opposition between determinate and indeterminate, since this is where the "source" lies. The connotations of these correlates A and B are reciprocally inverted, but since A comes "before" they are not cotemporal and they comprise an asymmetry. Moreover, there is (insofar as one can say it "exists") but one single *wu*, but one single void because it is a question of the continuous and simple, while there are as many *you* as there are existences within the multiplicity. Consequently, their relationship is not the same as that which relates good and bad, high and low. We will conclude below that there is really a hierarchical relationship between the two.

Dao and *Wu* 物 (beings)

The question was raised of knowledge of the relationship of the *Dao*, which produced the world, to its product, in other words, of the *Dao* to beings. The commentators' position on this subject is nuanced. First, attention must be paid to the term "production," which I have used for lack of a better alternative, to avoid the use of "creation," which might make one think that something new is appearing. Now, the terms most frequently used by Chinese texts are either *hua* 化

"transform" or *sheng* 生, which signifies at the same time "to beget" and "to give life." This last term must be understood in the Chinese context where the notion of filiation is strongly dominated by that of continuity.[18] That the *Dao* was "cause" does not imply that the world is its "effect," because here it means nothing more than that the world is its unfolding, its manner of appearance. The *Dao* is "cause" in the sense of motion, not of creation *ex nihilo*, something that will become clearer further on in my explanation.

One sees why the commentators take varied positions, and why one sometimes encounters ambiguities in the writings of a single author. One may hold to the notion that the term *Dao*, on the one hand, indicates metaphorically the foundation, *ti* or *ben* 本 (the source, the root), and at the same time that it only designates its production, the world, which would be its *mo* 末 "branch tips." We have seen that some pose the equation: the *Dao* is individual beings, or even it is the name given to beings in their entirety. The *Dao* does not have a present or a past, it is constantly at the root of beings, states Du Guangting (19.6b). The relation of *Dao* to beings is very often compared to that between fish and the water that surrounds, fills, and nourishes them. For Wang Pang, the *Dao* is never separated from beings, but if one considers it from the point of view of the multiplicity, it is the unfathomable source for them (706.1.15b); however the same Wang Pang also says that the *Dao* is "distant" from beings (706.2.26b). All people have the *Dao*, according to Su Che among many others, but it must not be confused with beings, no more than it may be separated from them (1.5a–b). The *Dao* and "forms," says Du Guangting, are two complementary moieties (11.8a), which implies that they are distinct but located on the same level. Generally however, commentators, such as Dong Sijing (2.7b), place the *Dao* above the world, which is perfectly logical since it exists before the world. At the same time, the *Dao* has existed ever since in the world, as Du Guangting has said (the image of the root and the flowers is adapted well here); so this "beyond" must immediately be made up for by a contrary affirmation. The problem of the relationship between the *Dao* and the physical world that had been posed regarding the "Great Appendix" of the *Yijing* (especially starting in the Song dynasty, but also earlier) had evidently reemerged for these commentators: is the *Dao* "before" the physical world ("before forms"), as stated in the "Great Appendix," a term that has been translated as "metaphysical"? What is the nature of the difference between the "metaphysical" Dao and the physical world? Some commentators distinguish between what is "before forms" (metaphysical) and nameless, which is the Dao,[19] and that which is "of forms" and possesses names such as de, "efficacious virtue" (Wu Cheng), or the breath that comprises "signs" (Dong Sijing 1.3a and Wu Cheng). Others distinguish between the Dao which is not practicable (not "daoable") and that which is (Zhao Shi'an, 724.2.1a). But all do affirm that one cannot exist without the other.

The universal presence of the Dao (and the cyclical movement the Laozi assigns to the Dao in chapter 25, etc.), is named "principle" li, the positive aspect of wu, by Wang Bi. Beings are begotten and sustained by the Dao, and this is neccessary for their life (Heshanggong, chapter 39). In a somewhat different vein, Du Guangting, for example, emphasizes, along the same lines as Wang Bi does, that as counterparts beings are neccessary to the manifestation of Dao (11.7b), which is to say of Dao insofar as it is visible and intelligible, and as it is an extrinsic denomination. These positions taken by the commentators do not oppose each other, rather they emphasize the paradoxical nature of the the Dao, which at the same time is and is not what it produces: the world is Dao, and the Dao at the same time is another thing insofar as it is "that by which" the world exists.

The problem may be explained in two ways that illustrate the same thing. Either as the relationship of producer to its product (or begetter to the begotten), or as that between the actor and the action. Now, there is no actor without action, since the action makes the actor in the same sense that the actor makes the act, and to say that a producer "produces" or is "in" its production, is a tautology and does not make sense. This is a problem well known to Daoists and Buddhists. The division between producer and production is artificial and of completely relative value (although in a different way than the division between beauty and ugliness): it does not exist except as seen from the perspective of the multiplicity, as Wang Pang has said. This view represents the majority of interpretations that have been made by commentators to the Laozi. It follows that there cannot be, as in Western metaphysics, a distinction between operant power and its operation. The distinction is made between the hidden Dao, "interior," shut in on itself, and the manifested Dao, "exterior," which displays itself (the first chapter of the Laozi particularly lends itself to exegesis along these lines).

The One

Thus, there exist two notions of the *Dao*: one that is indeterminate, and the other which is at the same time the source of all things and its production. Likewise, there are two notions of the primordial unity.[20] One is indistinct and simple, equivalent to the void (Wang Bi); it precedes all determination and all existence and is "not a number" because it is the origin of numbers. The other One is the "beginning" of the world, the first number—in other words the unique One, all alone and outside of any series, and the first One that begins the series. Thus, two apparently contradictory notions are brought together by the many hesitant commentators: the One in the *Laozi* that is begotten by the *Dao*, and the One that is the *Dao*. The One that is *wu*, in the sense of pure and simple negation, and the One that is the origin of beings. But this raises a set of difficulties of which the Chinese are well aware and which are not limited to this particular way of thought. E. Bréhier, for example, in his exposition of the themes that concern Neo-Platonism, says of the "non-being" that is the source of all beings:

> As soon as you try to determine and pin it down through thought, you make it into a being. From then on, it is no longer the origin. Because it is a being one must ask anew what is its origin. If, by contrast, you leave it completely indeterminate, it appears to be no different from a pure non-entity, and consequently it is no longer the origin of being. You have to simultaneously impose and withdraw the determinations which are applied through thought; imposing them because the origin is not pure nothingness, and withdrawing them since it is truly an origin and not solely a term designating a reality.[21]

On one hand, the absolute and transcendant One is empty, amorphous, and cannot admit of any determination under penalty of becoming dual. On the other hand, the dynamic and productive One (which begets Two) is included in the process of the advent of the world, in a chain of successive begettings which form a genealogy, and is constitutative of the unity of the cosmos and of each thing in itself. Not all commentators have made this distinction, but several make note of it. Du Guangting distinguished in this way between the One that is void and the foundation of the world and the One that is a number, that begets Two, and that is the harmony and the center of the cosmos (31.2b, 31.1a, and 33.2a). Yan Zun places this One on the border between absence and the emergence of the multiplicity, by saying that it is *wu* in relation to spirit, but *you* in relation to *Dao*; in terms of its existence, it is empty but also full, *wu* and *you* (7.9a–b). Heshanggong, by contrast, does not see in the One anything but its activity and defines it as being like *Dao*'s efficacious virtue, *de* (chapter 15, chapter 51). Wang Bi, by contrast, identifies the One with the void in several instances.

Wu and You

Practically all commentators have proposed an identity between *Dao* and *xu* 虚 "void" or *wu*. Sometimes the term *wu*, which Wang Bi was the first to systematically bring to the fore in speaking of the *Dao*, has been translated as "substance."[22] However, as Alan Chan has indicated, in the case of Wang Bi (and I would add, also for the authors who came after him,) *wu* in fact implies that one should not reify the *Dao*, not make it into a being, as Bréhier would say, and it connotes the transcendent and unknowable aspect of the *Dao*. It is neither the substance nor the actor behind the world, nor yet its foundation; it does not concern ontology and even less theology (except in the case of a commentary like the *Xiang'er*, for example, which personifies the *Dao*). At the same time, the terms of *wu* and *xu* preserve the especially concrete sense of receptivity given in the *Laozi* (chapter 11) which does not seem to incorporate any metaphysical sense: these terms connote emptiness that receives, which allows one given part to contain another. In much the same way, the gaps in gears are necessary to allow them to run the machine. All these senses are present in this term.

Wu therefore has a sense which is eminently positive: it is the absence of any determination. On this occasion the Chinese, as Spinoza did, performed a reversal and showed that all determination (and therefore all affirmation) involves negation. *Wu* is therefore, as Graham has said, the positive complement of *you* "there is something which is determined." Because it cannot be identified with nothing, the *Dao* is all things. Because it is "empty," it can "respond," which is to say it may take the aspect that suits it at each place and time: "To respond," says Du Guangting, "is to be empty"

(6.3a). It is the receptivity of the *Dao* that guarantees its inexhaustible possibilities (we note that the suppleness of the *Dao* which is exalted in the *Laozi* is most often understood in this sense). In this manner, the *Dao* is the totality of the world, at once the possible and the real, and therefore the perpetually renewable real. But *you* also has a positive sense since it connotes the power or the manifestation of the *Dao*: because it produces all the things in the world, it cannot be called *wu* (see for example, among others, Du Guangting, 19.2b).

Since the Song, as the second and third phrases of the first chapter of the *Laozi* were first punctuated after *wu* and *you*,[23] the expressions *changwu* and *changyou*, which have come to mean eternal and absolute non-being and being, have needed to be explained. They have been most often explained as signifying that *wu* as well as *you* are eternal as correlates of one another; each manifests itself by the other, and both issue from the same source, although they are differently named (Fan Yingyuan, 724.3.15a). Cheng Taizhi (724.2.30b–31a) is perhaps the most explicit on this point: *wu* begets *you* and cannot therefore be *you*, so it remains as eternal *wu*; in the same way there is an eternal *you* which begets beings, but it is not these beings—this signifies that it is a question of a *you* in the context of principle, which is the productive potential. The *Dao* is constantly nonexistent to the degree that it does not show itself, and constantly existent to the degree it does. Another way of saying this is that the manifestation of *Dao* is constant, but does not exhaust its nonmanifestation, which also exists constantly. This is the way that the theory of perpetual motion and its paradoxical "beginning," which have always preoccupied the Chinese, have been settled.[24]

However, if a distinction is made between the eternal *Dao* which is *wu* and the limited "forms" which are *you* (Du Guangting, 11.18a), it is no more than a manner of speaking, since there is always interpenetration and complementarity between the *Dao* and these forms, between *wu* and *you*. The forms that are *you* have no meaning except through *wu*, since it is the void that permits them to emerge, to take their place and to function; *wu* by contrast has no other sense because it shows itself and produces. *Wu* is the root and therefore *you* are the signs, the traces, according to the Chinese (see Du Guangting, 19.13b). Du Guangting distinguishes between *xiang* "image," which is the root and visible sign, the *miaoyou* 妙有 "the marvelous existence" in the obscurity of chaos, and *wu* 物 "things," which is *miaowu* 妙無 "the marvelous non-existence," which proceeds from the root (19.3a–b). A hierarchical relationship is thereby again affirmed, like that between the root and the leaves, in which the latter change color and fall, perhaps disappearing, while the former remains: "the root is superior to the flowers," says Heshanggong (chapter 40). The dialectic of Mādhyamaka was constantly used in order to establish the equality and convergence of *wu* and *you* as a form of reciprocal interpenetration; this was from around the fifth century, and not only on the part of the commentators of the Chongxuan school (e.g., Su Che, Shao Ruoyu, Bo Yuchan often appeal to this).[25] Since around the time of the Tang Dynasty, the notions of *ti* "foundation" and *yong* "function" have often been applied, notions whose beginning may be seen in the work of Wang Bi and were subsequently developed by the Buddhists. Some commentators, including Wang Bi for example, had a tendency to incline toward the side of the indeterminate and unknowable *Dao* (the apophatic way of the mystics). By contrast, certain Confucians inclined toward the side of *you* ("beings"), arguing from the perspective that it is useless to speculate on the unknowable, and that the most important thing is to manage the world. But all of them sought to equalize these two aspects of ultimate truth; they tried at the same time to "impose and withdraw the determinations," as Bréhier said, or to "know the white and preserve the black," as the *Laozi* has it.

The Seed

In effect, this *wu* is not tenable in its most radical purity. It has a paradoxical nature. This absence, this indeterminate and empty *Dao*, involves a presence (and therefore a determination). Chapter 21 of the *Laozi* is always invoked as an illustration of the relationship between the *Dao* and what it produces: in being indistinct and obscure, the *Dao* contains the germ of this production. Everything in the world exists as potential in the *Dao* even if it is in another form, in the domain of an alternate reality. This notion of seed permits one to avoid the "efficient cause" which the West has had recourse to, which posited a cause more perfect than its effects, and which runs contrary to immediate observation. But it is paradoxical: the *Dao* is empty yet contains the world, which is not nothing. It contains it as the mother contains a child; this is why it is the "mother." Its relationship to the world is one of begetting, which is seen by the Chinese as both an interlocking and as an identity: we beget what we potentially are.[26] Then, is the world eternal? In general the commentators say no: by the relationship of the *Dao* to the world, beings are limited (among others reasons because they are multiple) whereas the *Dao* is not. Perhaps we might think the world is eternal "in the *Dao*," that its seed is eternal. The question has only been posed without being fully fathomed.

The counterpart is the paradoxical aspect of this *wu*, which, in terms of the origin of the world, contains something (at least virtually), has been underlined.

Ming 名 and Wuming 無名

Wu, the absence of determination, is therefore the absence of being named. Commentators, faced with the reticence of the *Laozi* to name the *Dao*, have not made this into a problem of language in the sense intended by Hansen. As I have said, the name of the *Dao* limits itself to connoting its *esse objectivum*, and not what it is "in itself." None propose, as does Hansen, that one must distrust language. At most, they point out that language is limited and cannot therefore express the totality (Wang Bi, chapter 25). Language determines, distinguishes, and cannot be applied to things that are indistinct (Su Che, 691.1.1a). Language is incapable of expressing contradictions. As Wang Bi says, one would like to *say* that the *Dao* is *wu*, yet beings also exist. One would like to *say* that the *Dao* is *you* and yet it is imperceptible (chapter 14). Language fails to express the absence of all things, says Du Guangting, and this is why the *Laozi* speaks of obscurity and the indistinct (14.6B). Moreover, remarks Wang Bi, among others, *Dao* precedes language; in terms of its origin, it is "nameless." Lü Huiqing (1.1a–2b) and others have also made this remark, as have Graham and Schwartz.

Another reason why the *Dao* might not have a name is that it has all names; it is both anonymous and polynomous (Du Guangting, 6.3a), or yet, because it is in the process of changing, it has neither a fixed form or place, as we shall see further on. It is not only that naming determines it by specifying one of its forms (its presence) by indirectly excluding others (this is also a problem that has been encountered in Judeo-Christian theology) but it is also that according to Chinese logic, the fact of not having a name leaves open all possibilities. Here, they apply the logic of the dynamic of opposites; the same cannot beget the same (unless it is the tautological case of not begetting), all arising requires the stimulus of the other ("what begets is not begotten" according to the *Zhuangzi* 17/6/42; the *Huainanzi* and Wang Bi cover the same ground). This is the way the original character of the difference was stated (in Chinese cosmology the world is founded on the division into two); in the same way its necessity is both ontological and logical.[27]

Only the Nameless can accomodate all names, only the Formless can take on all forms. This is the positive aspect of indeterminacy. However, this poses a problem, since it means that there is a continuity, indeed, an ontological identity, between the *Dao* and beings, between the begetter and the begotten. The two tendencies confront each other in this way: the one that affirms identity (this is the thesis of Wang Fuzhi, for example, for whom there never was a Formless) and the one that affirms their alterity. The dialectic of Mādhyamaka permits a resolution of this problem.

Language is therefore not the sole cause here, nor is discursive thinking, which orders and categorizes. As soon as thought attempts to "name," which is to say determine, one forms a "name" for the unlimited *Dao*, a determining limitation. This is not a problem of language, but of two distinct and contradictory orders and a thought process that does poorly in apprehending them at the same time and on the same level.

These two orders are distinct but not incompatible. Sima Chengzhen, among others, was interested in showing a relationship that connected indeterminate reality, the *huncheng* 混成, the original state of the *Dao* (chapter 25) which is the *ti* ("foundation") where nothing may be perceived, and the "Great Image" (chapter 35) which is a visual representation and a name: "When we speak of reality, the name is not exterior to it," he says, "therefore one may connect the name to its reality. But when one considers the name from the point of view of discrimination, reality is exterior to the name and cannot therefore be connected to it. Reality and name are only one and are connected" (1035.4b). In other words, depending on the case, one may give priority to the real aspects from the content of a name, the name as it retrieves the reality, or else one can adopt a point of view that emphasizes the distinction between the indeterminate reality and the determinate name it is given; but it is stipulated that the reality is connected to the determinate forms it takes, even though this seems to be distinct insofar as it is determined. And he adds later that it is the name that arouses reality and "makes it arrive," so that it is distinct from it. The *Laozi* also says that this Great Image is "formless" (chapter 41): so it remains hidden. This is its own way of appearing; one can only discover the *Dao* as something that remains hidden. We will return to this question as the occasion presents itself and we will see that some value, either anagogical or "practicable," is accorded to names.

Ziran "Spontaneity"

The production of the world by the *Dao* is marked by its own unique mode of action: it is action that is not an action, a *ziran* (spontaneous) act. Spontaneity is a concept that occupies a central place for certain commentators (e.g., Wang Bi), and one finds them giving it several senses and explaining it on several levels.

The *Dao*, says the *Laozi*, is ruled by *ziran* (chapter 25). For Heshanggong, Lü Huiqing (2.10b), and several others this signifies that it has no rules. Wang Bi understands it this way: the *Dao* changes according to circumstance (it is square with the square, round with the round), and it obeys nature (chapter 25). These two apparently different readings can be reconciled if one understands, with the Chinese, that *ziran* is "things as they are": if the *Dao* is things as they are, one may say *that* is its rule, which is also not a rule because it is a fact.

On one hand, *ziran* means that the world is produced without intention, without a preliminary plan. The notion of the "divine idea," which arose in Christianity, heir to a similar idea in Platonism, is absent. The question, which Christianity and Islam pose, of knowing "why" God felt the need to make the world, or in what sense He could have had some "desire" to do so, is simply not raised. This is because "it is like that," because "it is thus." *Ziran* connotes an observation and, in a way, signifies that one hits a wall with respect to the human spirit. *Ziran* is the limit that cannot be surpassed, and so is the final term. *Ziran*, says Wang Bi, "is a word for not naming, a term which refers to the final basis" (chapter 25). "*Ziran* is the absence of *you*, of beings, and the absence of names" (Wu Cheng, 704.2.9b).

This spontaneity is seen by the commentators to apply to both the action of *Dao* and to the development of the world (which are one under two aspects). The *Dao*, they say, "conforms to the natural aspects of things" (Wang Pang 706.4.23a). Once its action is accomplished, the *Dao* recedes, which is to say that it does not interfere: the *Dao* has no relation of dependence to its production, it remains unchanged (neither full nor empty); it can give rise to and transform beings without being implicated therein ("without entering into beings," according to Cheng Taizhi, 724.2.31a–b). Correspondingly, it does not maintain beings dependent upon it (it is content to support and continue them). This could have left a place for a notion of freedom (in the Christian sense of human freedom of choice *vis-à-vis* God's, an idea that has been very problematic, as we know). However, *ziran* instead has taken the sense of self-creation. The *Dao* is eternal and present at all times and in all things, and the world constantly recreates itself by drawing on its source. Guo Xiang, in the fourth century (he is commenting on chapter 2 of the *Zhuangzi* but the issue is the same), formulates this dilemma well: Is there something that created things? If there is, is it possible that something (determinate) made all things? If not, how could something that is not a thing make something that is? So the *Dao* is each thing that has created itself, and *ziran* designates the absence of any external operator, the capacity to be *ran* (so) *zi* (by itself). Du Guangting takes the same position: "The foundation has no operator, this is why one calls it *ziran*" (21.4b). The world is eternal to the extent that it is identified with the *Dao* and has created itself, a position taken by almost all the Chinese commentators (this doesn't mean that Heaven and Earth as we know them are eternal, they exist for only a moment). Moreover, for Wang Pang *ziran* indicates what is "above beings" (706.4.13b); this will be a transcendent dimension (in the sense of being above the world of the senses, so the source is beyond the known world) of this source of life which is in them.

Fan "Reversal"

The *Laozi* states (chapter 40) that *fan* (reversal) is the movement of *Dao*. Our contemporary exegetes have spoken in this context of a "reversal of values" or at least of a new way of evaluating established values by balancing things with opposing values. According to Graham and Hansen, the *Laozi* shows that the act of distinguishing begets *ipso facto* a pair of correlatives that cannot oppose each other because they are complementary (this is part of the logic of *yinyang* thinking). As a result, Graham thinks this may reveal a tendancy to anarchy in the Daoist thesis (since everything is worthwhile). LaFargue, on the other hand, thinks that the *Laozi* conceives of a hierarchy of values, with organic harmony as a supreme good (indeed, there cannot exist a harmony without a hierarchy), and that the *Laozi*'s discourse, determined by mystical experience, interprets a conviction that is based on a value judgment. It seems that these two positions cannot be reconciled: on one hand we have the process of distinguishing knowledge, whether it be intellectual or affective, leading to a dichotomy that does not correspond to reality and which must be rejected (Graham and Hansen). On the other hand, another sort of knowledge (mystical) is proposed which harmoniously and hierarchically reconciles opposites (LaFargue), whence come the paradoxical formulas of the *Laozi*: non-action that acts, formless form, a great image that is not an image.

The Chinese commentators have understood these passages in what appear to be different ways, but in fact they are reconcilable—they are simply different ways of formulating and approaching the same idea.

Fan indicates the return to the root: "*fan* is the root," says Heshanggong plainly (chapter 40), it is "to return to the root," says Lin Xiyi (2.5a), "to return to the beginning," says Deng Yi (2.14a). Shao Ruoyu (3.7a) speaks of "returning *xin* 心 (spirit) to the interior, Li Yue (2.6a) suggests "to return to the empty spirit," and Su Che (3.4b) and several others "to return to *xing* 性 (nature)," to the original self; this in a context where the *Dao* is identified with this spirit or nature. It is therefore the same thing as returning to the origin.

A different nuance becomes clear with those commentators who appeal to the principles on which Chinese cosmology is based and evoke the reversal of a force that, when it arrives at its apogee, then declines; it leaves its position due to a contrary/complementary force in cyclical alternation ("like a ring") (e.g., Chen Xianggu 1.8a and 2.3b; Zhang Sicheng 2.2b). Lin Xiyi (2.5b) belongs to this group as well as the first, which shows that the two explanations do not contradict each other in spirit; rather they complement each other.

Another interpretation appeals to the dialectic of the Same and Other which was invoked above. Lu Xisheng (3.5b) broadens the question from the cosmological plane to the metaphysical one, by saying that it is by this reversal that form begins from the Formless. This touches on reversal, spoken of above, which consists of the attribution of a positive value to indeterminacy and a negative value to determinacy, contrary to what one perceives under a naïve view of things. Formulating the same truth in another way, Wang Bi understands *fan* to designate that by which the cause of a thing is not the same as the thing itself, but rather its opposite: that which is high takes a seat on that which is below, *you* cannot be put into action except in *wu* (chapter 40). He adds that *fan* is the "*Dao* of *ziran*" (chapter 25), which is to say that it is a natural law. But this law, for Wang Bi, is the same thing as the movement of renewal of the source and so also within the void. This way of looking at it reunites those commentators previously mentioned. In general, the Chinese commentators understand *fan* in a broader sense than our contemporary interpreters, but the two interpretations do not contradict one another.

Changdao 常道, the Constant Dao

Let us linger on the different interpretations of the first line of the *Laozi*: "The *Dao* (the Way or the Word) (or the *dao*s) which may be *dao*'ed (walked, or spoken) is not the *changdao* (constant *Dao*)."

Our contemporary exegetes understand this phrase in several different ways. For Graham, "constant" does not indicate the *Dao*'s unsayable character but instead the inadequacy of words; it is necessary to counterbalance all assertions with contrary assertions.[28] In this way, there is and there is not a constant *Dao*. Hansen would like the word *dao* to be read as a plural substantive noun. This is why he translates this phrase: "Ways that can be told are not constant ways."[29] The *Laozi* would discredit all norms. Schwartz's interpretation is traditional: there is on the one hand an unnamable and ineffable *Dao*, and on the other hand that of which one might speak.[30] LaFargue adopts a similar sense of the term: the opposition is between the mind with neither concepts nor distinct perceptions, where the *Dao* resides, and the mind that discriminates.[31]

Let us now look at how the Chinese have understood this phrase, and in particular the meaning they have given to *chang*.[32]

For the most part the Chinese commentators have given it the meaning "invariable," "lasting," even "eternal" ("without beginning or end") (e.g., Chen Xianggu, Chen Jingyuan, Li Yue). They, and this is true for the majority, contrast the invariant *Dao* with changing *dao*s. The *dao*s are normative speech or guides to behavior, which may be followed, but change along with circumstance and subject, and fall into disuse (Chen Xianggu, Zhang An, Wang Anshi, Dong Sijing, Wu Cheng, Peng Si, Shao Ruoyu, etc.) Lü Huiqing stipulates that the *Dao* that cannot be followed is an ecstatic one which "forgets the self and others." Some propose that one can only speak of the changing *dao*s and not of that which does not change because it exists before the world (Du Daojian, Wu Cheng). The *Han Feizi* contrasts beings, which live and die, with what lasts as long as the universe (chapter 20). Chen Xianggu contrasts the *dao*s, which one speaks, with the *Dao*, which no speech can exhaust. Wang Bi contrasts the absolute *Dao* with the mundane *dao*s, Su Che the *dao*s of Confucian virtues, each with its specific nature, and the *Dao* without specificity. These are nuances of detail. Fan Yingyuan went the farthest in his interpretation of *chang* (724.3.15b); the term connotes an absolute that is above *wu* and *you* and offsets the imperfection that is spoken of in terms of *wu* and *you*.

Other commentators place the accent on the constant *Dao* as a universal norm. The *Dao* comprises a rule, an invariant, says Wang Pang, which, thanks to *li*, the organizing principle, is reliable (2.28b); thus, it allowed one to govern yesterday in the same way that one does today (2.30b). The *dao*s which can be followed are all the *Dao*, maintains Lü Huiqing, but there are also some *dao*s that move away and roll downhill, and so they are not the *changdao*.

Many commentators have emphasized that one may nevertheless speak of the *Dao*, at least in a relative way. Lu Xisheng, after having contrasted the *changdao* with *li*, the principle of things, which, along with numbers are only its *yong* ("function"), lends names value in an anagogic way: they are the *yong* of *Dao*, they rely on it and permit the search for the *ti* ("foundation"). But, he explains, this task situates itself in the domain of beings that change, not in that of the constant Name.

The position of Chen Jingyuan and Du Guangting is completely different: the *Dao* is not constant; it changes with circumstances; its constancy resides in its incessant change. It is unfathomable because it has neither fixed location nor name. For Cheng Jingyuan, one may follow it in the embodying *ti* of the Confucian virtues. That it has no name is proof of its duration, and that it has a significant name shows that it may be practiced. In sum, the same *Dao* that has names has none, it is both imperceptible and may be practiced. According to this interpretation, the first line of the text should be translated: "The *Dao* may be practiced, but it is not constant." One finds the same idea in Li Daochun's 李道純 (fl. 1288–1290) understanding of the *yi* of the *Yijing*, which is both *chang* and changing.[33] The mid-seventh-century *Daojiao yishu* 道教義樞, commenting on this phrase, insists on the fact that *chang* does not signify that there is a *changdao* outside of the *daos*, but rather that one must not focus on any constant *Dao* because each *dao*, i.e., each guide to behavior, changes with the situation in the same way that a prescription must change with the illness (an idea borrowed from Buddhism).[34] Not to reach the *Dao* (to recognize its inaccessibility because of its multiplicity and being in flux) is to reach it. These commentators seek to reconcile the Chinese view of a world in perpetual mutation and renewal with the possibility of saying something about it. Moreover, they also want to accord with the *Laozi*'s counsel of pliancy, a pliancy the *Huainanzi* applies on the political level with the contradictory idea of something that does not vary. To speak presumes the existence of some fixed being. Now the *Dao* is both in motion and unfathomable, so one may not speak of it. However, one may give it a name implying a conducting wire in the middle of its mobility. If it only had mobility, one could say anything and its opposite, and nothing could be said.

Chang has also been understood as meaning "ordinary": the subtle and marvelous *Dao* is not what ordinary people call *dao* (Yu Qingzhong, 724.4.1a). The interpretation of Sima Guang is audacious: ordinary people maintain that one may not speak of the ineffable *Dao*. Laozi, by contrast, says that one may speak of it, but that it is not the *Dao* of ordinary people. This interpretation gives us: "The *Dao* which may be spoken is not the ordinary *Dao*." Shi Tan objects to this understanding of *chang* (724.4.20a–b) saying it does not tally with the sense of *chang* in chapter 16 of the *Laozi*; there we are told that one is illuminated when one knows *chang*.

Order, Efficient and Final Cause

This notion of *chang* is connected to a conception of order which Schwartz has noted is difficult to reconcile with a mystical point of

view. The cosmos, for the Chinese as for the Greeks, is characterized
by the order that presided over its development. The *Dao* as producer of the world is therefore an orderly principle. We have here
an aspect of the *Dao* that may hardly be detected in the *Laozi*,
except through the important notions of harmony and unity, as well
as by this adjective *chang* joined to the *Dao*. This sense of order
clearly corresponds to the Chinese vision of the world and so may
not be left out of our interpretation. The production of the world is
an ordered display. The *Dao* acts through a natural order, which
some call *li*, and which is also one of its aspects. This order is a
"master" and foundation, as Wang Bi emphasizes, e.g., "*Dao*," he
says, "is possessed of a great constancy, the *li* (principle) has great
aim. . . . Events have a foundation and beings have a master" (chapter 47). "The *Dao* has constant rules, its *li* is very reliable," says
Wang Pang (706.2.28b), who appeals to the adjective "reliable" that
the *Laozi* accords to the indistinct *Dao* (chapter 21). The "that by
which" that returns back to the mother indicates the existence of a
unique and motive order.

Contrary to the pre-Han and Han Chinese conception of Heaven
or the Christian God of, say, Duns Scotus, there is no superior power
that intervenes in the world. This notion of order is correlated to
spontaneity; the order of the *Dao* shows itself naturally as if by an
internal logic and force. They are then reconciled with the concept of
operative efficiency and the absence of an external cause of existence. However, this notion of a driving order, of the "Way" which
implies an orientation in the world's unfolding (which is not teleo-
logical, but which implies a serial order that the process of the
display follows), plays a role very close to that of the cause of a vital
movement. The ten thousand beings do not find their reason for
being anywhere but in this Way or in this order, which "justifies"
("corrects," *zheng*) their existence.

So the world in its "correct" display does not separate itself from
the *Dao*, it is the same action, the manifestation of an interior vital
creative principle, direct and immediate. It results in a pantheism.
However, in an inexplicable way, it happens that people "separate"
themselves from the *Dao* when they behave without taking into
consideration the order of the universe. This happens when they
"forget" the source of the world. So they must return to it. This
possibility of being lost is paradoxical since the *Dao* is everywhere
and one cannot separate oneself from it; however the Chinese do not

attempt to explain this. They only, following the *Laozi*, make this observation.

The Mystical Way

It remains to say a few words about the mystical interpretation of the *Laozi*, present in many commentaries, including Confucian and Neo-Confucian commentaries. Some commentators, such as Lin Xiyi, do not make any appeal at all to mysticism, others make it one of several keys to possible readings, and still others place it on the first level. If the dialectic of Madhyamaka (which has often been said—with just cause—to have been born of a mystical experience) is in effect a system that seeks to allow the conception of two distinct truths at the same time, mystics attempt to do the same thing, except that they appeal to a different kind of knowledge. This illuminating knowledge is often called *huizhao* 回照 by the Chinese (e.g., Du Guangting, 14.2a); it is acquired by "reversing the light" *huiguang* 回光 toward the interior (Fan Yingyuan, 724.3.14b). It is the work of the *xin*, which in this context designates what one may call the "spirit" rather than the heart-mind, the organ of both intellectual and affective knowledge. The object of this knowledge is an original self similar to that of *gnosis*, which, depending on the case, is called *xing* 性 (Huizong 1.19b, 3.3b; Lu Xisheng, *passim*) the "nature," or *xin*, identified with *Dao*, with primordial breath, or with the initial unity (Du Daojian, 1.5b; Lü Huiqing, ex. 2.10a; Lin Xiyi, ex 2.5a; Zhang An; Su Che 1.10-a, 14b, 15b, etc.). This knowledge is "forgetting all things," a technical term designating the forgetting of the distinction between self and others, the *Dao* and beings, in a unitary fusion. This mystical knowledge is also the fusion of movement and quietism brought close to the original state of chaos; so it is not quietism, but a radiant action (Su Che, 17b–18b). Several commentators have also drawn on vocabulary and concepts from interior alchemy (Li Lin, Deng Yi) and others, as we know, interpret several passages from the *Laozi* in terms of breathing techniques.[35]

Conclusion

It is possible to speak of a general consensus among the interpretations of the *Laozi* on a certain number of points, summarized well by

Dong Sijing (preface, 4b): non-action, *ataraxia*, spontaneity, action answered by the void of receptivity, absence of desire and social action which "anticipate Heaven," governing oneself and the state; to which one may add: forgetting oneself and others as well as all opposites, in praise of pliancy. Great Neo-Confucian thinkers like Su Che and Lu Xisheng were "drawn" by the text and had to make allowances for themes that were not truly of Confucian inspiration, like *ataraxia* and the correlativity of opposites.

It also appears that, as Schwartz has said, Daoism was most interested in defining the mysterious region where *wu* and *you* are articulated one from the other.[36] The commentators have not sought to highlight the *Laozi*'s inherent ambiguities but on the contrary to maintain them and to place value on the paradoxical nature of the *Dao*, while reconciling the opposites. Their *Dao* surpasses the oppositions between the determinate and indeterminate, between constancy and change, between speech and silence. If *not A begets A*, this implies that the *not A* that begets is not completely different from the A that is begotten, neither ontologically nor logically but only formally and ephemerally. In this sense, *A equals not A*: the principle of contradiction is not excluded on the worldly level, but it is not worthwhile for the *Dao*. In this way, the form of thought has gone beyond language and discursive thinking.

The *Dao* is situated "before" the world, the latter occupies a position subordinate both logically and chronologically. Thus arises the insertion of time, which supposes the cosmological linearity necessary to institute an order. But this linearity is compensated for by a circularity, a possibility of "returning" to the beginning, which is a reversibility contrary to the idea of time, a turning in on itself: "before" could meet again "after." The origin arises both in the past and in the present, this is the rule according to which there is no first term, just as Lü Huiqing (1.17a) among many others has said. The point of departure and the point of arrival are limit points beween "there does not exist"—before movement—and "there exists"—movement. They pertain to both while not being located in either of the two, since the point of departure and the point of arrival are as incompatible with movement as with rest. This is the well-known aporia of the beginning of something.

This liminal position of thought ineluctably involves ambiguity, and can only be expressed in that way. So the question is not, as LaFargue says, of an ambiguity born of imperfect comprehension; it is an inherent part of the intention of the *Laozi* as "threshold thought." Two modes of reality are simultaneously taken to be true, even if they contradict each other. Both are "allegorical" modes, in the sense that each returns to the other and is only complete once it returns there. What is not said, or what is said obscurely, belongs to the truth; that which is beyond appearances or contrary to it is at the same time expressed by it. The inadequacy, the open-ended nature of language and thought (and even of behavior, as we see with the *Laozi*'s clumsy and timid saint) all survive by being subsumed.

In this way of thinking, the ideas *ben* or *ti* "foundation" and *mo* ("branch tips") or *yong* ("function"), which permit the two aspects of the *Dao* to be connected while distinguishing them, merit being compared to its quiddity and practice. The aspects of invariance and fluctuation of the *Dao* may also be compared with the notions of "substance" and of "accident" (this last term in the sense Porphyre gives it of "what can appear or disappear without destroying its subject"). The difference from the thinking of Aristotle and his successors is that for the Chinese these "accidents" are necessary and constant (although limited by their diversity and multiplicity, which are, however, equally necessary and constant); they are not contingent, they are grounded in essence, belonging to the *Dao*; they are not a "quality" but a putting into form. If the *Dao* is a substance, it is not in the sense that it remains underlying the accidents, but in that which gives rise to these accidents and shows itself in them. In contrast to Westerners who have sought to analyze, cut up, and distinguish between substance and accident, etc., the Chinese, while admitting similar distinctions, have sought to synthesize. Emphasizing the completely relative value of these distinctions and their basic underlying unity, they attempted to find the means to think of the one and the multiple as two sides of the same coin. But this topic warrants a whole study of its own and falls outside the scope of this article. We may add that the Chinese seek to maintain the equivocal nature of being, a direct correlate of their predilection to admit into evidence the relationship between given terms. Or at least they make an effort to keep the two on equal ground: on one hand the synthetic unity of the things of the universe, fruit of a primal perception (the return to the origin), and on the other hand, their multiplicity and the analysis of distinctions, the object of worldly experience.

The different readings of the *Laozi* pose the very problem of interpretation that has already caused much ink to be spilled, and to which I shall only allude. Must one, with LaFargue, consider that a work is written for a specific audience, and interpret it according to a reconstituted historical and psychological situation (something that is always a temptation)? To what degree is a text independent from its relationship to interpretations made of it? What is the influence of the mental attitude, often unconscious, of the receptor? What is the place of one possible meaning with respect to all the other possible meanings of the text? What importance must be given to the use an individual or group has made of a text? (I have not spoken, as it would be possible to do, of the use of the *Laozi* by the Legalists, by the HuangLao movement, or by the Celestial Masters, or for carrying out the art of war, as in the case of Wang Zhen, because it would have taken too long.) Is the variety of interpretations a result of authorial intent (if such a thing may be recovered) in the work, or of the intention of the reader? To what degree may one choose not to consider the receptor of the text and so pretend to give the text an absolute and singular meaning or simply a more probable meaning than others? A book is a dialogue, a game of relations. The reading modifies the book which in turn modifies the reading. Groups of readers and readings emerge from these diverse interpretations.[37]

The *Laozi* gives the impression of having, both by its form and by its aim, opened the door to mutiple interpretations, and this is its success: it is stimulating. Chinese commentators have shown themselves to be rather free, since one can see in them, like Deng Yi, several different interpretations being advanced on several different levels (literal, philosophical, and mystical/alchemical). Zhao Shi'an distinguishes three possible planes of applying the *Laozi*: one according to the way of non-action (which is the way of "total forgetting", the mystical way), another according to longevity techniques, and a third according to politics. Guan Caizhi interpreted the *Laozi* by systematically juxtaposing citations from the *Zhuangzi*, *Huainanzi*, and *Liezi*, which to his eyes best illustrated its thinking. Du Daojian understands the *Laozi* in light of the work of Shao Yong. Lu Xisheng tried to reintegrate the *Laozi* into Confucianism by showing those aspects that accorded with the *Yijing*, *Liji*, and *Lunyu*. Su Che and Wang Pang wanted to set free the unitary inspiration on which Daoism, Buddhism, and Confucianism were based, attempting a synthesis that might still maintain their differences. Numerous anthologies have been made comparing, phrase by phrase and chapter by chapter, the different interpretations that have been given the *Laozi*. Dong Sijing discusses them often. The flood of discourse which the *Laozi* has produced is inscribed in the immense conversation Chinese thinkers conducted across the frontiers of time and schools, and has benefited from the interactions that are produced in this way. One can find within it the entire history of Chinese thought, the signs of its different currents as well as the themes they have debated. The "naive" interpretations, the most elementary, which attempt to develop the presumed meaning of the text, rub shoulders with critical interpretations that examine certain ambiguous points (of which I have presented only a few examples), taking back or rejecting previous interpretations, even when they are traditional or canonical (indeed, the canonical ones are several). At the same time, there has been an effort by nearly all the interpreters to integrate this thought with more general Chinese thought.

Even though, as Valéry has said, there is no "true" sense of a text, the Chinese have come up with a certain coherence in the general trend of interpretations that have been given to the *Laozi*, even precisely in their ambiguity. If one maintains, as Graham suggests, that all interpretations are valid, this reduces to a statement that the text itself signifies nothing.

It must be noted in this regard that there is a fundamental difference between Daoism and Confucianism. The latter has always been concerned with the preservation of a body of doctrine, and developed under the form of commentaries and exegeses of canonical texts, commentaries and exegeses that in turn became canonical texts. At first there was the Five Classics, with a Confucius who "did not create" but only transmitted. Then came the Four Books and a Neo-Confucianism that pretended to return to the texts and rediscover the original path and true spirit of the Classics. Then, in turn, the great Neo-Confucians of the tenth and eleventh centuries became reference figures.

There never were, as appeared regularly in Daoism, new texts that made neither reference to earlier texts nor to already constituted doctrine. Such texts took their authority from revelation, which gave them an original stature and released them from dependence on their antecedents. Perhaps this is also the reason that there never was a body, properly speaking, of Daoist doctrine to defend, nor yet a "correct sense" (*zhengyi* 正義). It also explains why the *Laozi* and *Zhuangzi*, and other Daoist texts, could have been commented on by people of such diverse orientations.

─────────────── APPENDIX: ───────────────
MAJOR COMMENTARIES TO THE LAOZI

The dates in parentheses indicate the general date of the commentators or that of the commentary for which they are known. The second number indicates the number of the work in the catalogue of the *Daozang* published by the École Française d'Extrême Orient.

Bo Yuchan 白玉蟾 (ca. 1134–ca. 1239) Grand master of interior alchemy.

Chen Jingyuan 陳京元 alias Chen Bixu 陳碧虛 (1072), *Daozang* 714, Daoist master and author of numerous commentaries and interior alchemy texts.

Chen Xianggu 陳象古 (1101), 683.

Cheng Taizhi 程泰之 (1069).

Chu Boxiu 褚伯秀 (1270) 734; Commentator on the *Zhuangzi*.

Deng Yi 鄧錡 (1298), 687.

Dong Sijing 董思靖 (1246), 705; Daoist master.

Du Daojian 杜道堅 (1306), 703; Daoist master.

Du Guangting 杜光庭 (907); Daoist master, ritual expert, and author of both religious and philosophical essays.

Fan Yingyuan 范應元 (early thirteenth century).

Guan Caizhi 冠才質 (1189), 684.

Heshanggong 河上公; legendary personality from the second century B.C.E., the commentary attributed to him could possibly date from the second century C.E.

Huizong 徽宗 (between 1111 and 1118), 680; Emperor.

Li Lin 李霖 (1172), 718.

Lin Xiyi 林希逸 (1261), 701; scholar and commentator also on the *Zhuangzi* and *Liezi*.

Li Yue 李約 (ca. 810), 692.

Lu Xisheng 陸希聲 (ca. 890), 685, Confucian scholar trained also in the study of the *Yijing* and the *Chunqiu*.

Lü Huiqing 呂惠卿 (1078), 686, minister.

Niu Miaozhuan 牛妙傳 (1280).

Peng Si 彭耜 (1229), 707; alchemist and disciple of Bo Yuchan.

Shao Ruoyu 邵若愚 (preface dated 1135), 688.

Shi Tan 石潭, (thirteenth century), alias Ding Yidong 丁易東, author of studies on the *Yijing*.

Shi Yong 時雍 (1159), 696.

Sima Guang 司馬光 (1019–1086), 683, Prime Minister.

Su Che 蘇徹 (ca. 1100), 691, scholar and statesman, brother of poet Su Shi 蘇軾.

Wang Anshi 王安石 (1021–1086), statesman.

Wang Bi 王弼 (226–249), one of the most eminent members of the WeiJin movement known as *Xuanxue* 玄學 ("Mysterious Learning").

Wang Pang 王旁 (1042–1076), son of Wang Anshi. Although Wang Pang's commentary is lost, the most complete fragments are preserved in *Daozang* no. 706.

Wang Zhen 王真 (809), 713.

Wu Cheng 吳證 (1247–1331) 704, scholar of the Hanlin Academy, disciple of Neo-Confucianist Lu Xiangshan 陸象山, also author of a commentary on the *Yijing*.

Xiu Xiu'an 休休奄 (1288).

Yan Zun 嚴遵 (attributed to Yan Zun, scholar of the *Yijing*, 53–24 B.C.E.), 693.

Yu Qingzhong 喻清中 (1299), disciple of Shi Tan.

Zhang An 張安 (probably before 1116), wrote a subcommentary to that of Huizong, 681.

Zhang Sicheng 張嗣成 (1322), 698, thirteenth patriarch of the Celestial Masters tradition.

Zhao Bingwen 趙秉文 (fl. 1185–1232), 695, author of many commentaries to the classics.

Zhao Shi'an 趙實奄 (1152), Daoist ritual master.

NOTES

1. A. C. Graham, *Disputers of the Tao: Philosophical Argumentation in Ancient China* (LaSalle: Open Court, 1989), 300.

2. Benjamin I. Schwartz, *The World of Thought in Ancient China* (Cambridge and London: Belknap Press, 1985), especially "The Ways of Taoism," 186–254.

3. Graham, "Lao-tzu's Taoism: The Art of Ruling by Spontaneity," in *Disputers of the Tao*, 215–235.

4. Chad Hansen, "Laozi: Language and Society," in *A Daoist Theory of Chinese Thought* (New York: Oxford University Press, 1992), 196–230.

5. Michael LaFargue, "Hermeneutics: A Reasoned Approach to Interpreting the Tao Te Ching," in *The Tao of the Tao Te Ching* (Albany: State University of New York Press, 1992), 190–216.

6. I will only refer to those passages in which the *Dao* is specifically named, in order to avoid the places where the *Laozi* speaks of a "Heavenly Dao" which may be applied to the art of government.

7. The two Mawangdui manuscripts have *zhu* 注: the point of convergence.

8. Here I combine the translations of M. LaFargue and C. Chan.

9. *Encyclopédie philosophique universelle*, (Paris: Presses Universitaires de France, 1990), 6.

10. Although it also happens frequently enough that these commentaries attempt to isolate tendencies common to the *Laozi* and other Daoist, Buddhist, and Confucian thinkers.

11. References represent the number of the work in the catalogue of the *Daozang* 道藏 published by the École Française d'Extrême Orient, followed by the number of the chapter and the page. The first is specified only when it concerns an anthology, but is not when it concerns an anthology listed in the Appendix. References to the commentaries of Wang Bi (226–249) and Heshanggong only include the chapter number of the *Laozi* because of the existence of the numerous editions of these works.

12. Wing-tsit Chan, *The Way of Lao Tzu* (Indianapolis: Bobbs-Merrill, 1963), 105.

13. For Sima Chengzhen (647–735), see *Daozang* no. 1035.11b.

14. For a brief overview of this question see I. Robinet, "The Place and Meaning of the Notion of Taiji in Taoist Sources Prior to the Ming Dynasty," in *History of Religions* 29 (1990): 373–411, esp. 386–389.

15. Rump translates: "For in general there is always a cause whereby things are produced and achievement completed. Since they are caused by something, they are all caused by *Dao*" (Ariane Rump and Wing-tsit Chan, *Commentary on the Lao Tzu by Wang Pi* [Honolulu: University of Hawaii Press, 1979], 147). The translation of Alan Chan is more precise: "For things that are born, and for efforts that are made complete, there are always causes. As there are causes, then none is not caused by *Dao*" (Alan K. L. Chan, *Two Visions of the Way, A Study of the Wang Pi and the Ho-shang*

Kung Commentaries on the Lao-Tzu [New York: State University of New York Press, 1991], 52).

16. *Encyclopédie philosophique universelle*, II. p. 1616.

17. Chan, *Two Visions of the Way*, 68.

18. This continuity is all the more marked since, as we have said, *Dao* is sometimes identified as the primordial breath, which for all Chinese at least prior to the eleventh century was the dynamic substance, neither material nor spiritual, of which the entire universe was made.

19. Wang Fuzhi (1619–1692), for example, is opposed to this idea, arguing that from the moment one speaks of "before forms," this supposes that the notion of form already exists. See his *Zhou Yi waizhuan* 周易外傳 (Peking: Zhonghua, 1967), 203.

20. Perhaps two traditions (that of the *Laozi* and that of the *Yijing*, or of the *Xici*, its "Great Appendix"), but in fact two complementary conceptions, which one also finds in Western thought. We note that China developed henology, a science of the One, rather than ontology as the West had. For more detail on this subject, see my article "Un, Deux, Trois," in *Cahiers d'Extrême-Asie* 8 (1995): 175–220.

21. E. Bréhier, "L'idée de néant et le problème de l'origine radicale dans le néoplatonisme grec," *Revue de métaphysique et de morale* 26, no. 4 (1919): 443.

22. E.g., Paul Lin, *A Translation of Lao Tzu's Tao-te ching and Wang Pi's Commentary* (Michigan Papers in Chinese Studies, no. 30) (Ann Arbor: Center for Chinese Studies, 1977).

23. Instead of reading, "in the *chang* (permanent) state of *wuyu* (non-desire), we contemplate its mysteries, in the *chang* (permanent) state of *youyu* (desire), we contemplate its approaches," one started to read (Sima Guang seems to have been the first to do so): "For the *changwu* (the permanent *wu*) we contemplate its mysteries, for the *changyou* (permanent *you*), we contemplate its approaches." As we know, the versions of the *Laozi* found at Mawangdui undermine this theory.

24. See I. Robinet, "*Primus movens* et création récurrente," in *Taoist Resources* 5, no. 2 (Dec. 1994): 29–69.

25. See I. Robinet, *Les commentaires du Tao To king jusqu'au VIIe siècle* (Paris: Collège de France, Institut des Hautes Études Chinoises, 1977), part 2. It is a question of not inclining toward *wu* nor toward *you*, because these two notions are both equally true (in the sense of their utility) and false.

One is thereby maintaining them whole and not considering them except as having a relative and analogical existence.

26. Robinet, *Les commentaires du Tao To king jusqu'au VIIe siècle*, 97.

27. The *Huainanzi* says so: "Cold cannot give rise to cold, heat cannot give rise to heat; only what is neither hot nor cold can give rise to heat and cold. This is why what has form issued from the Formless." See the edition of Liu Wendian 劉文典. *Huainan honglie jijie* 淮南鴻烈集解 (Shanghai: Commercial Press, 1923), 16.13a.

28. Graham, *Disputers of the Tao*, 221–222.

29. Hansen, *A Daoist Theory of Chinese Thought*, 216.

30. Schwartz, *The World of Thought in Ancient China*, 197.

31. LaFargue, *The Tao of the Tao Te Ching*, 95.

32. References, except where otherwise noted, are all to commentaries to the first sentence of the *Laozi*, therefore chapter and page numbers will be omitted.

33. Li Daochun, *Zhongheji* 中和集 (*Daozang* no. 249), 249.1.7a–b.

34. Meng Anpai 孟安排, *Daojiao yishu* (*Daozang* no. 1139), 1.3a.

35. In particular the *Jiejie*, see I. Robinet, *Les commentaires du Tao To king jusqu'au VIIe siècle*, 49–56.

36. This is not only the case for *Laozi* and *Zhuangzi* which Schwartz had in mind, but also for other currents of Confucianism. See Robinet, "*Primus movens*," and *Introduction à l'alchimie intérieure taoïste, L'unité et la multiplicité* (Paris: Le Cerf, 1995).

37. For details on the different forms and diverse tendancies in interpretation, see Robinet, "*Primus movens*."

Re-exploring the Analogy of the Dao and the Field[1]

Robert G. Henricks

When I lecture on the *Laozi*, lecture one is always concerned with issues of dating and authorship; in lecture two, I try to explain what the author means by the "*Dao*,"—the Way. In doing this, I develop an analogy between the *Dao* and a field. With this image, students can easily move from the concrete to the abstract; they can "see"—in their mind's eye—what the *Dao* is, how it works, and how the *Dao* is related to the ten thousand things. Thus, for my contribution to this volume, I can think of nothing better to do than to work through that analogy, letting the analogy be more publicly known.

Let us begin with our primary question: What does Laozi mean by the *Dao*? We can answer this in a number of ways, for in the *Laozi*, the Way is 1) a cosmic reality, and it is 2) a personal reality, and it is 3) a way of life; *or*, it entails a way of life; *or*, we might want to say Daoists recognize that things tend to happen in certain ways. (One of the things I mean by this will become clear as we proceed.)

In saying the Way is a "cosmic reality," I mean that for Laozi, the *Dao* is that reality, or that level of reality, that existed prior to and gave rise to all other things—heaven and earth, the physical universe, and all things in heaven and earth, what the Chinese call the "ten thousand things" (*wanwu* 萬物). The "ten thousand things" is a phrase that refers collectively to the various genera and species of living things—birds, animals, trees, flowers, fishes, insects, and so forth; a human being is simply one of the ten thousand things.[2] All of these things come forth from the *Dao* in the way that babies emerge from the womb.

In saying that the Way is a "personal reality," I mean that having given birth to the ten thousand things, the Way continues to be *present* in each individual thing as a kind of energy or force—the life force, perhaps. And as an energy or force it is not static; rather, it is constantly pushing each individual thing to grow and develop, and to grow and develop in a particular way—in a way that is in accord with its "nature" (*xing*). The most important thing to do in Daoism is to be who by nature you are. However, we must bear in mind that the word *xing*, "in-born nature," never occurs in the *Laozi*. *Xing* as the thing that distinguishes one species of thing from another—that which makes a thing what it is—and as an individual's unique allotment of talents and skills, is the focus of Daoist reasoning for the first time in the writings of the "Primitivist" in chapters 8, 9, and 10 of the *Zhuangzi*.[3]

The *Dao in* things in this way is what Daoists mean by "virtue," (*de*)[4] The *Laozi* itself never says this as such, but we can find words of this sort in the *Zhuangzi*. Chapter 12 of that book, in a passage intent on defining and distinguishing in a Daoist way virtue (*de*), fate (*ming*), physical form (*xing* 形), and nature (*xing*) tells us that:

> In the Great Beginning, there was nonbeing; there was no being, no name. Out of it arose One (i.e., the *Dao*); there was One, but it had no form. Things got hold of it and came to life, and it was called virtue (*wu de yi sheng wei zhi de* 物得以生謂之德).[5]

In the *Laozi*, "virtue" is used in two different ways. There are places—the start of chapter 55 for example[6]—where it is used in this sense of energy or life force. There are other places, however, where it is used as the Confucians would use it—to refer to behavior that is morally good. Chapter 38 in the *Laozi* begins: "The highest virtue is not virtuous; therefore it truly has virtue" (*shangde bude shiyi youde* 上德不德是以有德). That is to say, *true* virtue lies in doing what is morally good with no ulterior motive; you are unconcerned with the fact that others might regard this as morally good.

To understand all that Laozi means by the *Dao*, we must look at a good number of chapters in the text. Especially important in this regard are chapters 1, 4, 6, 14, 25, 34, 51, and 52 (readers unfamiliar with these might quickly review the Appendix, "Key Passages on the *Dao*"). If we look at those chapters and try to compile a list of the traits or characteristics of the *Dao*, we would have to note the following things:

1) The Way is a single, "undifferentiated" reality. So the "One" reality that is the source of all differentiation in the world is itself undifferentiated (shapeless and formless); it is intangible and cannot be seen or heard or detected in any way. Moreover, it is 2) still and tranquil and empty. But the emptiness of the *Dao* is a womb-like emptiness, since it 3) contains the "seeds" or beginnings/essences of the ten thousand things. And as the source of material reality, it is 4) an inexhaustible source: at one point it is compared to a bellows (*nangyue* 囊籥); a bellows is empty, but when you work it, set it into motion, it is an endless source of air. (Also relevant is the opening line of chapter 4: "The Way is empty; Yet when you use it, you never need fill it again.")

The feminine nature of the *Dao* is clear throughout the text, and the *Dao* is explicitly called the "Mother" by Laozi in five different chapters.[7] But the maternal nature of the *Dao* is seen not only in the fact that it gives birth to all phenomenal things; that being done, it continues to feed and nourish *each* of the ten thousand things; it has no favorites. And it does this in a totally selfless way; it claims no credit for all it has done, and it does not try to own or control the things that it helps to develop.

Keeping these things in mind, what is the analogy of the *Dao* and the field? The field in the analogy would be a "natural" field, an untended field, one that is left to grow on its own; it is not a farmer's field which is cultivated for the raising of a particular crop. In the analogy, the field—the bland soil—is the *Dao*, and the "ten thousand things" correspond to the variety of grasses and wildflowers that would fill such a field throughout the spring and summer.

The analogy works out in this way. Were you to go to this kind of a field in the winter you would see something tranquil and still, and the field in the winter is "undifferentiated"; it is one in essence and color, either all brown or all white, depending on whether it is covered with snow. Did you not know any better, you might well conclude that the field is "empty" and barren, since there is no sign of life.

Nonetheless, if you return to that field in the spring, you would see that a transformation has occurred. The field that in winter was empty and tranquil, is now filled with all sorts of grasses and flowers: each *species* of flower (e.g., chicory, goat's beard, nightshade) is unique in color and shape and size, as is each *individual* plant of each species. You would now know that the field even in winter was in reality a fecund womb, containing within itself the roots and shoots of each of these things.

Moreover, the work of the field does not end with emergence of the flowers in spring. It—the soil—continues throughout the summer to nourish and feed all of these plants, providing them with minerals and water. In this way they develop and grow. In providing these things to the flowers, the field does so indiscriminately, providing for one and all alike; it has no favorites. It does not try to control the way each of the flowers matures. It claims no credit for all it has done; it never stands up and boasts "Look at the beautiful flowers I've brought into the world!" The field itself—the brown, bland, lackluster soil—stays in the background, lies unseen below the flowers; when we look at the field, what captures our attention are the colors and shapes and smells of the flowers.[8] We forget that the "invisible" soil is responsible for all of these things because we never see it *do* anything. (In the same way, people for the most part are unaware of the *Dao* as the source and provider of life, since it is invisible and never demands things from us in return.)

Wuwei—"to do nothing" or "to act without acting"—is a concept in Daoism that is well illustrated here by the field. The field appears to do nothing; all of this happens "by nature" (*ziran*—"it is so on its own"). And, having accomplished its deeds, the field—like the *Dao*—assumes none of the glory. The ideal ruler in Daoism, in like manner, is someone who is to the people who live in his state *as* the field is to the flowers, or *as* the *Dao* is to the ten thousand things. His aim is to see that all of the people who grow up in his land are nourished and fed, can grow and mature and reach a natural end to their lives, and to create conditions that will encourage each individual to be who he or she is by nature. But he does this by interfering with their lives as little as possible, acting unobtrusively in the background. And when he accomplishes his goals, he claims no credit for doing these things. The people will say "These things all happened to us by nature (*wo zi ran* 我自然)."[9]

No analogy is perfect, and the analogy of the *Dao* and the field—as my students have been happy to tell me over the years (!)—has its shortcomings as well. To note but a single example, the analogy seems to suggest a view of the world in which generation and dissolution of the world and all of its creatures is periodic, and when it exists the world passes through well-defined stages (like the four seasons). These cosmological notions are found in India, of course, in the idea of *kalpas* and *yugas*. But this is not the Daoist view. Creation—or emergence—for Daoists was an event that happened once in the past; though it is true that in some sense each new thing that is born (tree, insect, human) is thought to come from the *Dao*.

That point aside, the analogy is a good one, and one that helps us to understand a number of concepts in Daoist thought. I have suggested elsewhere that it might be *more* than an analogy, in that a good many things that Laozi says of the *Dao* are said in other religious traditions about "Mother Earth."[10] Relevant to this discussion, we must keep in mind that one of the names Zhuangzi used for the *Dao* was the "Great Clod" (*dakuai* 大塊, large lump of earth): "The Great Clod burdens me with form, labors me with life, eases me in old age, and rests me in death."[11] The stages in human life, here and elsewhere, are compared by Zhuangzi to the four seasons.[12]

I claimed at the start that the *Dao* is a cosmic reality, and a personal reality. The analogy of the *Dao* and the field helps us to see in what ways these claims are true. But what about this idea that the *Dao* is, or *entails*, a way of life, the idea that some events in the world tend to happen in certain ways?

One of the things I mean by this is well illustrated by the events that led to my "discovery" of this analogy, which I would now like to relate. In my first year of teaching—some twenty years ago— I offered the standard course on "Eastern Religions," a course that focused for the most part on Hinduism and Buddhism. I had reserved only two days to talk about Daoism—the last two days of the term. The next-to-last day I reviewed the problems of dating and authorship that we encounter with the text of *Laozi*. The last day of the term I would expound on the *Dao*.

I thought this would be easy to do since I had spent a good deal of time as a graduate student reading this text and its commentaries; I rather fancied myself as a specialist here. Having slogged through lectures on Hinduism and Buddhism, I was at last talking about something I really *knew*. It goes without saying that I wanted to compose a first-rate lecture; I wanted to impress the students with my knowledge and level of understanding; I wanted them to be as excited about the ideas in the text as I was. And, I hoped to find a way of discussing the *Dao* that would be accurate, comprehensive, and philosophically profound.

I quickly reviewed key chapters on the *Dao* in the text and started to write. Two or three hours later, after making a number of starts, I had really gotten nowhere with the lecture and found myself frustrated, confused, and disappointed. I concluded after a bit of soul-searching that it simply wasn't to be. It was the end of the term, and after writing new lectures day after day, I was simply exhausted; my creativity had been totally sapped. Though it involved loss of face, I would explain this to the class the next day, apologize, and assure them these materials would not show up on their impending final exam.

I felt good about this decision; I was resolved and I relaxed. I put all thoughts of the *Dao* out of my mind; I "emptied" my mind, in a way. I then had time on my hands, and it was a warm, early spring day. We lived out in the country; so I took my dog for a walk, my *Peterson's Guide to Wildflowers* in hand, since that was an interest I had at the time. We walked on a lane through the woods, a lane that led to an untended field. And there I sat down with my book to identify some of the flowers growing wild in the field.

I may have sat there five or ten minutes before it dawned on me that I was sitting, in a sense, on the *Dao*! And all of a sudden the mind I was sure was *exhausted* felt fully *renewed* and filled with creativity; the mind that was *empty* of thoughts on the *Dao* was now *filled* with those thoughts, as I saw point by point how the analogy worked. Fitting to cite here are Laozi's words in chapter 22:

> When emptied, you will be full;
> When worn out, you'll be renewed;
> When you have little, you'll attain much;
> With much, you'll be confused.[13]

The point that is illustrated by this experience is the Daoist point that in certain cases at least, it is only by "*not* seeking that you will find"; you have to "do the opposite thing," do the reverse of what your mind tells you to do, to achieve your goal.[14] In the end I found what I was seeking—a way to present "the Way" to others in a very short period of time (a one-hour lecture), in a way that would tell them a lot about the *Dao* and its relationship to the ten thousand things, and a lot about Daoist thought in general. But I found that *only* when I sincerely gave up the quest.

Still, I would have to admit that *what* I found was not exactly what I had in mind: I was hoping to dazzle my students with profound philosophical discourse; instead, I would present them with a simple, concrete image from nature. I would also have to admit that the "I" that made this discovery was not the same "I" that initially set to work that day on a lecture. *That* I wanted to impress with concepts and terms it had created by force of its intellect; *this* I was quite content to present the students with an analogy that could be discussed in nonphilosophical terms. And *this* I felt that when all was said and done, it had nothing to do with "creating" that image: the ideas had flowed forth, as it were, from the mind on their own; "I" did not own them or make them.[15] "I" was an observer who had taken some notes while my mind, like an internal movie projector, presented a show.

Needless to say, Laozi's words at the end of chapter 7 have assumed new significance for me ever since that day:

> Therefore the Sage:
> Puts himself in the background yet finds himself in the foreground;
> Puts self-concern out of his mind, yet finds that his self-concern is preserved.
> Is it not because he has no self-interest,
> That he is therefore able to realize his self-interest?[16]

My "self-interest" was in finding a way to describe the *Dao*, but I had found that only when I stopped worrying about my "self-image."

Let me close by noting one final way in which this analogy can be very instructive. If there is one thing that is clear from the analogy, it is that for each flower that grows in the field, for it to be 1) what by nature it is (i.e., for a sunflower to realize its "sunflowerness" or a buttercup to realize its "buttercupness"), for any plant to exhaust the possibilities of its genetic makeup, and 2) for it to live out its natural term (and for wildflowers, length of life varies with species and for each individual in each species), there is one condition that has to be met—it must keep its roots in the soil. In the Daoist view of things, this is exactly what we as humans fail to do. Something happens to each of us as we grow and mature, such that by the time we turn into adults, we have strayed from the Way. As Laozi puts it in chapter 53:

> Were I to have the least bit of knowledge, in walking on a Great Road (*da dao* 大道, i.e., the "Great Way"), it's only going astray that I would fear. The Great Way is very level; but people greatly delight in tortuous paths.[17]

We might paraphrase here—the easiest thing in the world ought to be to be who by nature you are; yet we all seem to delight in trying to be something or someone we're not.

As a result, if we as humans are to be who by nature we are and live out *our* natural years—which will vary from person to person—we must, as adults, *return* to the *Dao*. We must reattach ourselves to that source of power, energy, and life that is the *Dao*. In a sense, we must draw our nourishment from the *Dao* once again, like the flowers that grow in a field, and like infants who suckle at the breasts of their mothers. Regrettably, in Laozi's estimation, those who will do this are few. In chapter 20 of the text, Laozi sets himself apart from the masses by noting:

> My desires alone differ from those of others—
> For I value drawing sustenance from the Mother (*Wu yu
> du yi yu ren er gui shi mu* 吾欲獨異於人而貴食母).[18]

APPENDIX:
KEY PASSAGES ON THE DAO

(All translations from Henricks, *Lao-tzu Te-tao ching*)

Chapter 1: "As for the Way, the Way that can be spoken of is not the constant Way. As for names, the name that can be named is not the constant name. The nameless is the beginning of the ten thousand things; The named is the mother of the ten thousand things."

Chapter 4: "The Way is empty; Yet when you use it, you never need fill it again. Like an abyss! It seems to be the ancestor of the ten thousand things."

Chapter 5: "The space between Heaven and Earth—is it not like a bellows? It is empty and yet not depleted; Move it and more [always] comes out."

Chapter 6: "The valley spirit never dies; We call it the mysterious female. The gates of the mysterious female—These we call the roots of Heaven and Earth. Subtle yet everlasting! It seems to exist. In being used, it is not exhausted."

Chapter 14: "We look at it but do not see it; We name this 'the minute.' We listen to it but do not hear it; We name this the 'rarefied.' We touch it but do not hold it; We name this 'the level and smooth.'"

Chapter 16: "The ten thousand things—side-by-side they arise; And by this I see their return. Things [come forth] in great numbers; Each one returns to its root. This is called tranquility. 'Tranquility'—This means to return to your fate."

Chapter 21: "The character of great virtue follows alone from the Way. As for the nature of the Way—it's shapeless and formless. Formless! Shapeless! Inside there are images. Shapeless! Formless! Inside there are things. Hidden! Obscure! Inside there are essences. These essences are very real; Inside them is the proof."

Chapter 25: "There was something formed out of chaos, That was born before Heaven and Earth. Quiet and still! Pure and deep! It stands on its own and doesn't change. It can be regarded as the mother of Heaven and Earth. I do not yet know its name: I 'style' it 'the Way.' Were I forced to give it a name, I would call it 'the Great.'"

Chapter 34: "The Way floats and drifts; It can go left or right. It accomplishes its tasks and completes its affairs, and yet for this it is not given a name. The ten thousand things entrust their lives to it, and yet it does not act as their master. It can be named with the things that are small. The ten thousand things entrust their lives to it, and yet it does not act as their master; it can be named with the things that are great."

Chapter 40: "The things of the world originate in being, And being originates in nonbeing."

Chapter 42: "The Way gave birth to the One. The One gave birth to the Two. The Two gave birth to the Three. And the Three gave birth to the ten thousand things."

Chapter 51: "The Way gives birth to them and Virtue nourishes them; Substance gives them form and their unique capacities complete them. The Way gives birth to them, nourishes them, matures them, completes them, rests them, rears them, supports them, and protects them. It gives birth to them but doesn't try to own them; It acts on their behalf but doesn't make them dependent; It matures them but doesn't rule them. This we call Profound Virtue."

Chapter 52: "The world had a beginning, Which can be considered the mother of the world. Having attained the mother, in order to understand her children, If you return and hold on to the mother, till the end of your life you'll suffer no harm."

──────────── *NOTES* ────────────

1. My paper entitled "The Tao and the Field: Exploring an Analogy" was published by St. John's University in 1981 in the series "St. John's Papers on Asian Studies" (No. 27)—hence the present title. Key features of the analogy are also reviewed in the introduction to my translation of *Laozi*, *Lao-tzu Te-tao ching: A New Translation Based on the Recently Discovered Ma-wang-tui Texts* (New York: Ballantine Books, 1989), xx–xxii.

2. Some scholars might well include inanimate things, inorganic things—clouds, rocks, rivers, etc.—among the ten thousand things. But when Daoists discuss the *wanwu* they always seem to mean *living* things. For example, in chapter 9 of the *Zhuangzi* we read: "The ten thousand things live species by species (*wanwu qunsheng* 萬物群生), one group settled close to another. Birds and beasts form their flocks and herds, grass and trees grow to fullest height." (Translation is by Burton Watson, *The Complete Works of Chuang Tzu* [New York: Columbia University Press, 1968], 105.) For the original see the Harvard-Yenching Institute's *Concordance to Chuang Tzu* (Sinological Index Series, No. 20), 23, line 8.

3. For the views of the Primitivist, see A. C. Graham's *Chuang Tzu: The Inner Chapters* (London: George Allen & Unwin, 1981), 195–217. Also useful on the notion of *xing* in Daoism is Harold Roth's article, "The Concept of Human Nature in the *Huai-nan Tzu*," *Journal of Chinese Philosophy* 12 (April 1985), 1–22.

4. Other popular and quite valid translations of *de* are "power" and "potency." I prefer the traditional "virtue" since in English this has the same ambiguity: "virtue" can mean inner strength; it can also mean moral conduct.

5. Translation is by Watson, *The Complete Works of Chuang Tzu*, 131–132. The passage continues: "Before things had forms, they had their allotments; these were of many kinds, but not cut off from one another, and they were called *fates*. Out of the flow and flux, things were born, and as they grew they developed distinct shapes; these were called *forms*. The forms and bodies held within them spirits, each with its own characteristics and limitations, and this was called the *inborn nature*. If the nature is trained, you may return to Virtue, and Virtue at its highest peak is identical with the Beginning." (Italics added for emphasis. For the original text, see the Harvard-Yenching *Concordance*, 30, lines 37–39.)

6. "One who embraces the fullness of Virtue, Can be compared to a newborn babe. Wasps and scorpions, snakes and vipers do not sting him; Birds of prey and fierce beasts do not seize him; His bones and muscles are weak and pliant, but his grasp is firm" (Henricks, *Lao-tzu Te-tao ching*, 132).

7. Chapters 1, 20, 25, 52, and 59. The passages in question read: "The nameless is the beginning of the ten thousand things; The named is the mother of the ten thousand things." (1) "But my desires alone differ from those of others—For I value drawing sustenance from the Mother" (20). "There was something formed out of chaos, That was born before Heaven and Earth. Quiet and Still! Pure and deep! It stands on its own and doesn't change. It can be regarded as the mother of Heaven and Earth. I do not yet know its name: I 'style' it 'the Way'" (25). "The world has a beginning, Which can be considered the mother of the world. Having attained the mother, in order to understand her children, If you return and hold on to the mother, till the end of your life you'll suffer no harm" (52). And "If you repeatedly accumulate virtue, then there is nothing you can't overcome. When there is nothing you can't overcome, no one knows where it will end. When no one knows where it will end, you can possess the state. And when you possess the mother of the state, you can last a very long time" (59).

8. But these colors and shapes can lead us astray. As Laozi says in chapter 12: "The five colors cause one's eyes to go blind. . . . The five flavors

confuse one's palate. The five tones cause one's ears to go deaf" (Henricks, *Lao-tzu Te-tao ching*, 210). The *Dao*—like the soil—may be bland and insipid, but it is in the *Dao* that the *true* flavor of life can be found. Relevant lines here may be found in chapters 35 (p. 256) and 63 (p. 148): "Music and food—for these passing travelers stop. Therefore the *Dao* has a saying that goes 'Insipid it is! Its lack of flavor' (*tan* [= *dan* 淡] *he qi wu wei ye* 談呵其無味也)" and "Act without acting; Serve without concern for affairs; Find flavor in what has no flavor (*wei wu wei* 味無味)."

9. As in chapter 17 in the text. "With the highest kind of ruler, those below simply know he exists. . . . He completes his tasks and finishes his affairs, yet the common people say, 'These things all happened by nature'" (Henricks, *Lao-tzu Te-tao ching*, 220).

10. See "The Tao and the Field: Exploring an Analogy," pp. 12–14.

11. Translation is by Watson, *The Complete Works of Chuang Tzu*, 85. For the original text, see the Harvard-Yenching *Concordance*, 16, line 24.

12. In chapter 18 of the *Zhuangzi*, he says of the life and death of his wife: "In the midst of the jumble of wonder and mystery a change took place and she had a spirit. Another change and she had a body, Another change and she was born. Now there's been another change and she's dead. It's just like the progression of the four seasons, spring, summer, fall, winter." (Translation is by Watson, *The Complete Works of Chuang Tzu*, 192.)

13. Henricks, *Lao-tzu Te-tao ching*, 232.

14. This is also the key, I think, to understanding Laozi's political views. If a ruler wishes to be "above" everyone else in the world, he should put himself "below" them; he should learn to be humble. If he wishes to win over all of the states, he should stop competing with them; he will win over the world because everyone will flock to his court. Hence the words in chapter 66: "Therefore in the Sage's desire to be above the people, He must in his speech be below them. And in his desire to be at the front of the people, He must in his person be behind them. Thus he dwells above, yet the people do not regard him as heavy; And he dwells in front, yet the people do not see him as posing a threat. The whole world delights in his praise and never tires of him. Is it not because he is not contentious, That, as a result, no one in the world can contend with him?" (Henricks, *Lao-tzu Te-tao ching*, 154).

15. My mind, in a sense, was functioning like the *Dao*. It is easy to see why the Mind is described like the *Dao* in Chinese Buddhism—it is the one source of all reality, both external reality, the "things" that we perceive to be other than ego, and internal reality, ego's feelings and thoughts. In Zen Buddhism, which is a very Daoistic form of Buddhism, the goal is to let those feelings and thoughts flow naturally from the mind without stopping

the flow by trying to control or own them or by seeing some feelings as "good" and others as "bad."

16. Henricks, *Lao-tzu Te-tao ching*, 200.

17. Henricks, *Lao-tzu Te-tao ching*, 128.

18. Henricks, *Lao-tzu Te-tao ching*, 226. The *Dao* as the "mother" of all humanity, from whom we have strayed and to whom we need to "return," though an abstract idea in the philosophies of Laozi and Zhuangzi, is transformed into a "goddess" in Chinese sectarian religion in Ming (1368–1643) and Ch'ing (1644–1922) times, a goddess who is worshipped under the name Wusheng laomu 無生老母, the "Eternal Mother" (literally the "Unborn, Old Mother"). About her Susan Naquin relates: "The story of the Eternal Mother was to be found in the literature of her sects. There she was described as the progenitor of mankind: she had given birth to a son and daughter who had married and were in turn the ancestors of all men. She had sent mankind, her children, to the 'Eastern world' to live on earth. To the Eternal Mother's great distress, her children soon 'indulged in vanity and lost their original nature.' 'All living beings were confused and lost in the red dust world; they had fallen and knew not how to return to their origin.' The Eternal Mother, seeing her offspring in this state, was filled with sorrow. '[She] weeps as she thinks of her children. She has sent them many messages and letters [urging them] to return home and to stop devoting themselves solely to avarice in the sea of bitterness. [She calls them] to return to the Pure Land, to come back to Mount Ling, so that mother and children can meet again and sit together on the golden lotus'" (Susan Naquin, *Millenarian Rebellion in China: The Eight Trigrams Uprising of 1813* [New Haven: Yale University Press, 1976], 9–10). The myth of the Eternal Mother is not purely Daoist. Mention of the "red dust world," the "Pure Land," and the "golden lotus," all reflect Buddhist influence. Also, the idea that humanity has somehow "fallen" from an original purity, might be Christian inspired. Finally, that a brother and sister once married give birth to the ancestors of all of the peoples that live in the world, originates in a flood myth of the Miao and Yao peoples, minorities that still live in southern China. (For more on this myth, see, for example, my article "On the whereabouts and identity of the place called 'K'ung-sang' (Hollow Mulberry) in early Chinese Mythology," *Bulletin of the School of Oriental and African Studies* LVIII (1995): 69–90.)

A Philosophical Analysis of the Laozi from an Ontological Perspective

Tateno Masami

Introduction

The *Dao* that Laozi talks about has been described as something "transcendent," beyond the grasp of human understanding, and as "the eternal and omnipresent actual reality" or "the original source of the myriad things"—that which offers the fundamental possibility for everything in the universe.[1] On the basis of such descriptions, the *Dao* is said to be beyond explanation. This is purportedly the reason why Laozi himself says, "The *Dao* that can be spoken is not the constant *Dao*" (chapter 1). And there are many such passages.

Clearly Laozi's *Dao* is something beyond the range of our ordinary, rational processes of thought. And so in terms of talking about it, the *Dao* is something for which we cannot possibly give an adequate logical account. However, Laozi's philosophy is not simply a theory or argument; fundamentally, it is something that arises out of the contemplation of the whole of our actual experience. And so we cannot simply replace *Dao* with some phrase like "actual reality" or "the original source of the myriad things," for from a philosophical point of view these offer no real explanation.

While Laozi's *Dao*, epistemologically speaking (in other words, in regard to the realm of "knowledge" or "words") clearly is "transcendent," if we take things one step further—to the ontological level—and carry out an ontological inquiry, it is by no means the case that the *Dao* is cut off from us and represents some absolute and infinite existence. On the contrary, the *Dao* is something that we must realize for ourselves through a profound exercise of personal understanding in the course of a regimen of physical discipline—in other words, through *practice*.[2] If this were not the case, then Laozi's calls for self-restraint, e.g., "Those who know do not speak, Those who speak do not know" (chapter 56), and his earnest appeals, e.g., "My teachings are extremely easy to understand and extremely easy to *practice*" (chapter 70), would be meaningless.

In what follows, I will first consider the epistemological aspects of Laozi's system of philosophical speculation concerning the *Dao*. I will then explicate his practical system of philosophical thought by focusing on the symbol of the content of his ontology: *de* ("power," "virtue," or "nature").

Section 1

From an epistemological perspective, the most fundamental world view within Laozi's system of philosophy is so-called "relativism." Laozi himself says of the phenomenal world:

> Everyone in the world knows the beauty of what is
>   beautiful,
> Only because there are things that are ugly.
> Everyone knows the good of what is good,
> Only because there are things that are bad.
> And so,
> What is and what is not give rise to one another,
> Difficult and easy complete one another,
> Long and short give form to one another,
> High and low slope into one another,
> Note and tone harmonize with one another,
> Before and after follow one another. (Chapter 2)

Through these examples, Laozi shows that for us human beings, there must first be beautiful and ugly and good and bad *things* in mutual dependence with one another before we can have notions of "beautiful" and "ugly" or "good" and "bad," etc. In other words, our conceptions of "beauty" and "ugliness," "good" and "bad," and the like are thoroughly relativistic. Absolute beauty or ugliness, good or bad, and the like do not exist. Since human understanding always works within the relativistic framework of "what is" and "what is not," "difficult" and "easy," "long" and "short," etc., it follows that human understanding cannot comprehend absolute truth.

Concerning this issue, the following passage may provide us with a record of Laozi's personal reflections on the limitations of human knowledge:

> To know that we do not know is best,
> Not to know what "knowing" is, is a disease.
> When one sees this disease as a disease,
> One is free from it.
> The sage is free from this disease.
> He sees the disease for what it is,
> And so he is free from it. (Chapter 71)

In other words, we ourselves must know that we cannot ever know absolute and universal truth. Not to understand the limitations of knowledge is a disease. But in realizing that this disease is a disease, i.e., by understanding the limitations of knowledge, the sage is free from this disease.

In summary, as long as we rely on human rational thought, our capacity for intuition and enlightenment will forever remain restricted within the confines of the type of knowledge generated by the relativistic framework of space and time and subject and object. As a result, we will never be able to reach the higher level of knowledge, where one makes contact and connects with the true world.

So then is there no way for us human beings to gain a sense of the true nature of this world? Laozi's answer is that there is a way: through the *Dao*.

Section II

Laozi believes that by passing through a practical regimen of training which involves a withdrawal into the innermost depths of under-

standing—in other words through *practice*—we can transcend and
pass far beyond the ordinary world generated by the modality of
mind and body and realize within ourselves (lit. "embody") the true
Dao. In regard to this practical regimen of training or *practice*, Laozi
makes the following pertinent and incisive remarks:

> The five colors blind our eyes,
> The five notes deafen our ears.
> The five flavors deaden our palates,
> The chase and the hunt drive our minds to madness,
> Goods hard to come by interfere with our activities.
> And so the sage is for the belly—not the eye.
> He discards the one and chooses the other. (Chapter 12)

Splendid colors (the "five colors"), enchanting music (the "five
notes"), a delicious banquet (the "five flavors"), and a pleasant
outing ("the chase and the hunt") draw and hold the attention of
our eyes and ears and thereby our minds. But such things are
thoroughly relativistic. What is more, they lead to excess, resulting
in blindness, deafness, madness, and other kinds of distress.

And so the sage shows no preference for the eye but is rather
for the belly. Being "for the belly" is a metaphor expressing the
active withdrawal of consciousness which accompanies the practical
regimen of training or *practice*. In such a program of meditative
cultivation, one concentrates one's spirit—i.e., the "energy" in the
expression *zhuanqi* 專氣 ("concentrating energy," see chapter 10) or
according to an alternative expression, the "field of cinnabar" below
the navel (the area approximately one inch below the navel). This
kind of spiritual regimen can be seen in the *practice* of Zen, Yoga,
and a host of other disciplines. We might say that it represents
the basic foundation for such spiritual *practices*. Through such
practice the sage is able to transcend the relativistic framework
of the ordinary phenomenal world and embody the *Dao* in the
innermost recesses of his own consciousness.

Here we must take special care to note that Laozi's *Dao* is not
simply what Kant called a *Grenzbegriff* ("limiting concept")—e.g.,
his notion of *Dinge an sich* ("things in themselves")—nor does it
simply represent a general category of knowledge such as we find in
epistemology, e.g., a transcendental concept like Descartes's *cogito*
("thinking"). Rather, Laozi's *Dao* is *true knowledge* concerning one's

real self, which is acquired through the cultivation of one's own consciousness.[3] Laozi describes this with both elegance and precision, in the following words:

> By concentrating your restless soul and embracing the
>   one,
> Can you keep them from leaving?
> By concentrating your energy and reaching the highest
>   suppleness,
> Can you be a child? (Chapter 10)

Expressions like "embracing the one" and "concentrating your energy" illustrate the practical nature of the *practice* of embodying one's true self which is the *Dao*. This is the process, mentioned earlier, of accumulating and unifying one's energy in the "field of cinnabar" in order to become a "child." The term "child" of course refers to an infant and an infant is not in any way constrained by the conceptual categories of space and time nor by notions of subjective and objective. And so the child is a symbol of the sage who embodies the *Dao*, a realm that is without space or time and in which subjective and objective are united as one. This is precisely the same realm referred to in the line from chapter 28 that describes how one is to "return to being a child."

The following passage makes the same basic point regarding the practical nature of this *practice*:

> Cultivate extreme tenuousness
> Preserve complete stillness
> The myriad creatures arise together
> And I watch them return
> They arise in mad profusion
> But each returns to its root. (Chapter 16)

Through *practice* the sage deepens his power of understanding. By embodying the "tenuous" and "still" *Dao*, which is his true self, deep within himself, he no longer regards the shifting variety of phenomena merely as sense objects. For him, the reality of the phenomenal world is revealed to be the truth that arises within himself. This is the "root" of the various phenomena. This *Dao*, which comes from within us, wherein the reality of the phenomenal world is embodied in the most profound regions of our understanding, is the practical and real knowledge that comes through earnest and disciplined *practice*.

However, here we must be sure to note that Laozi's way of thinking is not in any way a denial or rejection of the everyday world. Rather he insists that we must live our lives within this world but we must live them as embodiments of the *Dao* (lit. "as the *Dao*"). In other words, while on the level of epistemology the *Dao* is "nothing," in the end it is the truth of our very selves; it is never separated from the reality of human existence.[4]

When referring to the *Dao* as it exists in the actual world, Laozi calls it *de* ("power," "virtue" or "nature"). In what follows, in our effort to further explicate Laozi's notion of *Dao*, we shall explore his concept of *de*, the *Dao* as manifested in the world.

Section)))

In our effort to explain the ontological sense of Laozi's concept of *de*, let us first look at what he says about the *Dao* as manifested in the actual world (which is just another way of saying *de*):

> As a thing, the *Dao* is indistinct and elusive
> Indistinct and elusive, within there is a form
> Indistinct and elusive, within there is a substance
> Dim and dark, within there is an essence
> Its essence is pure authenticity,
>   within there is sincerity. (Chapter 21)

In this passage, although Laozi says that the *Dao*, as it exists in the actual world, is difficult to discern (because it is "indistinct and elusive" and "dim and dark"), he also says that it possesses a "form," a "substance," and an "essence." Moreover, because its essence is pure, sincerity comes into being. Put another way, this is nothing other than our being in the everyday world as the *Dao*. In other words, Laozi's *Dao* is not something that can be grasped through the kind of "knowing" one finds within the Kantian paradigm of intuition and reason. Rather, it is something each of us must understand for him- or herself through accumulated *practice* in which one actually embodies the *Dao* by engaging in an active withdrawal into the most profound regions of one's understanding. When one realizes the *Dao* one begins to appreciate truth for the very first time. In such a moment, precisely in such a moment, what Laozi calls the *Dao* is simply the true reality of each of us—the *Dao* as self.

It is very important to keep in mind that this *Dao* is not a direct expression of our individuality. Rather it is the way in which the *Dao* exists in the actual world. This *Dao* as self results from the cultivation of our *de*. It is what is referred to by the line, "One perfects oneself" (chapter 7). It is the fulfilled or perfected self.

We must remember that the *Dao* as it exists in the world, that is, the *Dao* as self, which comes into being when we realize the most profound parts of the self, is still from an epistemological point of view "nothing." If we want to talk about the actual existence of the *Dao*, we must say that it is *de*.

This is one reason why the *Laozi* is full of various metaphors. Let us consider the different ways in which the text uses words in its struggle to manifest the *Dao*, which is "nothing" and as such beyond words. In the passage quoted below, Laozi talks about the *Dao*, the true self realized in the individual person, which fundamentally transcends the ordinary relativistic world constructed by language. This is something that cannot adequately be grasped within the realm of language and through the use of reason:

> If looking we cannot see it, we call it ephemeral.
> If listening we cannot hear it, we call it rarefied.
> If grasping we cannot lay hold of it, we call it minute.
> These three cannot be fully fathomed,
> And so they are conflated and taken as one . . .
> Spinning off indefinitely, it cannot be named,
> This is called the shape without a shape,
> The form without a substance,
> This is called the indistinct and elusive. (Chapter 14)

We human beings cannot grasp the *Dao* through the kind of understanding that operates within the realm of our ordinary intuition and reason. On this level of understanding, the *Dao* is simply "nothing." If we want to make contact and connect with the *Dao*, we must embody it by enriching our understanding at the very depths of our being.

We can, through our ordinary external sensory perceptions, see, hear and touch this "formless" *Dao* or at least part of it. This is the ontological significance of *de*, the manifestation of *Dao*. In other words, *de* is the corresponding existing phenomenal expression of *Dao* in the realm of actual being. And so within our ordinary world, we can perceive the *Dao* manifested as *de* in various exquisite paintings. We can hear the *Dao* manifested as *de* in the musical compositions of the most gifted composers. And we can even directly feel the *Dao* in the performances of great martial arts masters.

We can summarize our analysis up to this point by saying that Laozi's *Dao* is beyond our perception, that is, beyond the realm of actual being. And yet this "nothing," which cannot be described in words, is manifested as actually existing *de*. This, the *Dao* as it exists in the world, can be described in logical terms. Nevertheless, these various logical descriptions of the *Dao* are not able to convey the fundamental nature of Laozi's *Dao* itself. We cannot forget that the key to Laozi's *Dao* is a physical regimen which involves an active withdrawal into the most profound regions of consciousness and the realization of the *Dao* as one's true self. By means of a projection of this self, we can realize the true character of the phenomenal world. (This is "perfecting the self." See chapter 7 quoted above.)

Section IV

Laozi's revelations are quite straightforward, which I fear may invite misunderstanding. He describes the truth of the knowledge we are led to by accumulating the *Dao*'s virtue (*de*) through *practice* in the following passage:

> What is well-established cannot be pulled out.
> What is held fast cannot be taken away.
> In this way, the sacrificial offerings of one's descendants
>   will never come to an end.
> Cultivate it in your person and this *de* will be genuine.
> Cultivate it in your family and this *de* will be overflowing.
> Cultivate it in your village and this *de* will be long-lasting.
> Cultivate it in your state and this *de* will be abundant.
> Cultivate it in the world and this *de* will be universal.
> And so, *guan* 觀 ("contemplate") yourself through
>   yourself.

Contemplate your family through your family.
Contemplate your village through your village.
Contemplate your state through your state.
Contemplate the world through the world. (Chapter 54)

If we embody the *Dao*, we actualize it as ourselves and then exist concretely as *de*. That it to say, by a deepening of the self through a progressive *practice*, we can grasp the true nature of the world by being what we really are. In the same way, by extending this, we can pass beyond mere "knowing" and directly perceive the real nature of the family, village, state and world.

In other words, through *practice* of the *Dao*, we can pass beyond the world of our ordinary relativistic way of thinking and directly embody the true nature of the world. When, in our own being, we exist as *de*, each of us is the *Dao*, and this *Dao*, just as it is, is the entire world.

Conclusion

Laozi is a philosopher. He looks with absolute frankness and honesty at the fundamental constraints on our possibilities for being, i.e., the constraints imposed by our relativistic view of the world. The reality we perceive is necessarily represented within a framework of space and time and subject and object. And so, according to Laozi, within our ordinary world, our normal cognitive faculties cannot perceive the absolute and universal truth of oneness.

But Laozi maintains that if we go behind the ordinary world, to the infinitely vast and profound realm of cognition in the depths of our own minds, we can directly embody the truth. Laozi called this truth the *Dao*.

The *Dao* is the most vivid and palpable truth of human existence. However, it is not simply some finite concept of epistemology. The *Dao* is something we must realize in our own selves through accumulated effort in a regimen of physical training. We might say it is true reality. Moreover, it is also said that through the cultivation of *de* one comes to completely embody the world; that is to say, one directly realizes the world in one's own self. In other words, according to Laozi, the *Dao* itself, just as it is, is actualized as the world. In ontological terms, we would say that the *Dao* is the external world. These ontological aspects of Laozi's thought in themselves are quite remarkable.

And so we see that Laozi's philosophical thought points to *Dao* and *de* and nothing else; these constitute the "perfection of the self." (See chapter 7 quoted above). To accumulate *de*, deepen one's understanding and become a sage, this is to perfect the self. This is the most poignant and sublime point of Laozi's philosophy. Given this, Laozi's teachings do not simply describe a technique for ordering the world nor are they simply a philosophical theory. They are the most fundamental source for the guiding, comprehensive truth of the world in which we human beings exist, and they have been handed down through an unbroken, living tradition for more than two thousand years.

Laozi is not just a philosopher, because the basis of his philosophical theory is the practical activity of *practice*, which entails one becoming the *Dao* through the exercise of *de*. But Laozi also is not just an accomplished practitioner, because the *practices* he advocates are always bolstered by frank and honest epistemological and ontological theories. So Laozi's philosophical system is a system of epistemology and ontology backed up by a regimen of self-cultivation. In this and precisely this sense is Laozi a philosopher.

———————— *NOTES* ————————

1. The *Dao* has been characterized in a variety of different ways, with examples too numerous to mention. However, my description of its general features is consistent with widely accepted views about its character. For a more precise and thorough discussion of this issue, which includes numerous specific examples, see my "Rōshi no Shi'i—Tetsugakuteki kanten kara no ichi shiron 老子の思惟: 哲學的觀點からの 一試論," *Kangaku kenkyū* 漢學研究 26 (1989): 1–15, and J. L. Schroeder, "On the Meaning of *Tao*," (paper presented at the fourth International Congress of the International Society for Chinese Philosophy).

2. I understand the character 行 as the word *gyō* as in the common Japanese expression *shugyō* 修行 "self-cultivation" or "*practice*." Specifically, it is a form of self-cultivation which entails a progressive withdrawal into the most profound depths of our essential nature through a physical meditative regimen of controlling one's *qi* 氣 "breath" or "energy." For a

study of this issue that provides a practical description of the process from a philosophical point of view, see Yuasa Yasuo 湯淺泰雄, *Shintai: Tōyōteki shinshinron no kokoromi* 身體: 東洋的心身論の試み (Tokyo: Sobunsha, 1977), Nagatomo Shigenori et. al., trans., *The body, self-cultivation, and ki-energy* (Albany: State University of New York Press, 1993), and my "Rōshi, Michi, Shichū no inja—Dōka shisō no tetsugakuteki kontekisuto 老子道市中の隱者—道家思想の哲學的コンラキスト" in *Shisō* 思想 864 (1996).

Translator's note: Throughout the essay the character 行 as the word *gyō* and no other character is translated as *"practice"* and the word is always italicized.

3. Translator's note: Kant argued that the concept of a non-sensible object or *noumenon* could validly serve to "curb the pretensions of sensibility." But since no actually existing object can be determined for such concepts, "they cannot be asserted to be objectively valid." (Quotations are from Norman Kemp Smith, trans., *Immanuel Kant's Critique of Pure Reason* [New York: St Martin's Press, 1965], 272.) Descartes employed the concept of *cogito* in the sense of thought or thinking in general. In neither case do these respective notions entail any particular *content* of thought. The author's point is that Laozi claims a specific, though unspecified and ineffable, content to the *Dao*.

4. Translator's note: The point here is that since the *Dao* is not any particular thing but rather the pattern and pulse of everything, there is no "object" for us to sense and hence nothing to "know."

Method in the Madness of the *Laozi*[1]

Bryan W. Van Norden

"The great square has no corners.
The great vessel is never completed.
The great note sounds muted.
The great image has no form."

—*Laozi* M 41

"Though this be madness,
yet there is method in't."

—Polonius, *Hamlet* II.ii

The *Laozi* has been an influential text, not only within its native culture, but also far beyond it. The German philosopher Martin Heidegger collaborated on a translation of it. Ronald Reagan quoted it. Director Sam Peckinpah's controversial film *Straw Dogs* takes its title from it. *The Simpsons* parodied it. And a translation of it was recently on *The New York Times* bestseller list.[2]

Although the *Laozi* lends itself to such diverse uses, I submit that it is a remarkably coherent text. Part of the reason for this coherence is that it is largely animated by a utopian social vision, out of which grow the text's concern with mysticism, cosmology, and what I shall call "the ethics of paradox." In other words, this mystical text is not only consistent, but many of its doctrines flow naturally from one core vision.[3] This essay is an attempt to sketch one interpretation of this core vision. In doing so, I immediately invite at least three major objections.

Three Methodological Objections

Some would object that it is illegitimate to look for coherence in the *Laozi*, because even if one takes seriously the notion of "authorial intent" (which many do not), there is no single author who is responsible for the *Laozi*.[4] However, there are other ways a text can be given coherence besides single authorship. Those who initially committed the sayings of the *Laozi* to writing must have been guided by some conception of what "belonged" in this work. Furthermore, once it became a written text, there developed native commentarial traditions that preserved and interpreted the *Laozi* for future generations. As philosophers such as Alasdair MacIntyre have stressed, traditions have their own coherence.[5] And these native traditions saw the *Laozi* as a coherent work. Thus, there is at least prima facie reason to believe the text has some sort of coherence.

Others would object that our effort to find coherence in the *Laozi* must assume that we can understand the text, and that to assume this is to ignore the character of the *Laozi* as a mystical work, and to impose on the text our own Procrustean Western rationality. Admittedly, in looking for coherence in a text, we are approaching that text with certain presuppositions. However, I think it is important to distinguish between "disabling" and "enabling" presuppositions.[6] A disabling presupposition is one that blinds us to certain aspects of the text. For example, linguist Deborah Tannen reports that men often systematically miscommunicate with women because of the male presupposition that reports of problems are always requests for solutions.[7] This is what I would call a *disabling* presupposition. However, it is impossible to approach a text (or anything else) without presuppositions of some kind. In the absence of all presuppositions, our experience would be nothing but (in William James's words) a "buzzing, blooming confusion." Presuppositions are *enabling* if, in the long run, they help us to communicate with others, and to understand and deal with the world around us.

Of which sort is the presupposition that the *Laozi* "makes sense"? I submit that this assumption is disabling only if we start from an overly narrow conception of what it is to make sense, and inflexibly maintain that conception even when it does not fit the text. For example, it would certainly be disabling to presuppose that the *Laozi* must be organized like Euclid's *Elements*. Less obviously, but equally disabling, is the presupposition that the *Laozi* must "make sense" in the way Western mystical texts do. Laozi was not Hildegard von Bingen.[8] In assuming that a text makes sense I assume minimally that it can be seen as the product of coherent human motivations and values that we can sympathetically understand (even if we do not, ultimately, share them).[9] I think that, in general, this should be our initial (but defeasible) hermeneutic assumption in approaching a text. However, I do not have the space to defend it here, so, if the reader does not agree with this general hermeneutic principle, I invite her to consider it as merely one strategy for reading this text.[10]

I also hold, more controversially, that the *Laozi* is coherent in the sense of embodying a noncontradictory world view, which we can accurately represent in a discursive essay. This is not the same as the previous kind of coherence. (For example, I may have a coherent intention to confuse you, in which case my utterances may be theoretically inconsistent.) However, I hope that my theoretical interpretation of the *Laozi*, which shows how various kinds of claims made in the text fit together, will seem compelling. In addition, I acknowledge that it is paradoxical to write something that is (like all the contributions in this volume) a discursive essay about a work that eschews a discursive style. We should keep in mind, though, that a text may admit of a theoretical reading even if its author(s) dismissed the value of theory.

Finally, some would object that my methodology seems to assume that there is such a thing as the one correct interpretation of a text. In fact, I make no such assumption. To begin with, readers from different fields can successfully read a text in different ways. The linguist, the social historian, and the philosopher should certainly learn from one another, but they will get different answers from any given text because they will ask different questions of it. Even from within one intellectual discipline, there are many different aspects of any complex text on which one can choose to focus.

Furthermore, we get better at asking questions of texts as the depth and breadth of human experience progresses. For example, the questions asked by Freudian and Nietzschean interpreters have only recently been framed. Nonetheless, I would insist that, focusing on certain aspects of a text from within one discipline, we can at least distinguish between better and worse interpretations. The fact that there is no one right interpretation does not mean that there are no *wrong* interpretations.[11]

The interpretation I propose here is certainly not intended as the final word on the *Laozi*. Perhaps the most important thing to remember about any presupposition is that it is defeasible. (Even the most wildly false presupposition will do only limited harm if we are willing to abandon it when it fails to do justice to the text.) Thus, we must be prepared for the possibility that the *Laozi* lacks any sort of coherence, or fails to make sense. In addition, there are many other aspects of the *Laozi* that one could profitably discuss from a philosophical perspective. (For example, I say nothing about the self-preservationist aspects of the text.) However, I will argue that my interpretation is more successful in certain respects than some rival interpretations.

The Core Social Vision

According to the *Laozi*, society is beset with a number of ills:

> The court is thoroughly deserted,
> The fields are choked with weeds,
> The granaries are altogether empty.
>
> Still there are some who
>   wear clothes with fancy designs and brilliant colors,
>   sharp swords hanging at their sides,
>   are sated with food,
>   overflowing with possessions and wealth.
> This is called "the brazenness of a bandit."
> The brazenness of a bandit is surely not the Way! (M 53)

One common response to social problems (we have seen it in our own time) is to call for a return to a kinder, gentler, and simpler era, before the corrupting influences of new ideas and new choices. I submit that this is precisely the sort of social vision that animates the *Laozi*:

> The more taboos under heaven,
>   the poorer the people;
> The more clever devices people have,
>   the more confused the state and ruling house;
> The more knowledge people have,
>   the more strange things spring up;
> The more legal affairs are given prominence,
>   the more numerous bandits and thieves. (M 57)[12]

Thus, the *Laozi* is critical of contemporary society for being too "sophisticated" (in a bad sense). Part of this sophistication is a tendency to recognize too many distinctions. Making distinctions leads to making evaluative comparisons. Making evaluative comparisons leads to envy, dissatisfaction, and competition, because to distinguish one thing as good automatically identifies other things as bad:

> When all under heaven know beauty as beauty,
>   already there is ugliness;
> When everyone knows goodness
>   this accounts for badness.
> Having and not-having[13] give birth to each other,
> Difficult and easy complete each other,
> Long and short form each other,
> High and low fulfill each other,
> Tone and voice harmonize with each other,
> Front and back follow each other—
>   it is ever thus. (M* 2)

In other words, I will not feel unattractive unless I compare myself to someone whom my community labels "beautiful." Similarly, it will not occur to me to lie unless "honesty" is labelled as a virtue. And society is not divided into "the haves" and "the have nots" unless someone has what are recognized as luxury goods.

The tendency of people to make such distinctions is embodied in (and reinforced by) linguistic distinctions: "As soon as one begins to divide things up, / there are names." (M 32) It is impractical to completely eliminate language and names. However:

> Once there are names,
>> one should also know when to stop;
> Knowing when to stop;
>> one thereby avoids peril. (M 32)

According to the *Laozi*, the corrupt state of society that results from these causes is not natural or inevitable. Unlike the descendants of Adam in the Judeo-Christian tradition, we can return to our antelapsarian state. The key is a ruler who allows the people to act naturally and unselfconsciously:[14]

> I take no action,
>> yet the people transform themselves;
> I am fond of stillness,
>> yet the people correct themselves;
> I do not interfere in affairs,
>> yet the people enrich themselves;
> I desire not to desire,
>> yet the people of themselves become
>>> simple as unhewn logs (*pu*). (M 57)[15]

The ultimate goal is to restore (in Philip J. Ivanhoe's phrase) a "primitive agrarian utopia."[16] Among the characteristics of this utopia are a lack of curiosity, envy, reflection, "higher culture," and self-consciousness. People lead simple but admirably contented lives:

> Let there be a small state with few people,
>> where military devices find no use;
> Let the people look solemnly upon death,
>> and banish the thought of moving elsewhere.
>
> They may have carts and boats,
>> but there is no reason to ride them;
> They may have armor and weapons,
>> but they have no reason to display them.
>
> Let the people go back to tying knots.[17]
> Let their food be savory,

their clothes beautiful,
their customs pleasurable,
their dwellings secure.

Though they may gaze across at a neighboring state,
  and hear the sounds of its dogs and chickens,
The people will never travel back and forth,
  till they die of old age. (M* 80)

The *Laozi*'s primitivism is thus of the "soft" variety. Soft primitivism depicts "a 'golden age,' in comparison with which the subsequent phases [are] nothing but successive stages of one prolonged Fall from Grace." In contrast, "hard primitivism" imagines "the primitive form of existence as a truly bestial state, from which mankind [has] fortunately escaped through technical and intellectual progress."[18] Those who believe in hard primitivism (such as *Mozi* and *Xunzi* in the early Chinese tradition)[19] emphasize the benefits of civilization and the power of the human mind. However, as the reference to abandoning writing in favor of "tying knots" suggests, the soft primitivist utopia of the *Laozi* has no place for intellectuals or higher culture:

Abolish sagehood and abandon cunning,
  the people will benefit a hundredfold;
Abolish humaneness and abandon righteousness,
  the people will once again be filial and kind;
Abolish cleverness and abandon profit,
  bandits and thieves will be no more.[20]
. . . .
Evince the plainness of undyed silk[21]
Embrace the simplicity of the unhewn log;
Lessen selfishness,
Diminish desires;
Abolish learning
  and you will be without worries. (M 19)[22]

Cosmology

Any political vision that, like this one, advocates the abandonment of intelligent, educated social administration owes us an explanation of how the universe is structured such that nonintervention will result in a well-ordered society. For example, social Darwinists think "survival of the fittest" gives an explanation of why society is better in the long run without government intervention. Likewise, advocates of *laissez-faire* put their trust in "the invisible hand" of supply and demand. A similar role is played in the *Laozi* by the *Dao* "Way":

> There is a thing featureless yet complete,
>   born before heaven and earth;
> Silent—amorphous—
>   it stands alone and unchanging.
>
> We may regard it as the mother of heaven and earth.
> Not knowing its name,
>   I style it the "Way." (M* 25)[23]

The *Dao* is that which, in the absence of human interference, guides human society (and the world as a whole) for the best:

> Of old, these came to be in possession of the One:
>   Heaven in virtue of the One is limpid;
>   Earth in virtue of the One is settled;
>   Spirits in virtue of the One have awareness,
>   The valley in virtue of the One is full;
>   The myriad creatures in virtue of the One are alive;
>   Lords and princes in virtue of the One become
>   leaders in the empire. (L* [1963] 39)[24]

The *Dao* may be described as "transcendent" in two ways.[25] It is *causally transcendent* because it creates, gives life to, and preserves Heaven, Earth, and the myriad things:

> The Way gives birth to them,
>   nurtures them,
>   rears them,
>   follows them,
>   shelters them,
>   toughens them,
>   sustains them,
>   protects them. (M 51)[26]

The *Dao* is also *normatively transcendent* because it is a paradigm for the human sage. The human sage is to act as the *Dao* itself acts:

> Humans
>   pattern themselves on earth,
> Earth,
>   patterns itself on heaven,
> Heaven
>   patterns itself on the Way,
> The Way
>   patterns itself on what is natural (*ziran*).
> (M* 25)[27]

Mysticism

In order for human sages to model themselves on the *Dao*, they must have some sort of "knowledge" of it (in some broad sense of that term). But the *Dao* is not an object of ordinary knowledge or ordinary language:

> We look for it but do not see it. . . .
> We listen for it but do not hear it. . . .
> We grope for it but do not grasp it. . . . (M 58/14)

Since the *Dao* is not an object of ordinary knowledge, if it is knowable at all, it must be the object of mystical knowledge.

"Mysticism" is a polysemous and disputed term in philosophy and religious studies. Here, I shall mean by "mysticism" the position that there is a kind of important, action-guiding "knowledge" (in some broad sense of that term) of the nature of the universe that cannot adequately be expressed in words.[28] The *Laozi* clearly is committed to a "wordless teaching" (V 43) of some sort:

> One who knows does not speak;
> One who speaks does not know. (M 56)

> If a *Dao* can be spoken of,
> It will not be a constant *Dao*;
> If a name can be named,
> It will not be a constant name. (V 1)[29]

In the modern West, social and political issues are typically seen as
sharply divorced from mysticism. However, it would be a disabling
presupposition to assume that the same is true of the Chinese
tradition. For the *Laozi* is both political and mystical. Indeed, since
the ideal of the *Laozi* is a society that is nonreflective and nonintel-
lectual, the text *must* hold that the most important kinds of knowledge cannot be put into words. For if the most important kinds
of knowledge *could* be put into words, there would be a role in
society for those who preserve, teach, and interpret these words. But
such intellectuals (primarily the Confucians) are excluded from the
Laozi's utopia.

Furthermore, although the *Laozi*'s utopia has no room for intellectuals, it does have a role for sage-rulers. Consequently, the text
must hold that there are some individuals with some special sort of
(nonverbal) "knowledge" that makes them fit to rule. Thus, we have
the minimal characteristics of mysticism that I identified: there is
an especially important sort of knowledge, but it cannot be put into
words.

Some other commentators on the *Laozi* use "mysticism" in a
more specific sense than I do, associating with it not only the features I specify above, but also the goal of achieving "mystic union
with the ultimate ground of reality."[30] However, "union" and "unity"
play importantly different roles in various sorts of mysticism. For
example, a mystic in Hindu culture may claim to pierce the veil of
illusion to see that "all is one," or "that are thou." In Jewish, Christian, or Islamic culture, a mystic might claim to have achieved (at
least temporarily) "union with God." In another culture, mystics
might claim to recognize that we are all parts of an organic (and
potentially harmonious) whole. These different mystical visions
assign importantly different roles and significances to "unity."[31] The
particular sort of unity advocated by the *Laozi* is suggested by the
following lines:

The Way gives birth to one: one gives birth to two; two gives
birth to three; three gives birth to the myriad creatures.

The myriad creatures carry *yin* on their backs and embrace
yang in their arms, mediating the *qi* so as to create harmony.

There are no words which the world detests more than "orphaned," "widowed" and "hapless," but kings and dukes in this
way describe themselves. (V 42)

The first part of this passage acknowledges that there is a genuine plurality of things that exist; in other words, it is not the case that everything is ultimately identical. However (as the second part of the passage explains), we can *achieve* a certain sort of unity—that of a harmonious whole. The alternative to this harmonious unity (as outlined in the third part of the passage) is to be "orphaned," "widowed," that is, cut off from the great family of which we are all (potentially) a part. Because contemporary rulers (who fail to model themselves on the *Dao*) are cut off in this way, both they and their subjects suffer the painful consequences.[32]

The Ethics of Paradox

The result of this mystic unity is paradoxical, in the classic sense of being contrary to ordinary opinions:

> Great straightness seems crooked,
> Great cleverness seems clumsy,
> Great triumph seems awkward. (M 45)[33]

This emphasis on paradox dovetails with the political vision of the text as described above. According to the *Laozi*, contemporary society is upside down. People misidentify true virtue: "The highest virtue is not 'virtuous'; hence it has virtue. The lowest virtue never loses 'virtue'; hence it is without virtue" (V 38).[34] Consequently, everything people do to dig society out of its current problems merely pushes it farther down. Furthermore, every self-conscious effort (*you wei* 有為) further removes society from the goal of unselfconscious action (*wuwei*). Thus, the truth cannot but sound ridiculous:

> When the inferior man hears the Way,
>   he laughs at it loudly.
> If he did not laugh,
>   it would not be fit to be the Way. (M 41)

In general, the ethics of the *Laozi* may be described as an "ethics of paradox." There are three aspects of the ethics of paradox, the first of which is *wuwei* or "non-action." As is now well known, *wuwei* is not quietism. Rather, *wuwei* is "unpremeditated, nondeliberative, noncalculating, nonpurposive action."[35] Since the ideal society lacks reflection and intellectual sophistication, the highest sort of activity must be *wuwei*.

A contrast with the views of two other influential philosophers (one Chinese and one Western) will be illuminating here. Consider what Immanuel Kant and Mengzi 孟子 might say about what I should do if my neighbor loses his wallet and I discover it. For all their many differences, they would agree that I should return the wallet to its owner. However, the two would disagree sharply over what the appropriate motivation is for returning the wallet. On the one hand, Mengzi would say that I should return the wallet out of my sympathy (*ce yin* 惻隱) with my neighbor's loss, or because I disdain (*xiu wu* 羞惡) to take what does not belong to me. On the other hand, for Kant, my returning the wallet has moral value only if I do it out of respect for the principle of justice. According to Kant, if I return the wallet out of self-interest (perhaps because I expect praise or a financial reward), or out of feelings of sympathy, disdain, or shame, my action lacks moral value.[36] The *Laozi* would be critical of either the Kantian or Mengzian position. The *Laozi* suggests that the best society is one in which there simply are no cash, credit cards, or other valuables to steal in the first place. The next best is the society in which I return the wallet because it simply would not cross my mind to steal it. Finally, for the *Laozi*, a society of Kantians or Mengzians—each of whom would act out of self-conscious (albeit different) moral motivations—is almost as bad as a society of those who act only out of a desire for fame or fortune. This is the significance, I suggest, of passages like the following:

> Therefore,
>> When the great Way was forsaken,
>>> there was humaneness and righteousness;
>> When cunning and wit appeared,
>>> there was great falsity;
>> When the six family relationships lacked harmony,
>>> there was filial piety and parental kindness;
>> When the state and royal houses were in disarray,
>>> there were upright ministers. (M 18)[37]

The second aspect of the ethics of paradox is a preference for *yin* over *yang*:[38]

Nothing under heaven is softer or weaker than water,
   and yet nothing is better
     for attacking what is hard and strong,
      because of its immutability.
The defeat of the hard by the soft,
The defeat of the strong by the weak—
   this is known to all under heaven,
     yet no one is able to practice it. (M 78)[39]

In order to have a handy label, I shall refer to this preference for *yin* over *yang* as the doctrine of "embracing the *yin*." In one couplet, embracing the *yin* is combined with an emphasis upon "reversal":

> Reversal is the movement of the Way;
> Weakness is the usage of the Way. (M 40)

Reversal, recognition of which is the third aspect of the ethics of paradox, is the fact that things tend to change over to their opposites. Thus:

> Things may be diminished by being increased,
> increased by being diminished. (M 42)[40]

D. C. Lau has suggested that there is a tension between reversal and embracing the *yin* (as these are normally interpreted):

[The doctrine of reversal] is usually interpreted as meaning that the *Dao* causes all things to undergo a process of cyclic change. What is weak inevitably develops into something strong, but when this process of development reaches its limit, the opposite process of decline sets in and what is strong once again becomes something weak....

The precept in the *Laozi* is that we should "hold fast to the submissive." But is the precept tenable if the cyclic interpretation is correct? If we are exhorted to hold fast to the submissive because in the conflict between the hard and the submissive it is the latter that emerges triumphant, is not this triumph short-lived if the submissive becomes hard in the hour of its triumph? This, if true, would make it impossible to put the precept into practice.[41]

Lau's insightful suggestion for resolving this problem is that "reversal" is an asymmetric process:

> [D]ecline . . . is inevitable. Nothing is said about development being equally inevitable. . . . In fact, not only is development not inevitable, it is a slow and gradual process, every step of which has to be sustained by deliberate effort.[42]

While Lau feels compelled to abandon the "cyclic" understanding of reversal, Chad Hansen has argued that the *Laozi* actually does not prefer *yin* to *yang*:

> The *Laozi* cannot consistently simply advocate another system of desiring which is the polar opposite of the conventional system. Its critical philosophical theories imply that we must eventually abandon all such systems, including the negative one.[43]

Hansen holds that the text therapeutically, as it were, exposes the reader

> to a *Dao* in which evaluations are reversed. [This] helps us see that the conventional *Dao* is not invariant. Our tendency is to desire or abhor certain things associated with certain conventional descriptions or names. The evaluations that typically go along with our names can be reversed; we could value a lower position, and disvalue wealth or beauty in certain circumstances or in the long run.[44]

The difficulty is that (unless Hansen regards the text as somehow "ironic"), his interpretation cannot do justice to the plethora of passages in which the *Laozi* explicitly endorses "embracing the *yin*."[45] The fact is that the *Laozi* does not merely argue that "we can *conceive* of a system of evaluation that completely reverses the standard, conventional attitudes."[46] Rather, it *advocates* such a system:

> If it is bent,
>   it will be preserved intact;
> is crooked,
>   it will be straightened;

is sunken,
    it will be filled;
is worn-out,
    it will be renewed;
has little,
    it will gain;
has much,
    it will be confused. (M 22)

Yet another way to understand the significance of reversal, embracing the *yin*, and *wuwei* is what I shall describe as the Legalist interpretation, since it seems to have been espoused by some thinkers in that movement:

Wuwei . . . has something in common with the Japanese wrestling technique called *jūdō* 柔道 , which is designed to enable the weak to overpower the strong. In *jūdō* one does not, or should not, take the lead in action, but remains quite relaxed, seeming to follow quite willingly the course taken by his opponent. But this passivity continues only until the opponent has, by taking the active role, placed himself in a disadvantageous position. When that moment arrives one acts, with all of the energy stored from his previous relaxation, and ends the contest (if his maneuver succeeds) at a single stroke.[47]

On this reading, the *Laozi* offers us advice about how to self-consciously navigate our way through a shifting and dangerous world. Situations change rapidly; those who were on top at one time may be on the bottom later. We must be on the lookout for "reversals," and make sure to ally ourselves with those who are on the way up (even if they are in the *yin* position now), rather than those who are on the way down (even if they are currently in the *yang* position). Furthermore, in conflicts, indirect strategies are the best. Rather than directly working for the downfall of our enemies, we should set them up for a fall.

The problem with the "strategic" reading is that it ignores the general aversion of the *Laozi* to self-conscious action. Consider these lines:

It is on disaster that good fortune perches;
It is beneath good fortune that disaster crouches.

> Who knows the limit? There is no straightforwardness. The
> straightforward changes once again into the crafty, and the
> good changes once again into the monstrous. (L* 58)

Crucial to understanding this passage is the rhetorical question,
"Who knows the limit?" The point is that any effort to self-
consciously anticipate the changes in the world is doomed to failure,
because no one knows the "limits" (i.e., the point at which reversal
will occur). Hence, one should eschew self-conscious thought and
rely on one's mystical insight into the *Dao*.[48]
   What is the significance, then, of reversal and embracing the
yin? Lau is correct, I think, in stressing the fact that cyclical change
is not "inevitable" in the *Laozi*: disaster "crouches" beneath good
fortune, but it does not "necessarily follow" it. Thus, after having
defeated what is hard by being soft, and what is strong by being
weak, one thereby will not necessarily become hard and strong
oneself (although this is a danger). Furthermore, it is at least possible that one can overcome the strong by being weak, yet avoid
becoming strong oneself, while maintaining *wuwei*; for "reversal is
the movement of the *Dao*." So if one models oneself on the *Dao*, one
will naturally follow the path of reversal, always staying with the
yin and avoiding the *yang*.[49]

Conclusion

My interpretation of the *Laozi* begins from what I hope is an enabling presupposition: despite the gulf of time and culture that
separates us from it, we can make sense of the *Laozi* as a coherent
text. In particular, I have presented one possible reading of the text,
according to which it has as its core a social vision in which humans
flourish in a primitive, unintellectual, unselfconscious utopia. Although this utopia will be restored and maintained by ideal rulers,
these rulers will not be highly educated philosopher-kings; rather,
they will be empowered by mystical insight into the *Dao*. It is this
Dao that makes everything function harmoniously, provided that
humans model themselves on it. Modelling oneself on the *Dao* involves "embracing the *yin*," and acting in an unselfconscious, or
wuwei, fashion.

So, if my reading is successful, the *Laozi* is a text we can understand. But to understand a text is not necessarily to agree with it. I can sympathetically understand why Achilles is enraged at his treatment by Agamemnon at the beginning of the *Iliad*. But I do not, and do not wish to, share the Mycenean Greek values that would allow me to actually feel his rage in a similar situation. Likewise, I do not, and do not wish to, share the overall vision of the *Laozi*.

The *Laozi* is a beautiful text. Only the heartless will fail to be moved by the depiction of the ideal society in chapter 80,[50] or the promise that, just as "Heaven and earth unite to suffuse sweet dew," so "Without commanding the people, equality will naturally ensue" (M 32). But we must not forget the aspects of primitive society that the *Laozi* does not emphasize. Most of the children in its "utopia" will die from diseases before they reach maturity. The adults will toil in the fields from dawn until dusk, with little time for leisure. In bad years there will be mass starvation. And unless one accepts the details of the *Laozi*'s cosmology, there is no reason to believe there will be no assault, theft, murder, and even the occasional witch hunt in this primitive society.

Angus Graham suggested that the *Laozi* "as philosophical poem has a structure which helps to illuminate patterns running through many branches of life. . . ."[51] There is much truth to this claim, and it helps to account for the enduring value and popularity of this work. The text can also play a valuable role in encouraging us to call into question the still-common assumption that *yang* is always preferable to *yin*. But we should also be aware that the *Laozi* expresses a synoptic vision which we would be ill-advised to adopt.

NOTES

1. I am indebted to Stephen Angle, Mark Csikszentmihalyi, P. J. Ivanhoe, and my colleagues at Vassar for helpful comments on earlier versions of this essay. Citations of the *Laozi* in this paper will be of the form "M 41," where an "M" indicates that the translation is from Victor Mair's translation of the texts discovered at Mawangdui, *Tao Te Ching* (New York: Bantam Books, 1990), but following the convention of this collection the "41" refers to the

chapter number in the Wang Bi text. An "L" refers to D. C. Lau, *Tao Te Ching* (New York: Alfred A. Knopf, Everyman's Library, 1994). I occasionally prefer Lau's earlier translation, *Tao Te Ching* (New York: Penguin Books, 1963), which I shall refer to as "L (1963)." An "*" following the letter indicates that I have revised the translation in some way. A "V" indicates that the translation is my own.

2. On Heidegger's interest in the *Laozi*, see Taylor Carman and Bryan W. Van Norden, "Being-in-the-Way," in *Sino-Platonic Papers* 70 (Feb 1996): 24–34. Reagan once quoted *Laozi* 60 in a speech: "Governing a large state is like boiling a small fish." Peckinpah's title comes from *Laozi* 5. The episode of *The Simpsons* was "Dead Putting Society" (7F08). Richard Wilhelm's Penguin Books translation went on *The New York Times* paperback bestseller list on September 10, 1995.

3. Thus, I agree with Chad Hansen when he claims that "[t]here is a central philosophical core linking these disparate elements" that make up the *Laozi*. *Language and Logic in Ancient China* (Ann Arbor: University of Michigan Press, 1983), 65. I also think Hansen is right in noting the importance for Daoism of the distinction between "knowing how" and "knowing that" (66), and in claiming that the *Laozi* assumes that "language not only makes distinctions and arouses desires, but does so largely through dichotomies" (69). I disagree, however, with several aspects of Hansen's interpretation, including his view that the core of the text "is a theory about names and language, knowledge, learning, desires, distinctions, and practical action" (65). My own view is that the central political vision is the core, which motivates the rest of the text. (I discuss other aspects of Hansen's interpretation below in section 5, "The Ethics of Paradox." For an overall review of Hansen's earlier work, see Philip J. Ivanhoe, "One View of the Language-Thought Debate," *Chinese Literature: Essays, Articles, Reviews* 9 (1987): 115–123.

4. See, e.g., Lau, *Tao Te Ching*, 1963 or 1994, Appendix 1, and A. C. Graham, "The Origins of the Legend of Lao Tan 老聃," in *Studies in Chinese Philosophy and Philosophical Literature* (Albany: State University of New York Press, 1990), 111–124.

5. See, e.g., Alasdair MacIntyre, *Whose Justice? Which Rationality?* (Notre Dame: University of Notre Dame Press, 1988), idem, *Three Rival Versions of Moral Enquiry* (Notre Dame: University of Notre Dame Press, 1990), and Jaroslav Pelikan, *The Vindication of Tradition* (New Haven: Yale University Press, 1984.)

6. Compare the distinction between "true prejudices" and "false prejudices" in Hans-Georg Gadamer, *Truth and Method*, 2nd rev. ed. (New York: Continuum Publishing, 1994), 298–299.

7. Deborah Tannen, *You Just Don't Understand: Women and Men in Conversation* (New York: William Morrow and Co., 1990), 49 ff.

8. I discuss some of the distinctions among kinds of mysticism below in section 4, "Mysticism."

9. Such "sympathetic understanding" is, of course, a matter of degree. We contemporary Western intellectuals cannot *fully* share the perspective of bronze age Chinese literati (nor, I would suggest, can men *fully* share the perspective of women on many topics). However, in each case, our assumption should be that we can achieve a *significant* sharing of perspectives. This assumption is part of what distinguishes our attitude toward fellow human beings from our attitude toward inanimate objects or many non-human animals. David S. Nivison makes a similar point in his "Golden Rule Arguments in Chinese Moral Philosophy," in *The Ways of Confucianism: Investigations in Chinese Philosophy* (LaSalle: Open Court Press, 1996), 76.

10. For a good discussion of hermeneutic issues, see Hansen, *Language and Logic*, chapter 1. The enabling assumption that a text "makes sense" is one formulation of what is commonly referred to as the "principle of charity."

11. Alexander Nehamas makes an argument for a related point: "The argument is sometimes made that a reading is 'only' or 'merely' an interpretation because an alternative could, in principle, always be devised. But this challenge is serious only if a better alternative is in fact devised, and in most cases this is not at all a simple task. The new alternative must be, according to some set of criteria, at least as satisfactory as the view it challenges" (*Nietzsche: Life as Literature* [Cambridge: Harvard University Press, 1985], 63). For further discussion of the limits of adequate interpretation, see Umberto Eco's contributions to *Interpretation and Overinterpretation* (New York: Cambridge University Press, 1992).

12. See also *Laozi* chapter 12.

13. I have changed Mair's "being and nonbeing" to "having and not-having." I worry that "being and nonbeing" (like Lau's capitalized "Something and Nothing") have inappropriate Hegelian or Heideggerian connotations. I take it that *you* 有 and *wu* 無 refer simply to "having [qualities, possessions, etc.]" and "not having [qualities, possessions, etc.]."

14. Such a ruler is the opposite of the Mohist technocrat who tries to self-consciously manage society in the light of "profit" and "harm." Benjamin I. Schwartz has some very insightful comments on the relationships among Mohists, Confucians, and Daoists on this issue in his *The World of Thought in Ancient China* (Cambridge: Harvard University Press, 1985), 189–191.

15. See also chapters 3, 17, 58 and 65. The "unhewn log" symbolizes the state before distinctions are made (i.e., before things are "chopped up" by human distinctions).

16. See P. J. Ivanhoe, "The Concept of *De* in the *Laozi*," in this volume.

17. That is, let them tie knots to keep records, instead of writing.

18. Erwin Panofsky, *Studies in Iconology: Humanistic Themes in the Art of the Renaissance* (New York: Harper & Row, 1972), 40.

19. See, e.g., Burton Watson, trans., *Mo Tzu: Basic Writings* (New York: Columbia University Press, 1963) 34 ff., and idem, trans., *Hsün Tzu: Basic Writings* (New York: Columbia University Press, 1963), 88 ff.

20. Although neither school is mentioned by name, there may be an attack on Mencian Confucians and Mohists in these lines. "Humaneness" (*ren* 仁) and "righteousness" (*yi* 義) are the two most important of Mencius's four "cardinal virtues." Likewise, "cleverness" (*qiao* 巧) and "profit" (*li* 利) are two terms with positive connotations for Mohists. (On the Mohist use of *qiao*, see Lisa Raphals, *Knowing Words* [Ithaca: Cornell University Press, 1992], 61–62 and 67–68.)

21. It is possible that this is a reference to *Analects* 3:8 (Harvard-Yenching text), in which, on one interpretation, "plain silk" (su 素) is the basic good character prior to refinement by the rites. The interpretation of *Analects* 3:8 is disputed within the Confucian school, though. See, for example, Dai Zhen 戴震, *Mengzi ziyi shuzheng* 孟子字義疏證, section 37. For a translation with helpful notes, see John Ewell, "Re-Inventing the Way: Dai Zhen's 'Evidential Commentary on the Meaning of Terms in Mencius' (1777)." Doctoral Thesis, History, UC Berkeley, 1990 (UMI Order No. 9126550). For a discussion of a more problematic translation of Dai's magnum opus, see Bryan W. Van Norden, "Review of Tai Chen on Mencius," *Journal of Chinese Religions* (1993): 148–150.

22. See also *Laozi* chapter 3.

23. Notice that chapter 25 specifically refers to the *Dao* as an entity or "thing" (*wu*), and says that this thing was "born before heaven and earth." Consequently, this passage seems to falsify Hansen's hypothesis that "*Dao*" never refers to a metaphysical entity in early Chinese texts. See his "A Tao of Tao in Chuang-tzu," in *Experimental Essays on Chuang-tzu*, ed. Victor Mair (Honolulu: University of Hawaii Press, 1983), 24–55. There are similar problems for Hansen's understanding of *Dao* in the *Zhuangzi*. See Philip J. Ivanhoe, "Was Zhuangzi a Relativist?" in *Essays on Skepticism, Relativism, and Ethics in the Zhuangzi*, ed. Paul Kjellberg and Ivanhoe, (La Salle: Open Court, 1996), 201.

24. Lau here takes *yi* to refer to a cosmogonic principle, possibly the *Dao* itself. (Lau, in turn, is following the Wang Bi commentary. See Ariane Rump and Wing-tsit Chan, trans., *Commentary on the Lao Tzu by Wang Pi* (Hawaii: University of Hawaii Press, Society for Asian and Comparative Philosophy Monograph No. 6, 1979), 119: "All things are produced by the One and this is why it is the master of all.") However, Mair's reading ("In olden times, these attained unity: / Heaven attained unity," etc.) is quite defensible. Lau's use of the phrase "in virtue of" for *de* 得 "to get" suggests the etymological and philosophical relationship between that term and the homophonous *de* "virtue." (For more on this relationship, see David S. Nivison. "The Paradox of 'Virtue'," in *The Ways of Confucianism*, 33.) Incidentally, the Mawangdui texts lack the line referring to the "myriad creatures."

25. David Hall and Roger Ames, in their much-discussed *Thinking Through Confucius* (Albany: State University of New York Press, 1987), argue that there is no notion of "transcendence" in early Chinese thought. Perhaps there is no transcendence in the sense in which they define that term; however, it seems that, at least in the *Laozi*, the passages cited here demonstrate that the *Dao* is "causally transcendent" in the sense that it creates, but is not created by, the other entities in the universe. (Note that the text never says that Heaven, Earth, the myriad creatures, or human beings "beget" the *Dao*.) Likewise, the *Dao* is "normatively transcendent" because it provides a paradigm for the sage (and not vice versa). Hall and Ames make much of *Analects* 15:29 (Harvard-Yenching text), which says "It is the human being who is able to extend the *Dao* (*ren neng hong dao* 人能弘道), not the *Dao* that is able to extend the human being," which they take to show that the "human being has an active, creative role in continuing, broadening, and extending the *Dao*, such that the *Dao* is historically composite and cumulative..." (Hall and Ames, *Thinking Through Confucius*, 229). However, the numerous uses of *hong* 弘 in the *Shangshu* 尚書 show that it means "to extend," not in the sense of "to modify and innovate," but rather in the sense of "to extend the prestige and influence of" something. Typical is the *Zhoushu* 周書, "Kanggao 康誥," in which a noble is instructed to *hongwang* 弘王, which James Legge correctly renders, "enlarge the royal *influence*" (*The Chinese Classics*, vol. 3, *The Shoo King*. [Rpt., Taipei: SMC Publishing, 1991], 387). For an excellent general discussion of Hall and Ames's book, see Stephen Wilson, "Conformity, Individuality, and the Nature of Virtue," *Journal of Religious Ethics* 23, no. 2 (Fall 1995): 263–289.

26. See also: "Everything under heaven has a beginning / which may be thought of as the mother / of all under heaven. / Having realized the mother, / you thereby know her children. / Knowing her children, / go back to abide

with the mother" (M 52). "In metaphorical terms, / The relationship of all under heaven to the Way / is like that of valley streams / to the river and sea" (M 32).

27. *Ziran* is literally "self-so," and describes what occurs without self-consciousness or external compulsion. It is thus closely related to the notion of "non-action" (*wuwei*), discussed in section 5 of this paper, "The Ethics of Paradox." For a discussion of the notion of *ziran* in the *Laozi*, see Liu Xiaogan's "An Inquiry into the Core Value in Laozi's Philosophy" in this volume.

28. Thus characterized, mystical states are related to both cosmology (which I discussed in the previous section of this paper) and ethics (which I discuss in the next section). There are, of course, other definitions of mysticism that one could offer, which draw attention to other important areas of religious experience in various cultures. I am only focusing on one limited aspect of what might be thought of as "mysticism." My characterization does stress what William James says are the two most important criteria of mystical states, and I think that mystical states are "action-guiding" is implied by what he says. (See James, *The Varieties of Religious Experience*, lectures 16–17 in his *Writings 1902–1910* [New York: Library of America, 1987], 343–344.) For a critical review of some recent work on mysticism, see Harold D. Roth, "Some Issues in the Study of Chinese Mysticism: A Review Essay," *China Review International* 2, no. 1 (Spring 1995), 154–173. See also Roth, "The *Laozi* in the Context of Early Daoist Mystical Practice" and Mark Csikszentmihalyi, "Mysticism and Apophatic Discourse in the *Laozi*" both in this volume. Mysticism in the way I define it is also committed to irrationalism or at least "anti-rationalism"; for characteristic of rationalism is a belief that linguistic accounts can provide knowledge. On the distinction between "irrationalism" and "anti-rationalism," see A. C. Graham, *Reason and Spontaneity* (London: Curzon Press, 1985).

29. Compare the Mawangdui version of the beginning of chapter 1 (*dao ke dao ye fei heng dao ye* 道可道也非恆道也) with the end of *Analects* 3:1 (*shi ke ren ye shu bu ke ren ye* 是可忍也孰不可忍也). I think the grammars of the two passages have suggestive similarities. *Analects* 3:1 is usually translated, "If this can be tolerated, what cannot be tolerated?" Cf. D. C. Lau, *Confucius: The Analects* (New York: Penguin Books, 1979). This suggests the corresponding translation of chapter 1 that I give above.

30. Schwartz, *The World of Thought*, 193. Compare Herrlee G. Creel, *What Is Taoism?* (Chicago: University of Chicago Press, 1970), 40: ". . . the early Taoists were mystics, intent like all mystics upon union with the Absolute, which in their case was called the Tao."

31. If the differences among these sorts of mysticism seem obscure, consider the following examples of unity and union: (i) Clark Kent is identical with Superman, (ii) East Germany united with West Germany to form one country, (iii) the notes in a Mozart concerto form a harmonious whole. (I draw here on Lee H. Yearley, "Three Ways of Being Religious," *Philosophy East and West* 32, no. 4 [1982]: 439–451.)

32. Ivanhoe (in correspondence) notes an alternative interpretation of the third part of the passage: taking on what "the world" despises is the mark of the sage and the *Dao*; even contemporary rulers recognize this on some level, so they try to tap into the power of the *Dao* by calling themselves these names. This is a very plausible reading, and one that fits in with some of what I myself say later about the "ethics of paradox" (see section 5, "The Ethics of Paradox"). However, I prefer the reading I give because, given the importance of the family in Chinese culture, I cannot believe even Daoists would use terms like "orphaned" and "widowed" to refer to good qualities (even metaphorically). Whatever reading of the lines in question is correct, I submit that my general interpretation of the *Laozi*'s "monism" is well supported by the other parts of chapter 42 that I quote.

33. See also *Laozi* chapters 41 and 78.

34. I am reading chapter 38 as making a distinction between true virtue and "virtue" (i.e., virtue as it is commonly understood). A more common interpretation of these lines (following the Wang Bi commentary) links them to the doctrine of *wuwei*: "The person of superior integrity / does not insist upon his integrity; / For this reason, he has integrity. / The person of inferior integrity / never loses sight of his integrity; / For this reason, he lacks integrity" (M). This reading is also quite plausible. (This passage is also discussed in Nivison, "The Paradox of 'Virtue'", 31ff.)

35. Schwartz, *The World of Thought*, 188. Robert G. Henricks also has a good discussion of this point. See his *Lao-tzu: Te-Tao Ching* (New York: Ballantine Books, 1989), xxvi, 260, and 265–266, n. 27.

36. For a valuable critique of Kant's views on the moral significance of the emotions, see Lawrence Blum, *Friendship, Altruism, and Morality* (London: Routledge & Kegan Paul, 1980).

37. See also *Laozi* chapter 38.

38. Lau comments, "*yin* and *yang* appear once and once only in the whole of the *Laozi* and there is no reason to suppose that they occupy an important place in the thought of the whole work" (Lau, *Tao Te Ching* [1963], 47). Although Lau is correct that these technical terms appear only once in the text, the *Laozi* does seem to show a preference for what those familiar with

the distinction recognize as *yin*. Hence, I do not think that it is out of place to use these technical terms in my exegesis. For more on *yin* and *yang*, see A. C. Graham, *Yin-Yang and the Nature of Correlative Thinking* (Singapore: Institute of East Asian Philosophies, 1986).

39. See also *Laozi* chapters 39, 43, 61, and 8.

40. See also *Laozi* chapters 63, 77, 78, and 22.

41. Lau, *Tao Te Ching*, 1963, 25–26.

42. Lau, *Tao Te Ching*, 1963, 27.

43. Hansen, *Language and Logic*, 68.

44. Hansen, loc. cit.

45. In addition to *Laozi* chapters 78 (quoted earlier in this essay) and 22 (quoted later in this essay), see also 39, 43, 61, and 8.

46. Hansen, *Language and Logic*, 70. Emphasis mine.

47. Creel, *What is Taoism?*, 67. Schwartz criticizes such an interpretation in *World of Thought*, 213–215.

48. This is not to deny that other early Chinese texts or philosophers may have assigned a different meaning to *wuwei*.

49. While acting in a *wuwei* fashion, one's preference for the *yin* would be natural and unselfconscious. Hence, it would be different from the artificial and self-conscious preferences the *Laozi* denigrates (see above, section 2, "The Core Social Vision").

50. Translated above, section 2, "The Core Social Vision."

51. A. C. Graham, *Disputers of the Tao* (La Salle: Open Court, 1989), 234.

An Inquiry into the Core Value of
Laozi's Philosophy

Liu Xiaogan

This article offers a view concerning the core value of Laozi's philosophy: that the most basic message and purpose of Laozi's five-thousand-word book, the *Daodejing*, is to point out the existence and advocate the further development of the ideal of *ziran er ran* 自然而然 ("acting naturally" or "letting things develop by themselves") in all human affairs. "Naturalness" is the core value of the thought of Laozi, while *wuwei* is the principle or method for realizing this value in action.[1]

Looking at the frequency with which various concepts are used, we see that the *Laozi* often discusses *wuwei* and *Dao* ("the Way"); from that we can conclude that these concepts are central to the book's argument. Nonetheless, the core value that actually informs this argument is "naturalness." The central question of Laozi's philosophy is the question of value: the issue of value permeates Laozi's views on nature, epistemology, methodology, and historiography, and finds application as well in the more practical realms of politics, military arts, social relations, personal conduct, and self-cultivation. Thus, while it is certainly not a gross distortion to view the *Laozi* as a manual for politics, military strategy or *qigong*,[2] such explanations of the text fail to penetrate the surface and get to the deeper, more substantial and unified principle that informs the philosophy of Laozi. A reverence for "naturalness" is the most distinguishing characteristic of the Daoist scheme of values and what most clearly separates it from Confucian theory, which extols hard work and striving.

It is necessary to make clear that the "naturalness" mentioned by Laozi and discussed in this article refers to the state of "acting naturally" or "letting things develop by themselves" and not "nature" in the sense of the natural world or the environment. From Laozi's reverence for the value of "naturalness" one could of course infer that he would be in favor of environmental protection and the preservation of ecological balance; however, Laozi himself never directly advocates an environmentalist position.

The recognition of naturalness as the core value of Laozi's philosophy is of more than purely academic interest; it also helps us to grasp the spiritual essence of Daoist philosophy. This in turn encourages us not only to apply Daoist thought to contemporary society, but also to adapt this ancient philosophy to the modern world.

Naturalness and Wuwei

As is generally known, "naturalness" and *wuwei* are two concepts that feature quite prominently in and are quite distinctive of Laozi's philosophy. One might even say that the question of whether or not a thinker employs and advocates the ideals of naturalness and *wuwei* could serve as a standard for determining whether or not the thinker is a Daoist or has been influenced by Daoist ideas. However, these two concepts are very difficult to place with any precision within the traditional philosophical framework—we have no way of finding an appropriate place for them in such realms as ontology, epistemology, methodology, or historiography. In passages such as, "The way models itself on naturalness" (chapter 25*),[3] or "The way never acts (*wuwei*) yet nothing is left undone" (chapter 37), naturalness and *wuwei* are apparently being used as attributes of the metaphysical "way," and would therefore seem to be cosmological and ontological concepts. Passages such as, "In pursuing knowledge, one does more and more each day; in pursuing the way, one does less and less each day" (chapter 48*), "Without looking out of the window, one can see the way of heaven" (chapter 47), and "One who knows does not speak, one who speaks does not know" (chapter 56) indicate that the principles of naturalness and *wuwei* have some relationship to epistemology. In lines such as, "Do that which consists in taking no action; pursue that which is not meddlesome. . . . It is because the sage never attempts to be great that he succeeds in being great" (chapter 63), they would seem to have some connection to the dialectic philosophy of mutual opposition which results in mutual completion. Passages such as, "I take no action and the people are transformed of themselves; I prefer stillness and the people are rectified of themselves" (chapter 57), or "help the myriad creatures to be natural and to refrain from daring to act" (chapter 64) indicate their possible application in the realms of political theory or the art of rulership, while the passage, "The strategists have a saying: I dare not play the host but play the guest; I dare not advance an inch but retreat a foot instead" (chapter 69), would seem to belong to the field of military strategy. The observation, "It is just because one has no use for life that one is wiser than the man who values life" (chapter 75), is a principle for self-cultivation. Naturalness and *wuwei* thus seem to cross over into all of the various divisions of philosophy, and find application in such realms as politics, military science, and personal self-cultivation. It is therefore quite difficult to find a place for them within the modern classification system of traditional philosophy, and consequently rather difficult to describe or analyze them with any sort of precision. Since there are no concepts or even areas of thought in traditional Western philosophy that correspond to the ideals of naturalness and *wuwei*, research on this subject within the discipline of the history of Chinese philosophy has been rather naive and superficial. This state of affairs is not at all appropriate when one considers the central importance these concepts have in Daoist thought, but it is a basic difficulty encountered when the framework of modern philosophical theory is used as a tool to analyze traditional Chinese philosophy. This fundamental problem is encountered particularly often in the study of Daoism.

One of the results of the superficial work that has been done on naturalness and *wuwei* is that the two concepts are very rarely distinguished from one another or examined in any depth. Generally the two concepts are conflated and used interchangeably. For instance, one scholar states, "The *Laozi* proffers one word—naturalness—to explain a state free of human effort, where things develop by themselves (naturally) and no one knows how this happens; this is simply a portrayal of *wuwei*, the central concept of the entire text of the *Laozi*."[4] *Wuwei* is here taken as the central concept in the

Laozi, with naturalness seen as merely a description of this state. Chen Guying 陳鼓應 also says that; "Naturalness/*wuwei* is the single most important concept in the philosophy of Laozi. . . . When Laozi mentions the idea of 'naturalness,' he is referring to a state in which not a bit of effort is applied and yet things unfold and develop of their own accord, whereas *wuwei* refers to the idea of following along with the way things naturally are and not adding any human effort."[5] This manner of speaking emphasizes the similarity between naturalness and *wuwei*, and seems to be suggesting that they can be considered as a "single concept." However, the author nonetheless goes on to note a distinction between the two concepts: naturalness refers to the state in which things unfold and develop of their own accord, while *wuwei* is the method for according with this sort of state. Lao Siguang 勞思光 also takes *wuwei* to be the central concept in the *Laozi*; he says, "The single idea *wuwei* is the central concept of the *Daodejing*."[6]

Why, though, would one say that *wuwei* rather than "naturalness" is the central concept in the *Laozi*? What after all is the primary message that the five thousand words of the *Laozi* are trying to convey? Before answering this question, we must first consider more carefully how the two concepts are related. Most scholars have treated naturalness and *wuwei* as if they were a single idea. However, in the final analysis, the two concepts are *not* entirely the same; they are consistent but not identical. "Naturalness" is a positive term used to describe the progression of a certain state of affairs or things, whereas "*wuwei*" is a negative term aimed at placing restrictions upon human activity. Naturalness is the most common way to describe the living presence and development of a particular state of affairs or things. While it can certainly be used in reference to human society, its use is not limited to this realm. *Wuwei*, on the other hand, is a type of description or prescription aimed at human activity; while it can also be used in reference to the inanimate world (for instance, to the way), such references inevitably convey a certain anthropomorphic flavor. When naturalness is used in reference to human social life, it is a description and approval of all spontaneous actions. *Wuwei*, on the other hand, while still preserving the emphasis on naturalness nonetheless imposes restrictions upon certain types of spontaneous actions—for instance, those motivated by desire for and pursuit of fame or profit. To sum up, naturalness and *wuwei* belong to the same overall system or direction of thought, but they are nevertheless not identical and cannot be used interchangeably in all situations.

The concepts of naturalness and *wuwei* can thus be used in reference to ontology, epistemology, anthropology, and even such disciplines as politics or military strategy, but nonetheless do not belong exclusively to any single domain. This being the case, what kind of concepts *are* they? To what range of questions do they apply? In the opinion of this author, the concepts of naturalness and *wuwei* apply to the question of value—the question of what we are to take as our highest value. The highest value—that Laozi both seeks and venerates—is naturalness. Naturalness thus serves as the core value of Laozi's philosophical system, while *wuwei* is the basic method or principle for action he recommends to realize or pursue this value. These two concepts are the focus of Laozi's emphasis and the most important component of the message his philosophy conveys. The concept of "value" most adequately and completely reflects the content and unique characteristics of the idea of naturalness, and as values are perhaps the most important and interesting elements of the various fields of thought mentioned above, it would not be at all inappropriate to utilize the concept of naturalness in such diverse fields as philosophy, political science, sociology, anthropology, and even military science. Similarly, the concept of *wuwei*—the method of realizing or actualizing this ideal of naturalness—encompasses an equally broad range of meanings, and can also be applied in many different areas of endeavor. In this way—looking at naturalness from the standpoint of value theory and at *wuwei* from the standpoint of methodology—we can avoid the difficulties encountered by approaches that traditionally have taken modern philosophy as their tool and analysis as their primary goal. Although value theory and methodology are also modern philosophical concepts of Western origin, they are nonetheless more appropriate methods for approaching the subject of naturalness and *wuwei*.

"Naturalness" in the Laozi

In classical literature, the concept of "naturalness" clearly originates in the *Laozi*. One finds no mention of naturalness in any of the earlier texts such as the *Shijing*, the *Zuozhuan* ("Zuo's Commentary"), or the *Lunyu*. In the text of the five-thousand-word *Laozi* itself, the word "naturalness" is mentioned directly in five passages, all of which clearly reflect the veneration and appreciation with which this concept is viewed by the author. Passages in which the idea of naturalness is described indirectly (without explicit mention of the term) can be found throughout the text. Naturalness serves as the central concept of Laozi's philosophy and penetrates all aspects of human life. For instance, chapter 17* of the *Laozi* advocates naturalness from the standpoint of the relationship between the ruler and the people:

> The best of all rulers is but a shadowy presence to his
>   subjects.
> Next comes the ruler they love and praise;
> Next comes one they fear;
> Next comes one whom they insult . . .
> Hesitant, he does not utter words lightly.
> When his task is accomplished and his work done
> The common people all regard my rule as natural.[7]

In Laozi's opinion, the best ruler does not force the people to do anything and makes no display of his own kindness or virtue—the people only know of his existence, and have no need to understand him. This is the "empty throne" ruler of the Daoist ideal. The next best ruler acts in ways that excite the admiration and affection of the people; this is the sagely ruler of the Confucian ideal. The next best ruler instills fear in his subjects; this is what is commonly referred to as a benighted ruler. Even worse is the ruler who inflicts hardships upon his subjects and earns himself nothing but insults and abuse. This is what is referred to as a violent ruler. An intelligent ruler is unhurried and at ease, and is a person of few words. All tasks are accomplished to his satisfaction and yet the people do not realize that he has done a thing, thinking rather that it all came about naturally. "Naturalness" here is a type of ideal state.

There is a significant problem of interpretation with regard to this chapter. Historically, most interpreters have been of the opinion that "naturally" here does not indicate that the ruler did nothing, but rather that the ruler's actions were accomplished imperceptibly, without the people being aware of them, or that they were accepted as if they had developed on their own. This type of interpretation raises an important issue: whether or not the value of "naturalness" can allow for the effect of external force. According to traditional commentaries, it would seem that the application of external force could count as "natural" as long as the people are not directly aware of it. If one accepts this interpretation, then the ideal of naturalness would not preclude the exertion of external force or acquiescence to the influence of such force, it would just preclude the use of external force in a *coercive* manner.

With regard to the last line of the chapter, traditional commentaries all render it: "The people all say, 'It happened to us naturally.'" This involves reading the word *wei* 謂 as an alternative for *yue* 曰 ("to say"); the phrase, *wo ziran* 我自然 ("It happened to us naturally") is thus read as a direct quotation introduced by *yue*.[8] The original meaning of *wei* is *lun* 論 ("to discuss, debate"). The *Shuowen* 説文 says, "*Wei* means *bao* 報 ("report, announce")," with Duan's 段 commentary reading, "*Wei* means to discuss people and events in order to determine the true state of affairs." The original meaning of *wei* is thus to "critically discuss"; according to this usage, the last line of chapter 17 should be read something like, "The people all regard my rule as natural." This means that the author in this case is speaking in the first person from the perspective of the ruler, the *wo* 我 (first person pronoun) here functioning the same way it does in chapter 20, where the text reads, "The multitude all have more than enough; *wo* ("I") alone seem to be in want." This manner of speaking clearly expresses the reverence the author has for naturalness, and this usage of the first person pronoun fully accords with a similar usage in chapter 67: *Tianxia jie wei wo da* 天下皆謂我大 ("The whole world says that I am vast").[9] This is how the line should be rendered; it would be inappropriate to render it: "Everyone in the world says *of themselves*: 'I am vast.'" The word *wei* appears thirty to forty times in the *Laozi*, and it would seem that it never serves to introduce a direct quotation. Whenever a direct quotation is introduced, it is indicated by means of *yue, yun* 云 or *you zhi* 有之, *you yan* 有言 ("it has been said").[10] In summary, then, if we take *wei* to mean "critically discuss" or "to judge," the line "The common people all regard my rule as natural" clearly reveals the author's reverence for the ideal of naturalness.

Chapter 17 emphasizes that the ruler should govern by means of naturalness, and allow the common people to fully enjoy a life without outside interference. This is applying the principle of naturalness to social relations, particularly the relationship between the ruler and the people. Chapter 51 goes on to give the principle of naturalness a metaphysical grounding:

> The Way gives them life;
> Virtue rears them;
> Things give them shape;
> Circumstances bring them to maturity.[11]
> Therefore the myriad creatures all revere the Way and
>   honor virtue. Yet the Way is revered and virtue
>   honored not because this is decreed by any
>   authority but because it is natural for them to be
>   treated so.
> Thus the Way gives them life and [virtue] rears them;[12]
> It brings them to fruition and maturity;
> Feeds them and shelters them.
> It gives them life yet claims no possession;
> It benefits them yet exacts no gratitude;
> It is the steward yet exercises no authority.
> Such is called the mysterious virtue.

The line, "Yet the Way is revered and virtue honored not because this is decreed by any authority but because it is natural for them to be treated so" is not commented upon by Wang Bi. In the silk manuscripts from Dunhuang, the word *ming* 命 ("decreed") is replaced by the word *jue* 爵 ("title of nobility"). This accords perfectly with Cheng Xuanying's commentary on the passage, which reads, "To be honored in the world one must have official rank and privileges, which do not endure long; the honor accorded to the Way and to virtue, however, has nothing to do with titles of nobility, and therefore always follows naturally." The position occupied by the Way and virtue comes to them naturally, and is not something endowed by other people. Heshanggong's commentary reads, "The Way never summons things; it constantly maintains naturalness, responding like a shadow or an echo." That is to say, the Way and virtue accord with naturalness and are *wuwei*; they do not issue orders to the myriad things, but rather passively shadow or echo them. These two commentaries, then, are in accord in this respect; where they diverge is in their interpretation of the three words *mo zhi ming* 莫之命[13] and not on the word *ziran* ("naturalness"). Whether we take *mo zhi ming* to mean, "The Way does not summon the myriad things," or, "No separate thing bestows the Way with an official position," "naturalness" is still the value being emphasized by the author. Laozi here is trying to emphasize that the lofty position of honor occupied by the Way comes to it naturally, and is not given to the Way by something or someone else. This natural respect for the Way is a model for the myriad things, the point being that a position of honor is not something that should be intentionally sought after. The Way's nourishing of the myriad things comes about naturally: having nourished the myriad things, it should not consider itself a nourisher, nor should it arrogantly dwell upon its achievements, nor—above all—should it seek to actively control or monopolize things: "It gives them life yet claims no possession; it benefits them yet exacts no gratitude; it is the steward yet exercises no authority." In this manner one can receive respect and remain graceful and composed, without being smug or self-satisfied, and will also refrain from complaining against Heaven or cursing others in the event that the public respect due one is not received. What Laozi is advocating is precisely this sort of attitude, where one simply accords with what is natural.

Chapter 64* further discusses naturalness from the standpoint of the relationship between the sage and the myriad things:

> Therefore the sage desires not to desire
> And does not value goods which are hard to come by;
> Learns not to learn,
> And makes good the mistakes of the populace
> In order to help the myriad creatures to be natural and to
>   refrain from daring to act.

The values of the Daoist sage are quite different from those of the Confucian sage or the common people. What the Daoist sage seeks is that which most people do not seek, and the Daoist sage looks upon those things treasured by the common people as mere floating clouds. When this conception of value is actualized in practice it manifests itself as "helping the myriad creatures to be natural," which means simply according with their naturalness. The "naturalness of the myriad creatures" is the ultimate state; the sage only fosters and preserves this type of "natural" state, and should not actively scheme to improve or ruin it. This passage is emphasizing the importance of naturalness from the standpoint of human beings' relationship to the myriad things. With regard to the line, "Learns not to learn, and makes good the mistakes of the populace," Heshanggong comments, "The sage learns what other people are unable to learn. Other people learn wisdom and cleverness, whereas the sage learns naturalness. Other people learn how to govern the world, whereas the sage learns how to govern himself, and holds firm to the true Way." Making naturalness the object and the content of learning is what distinguishes the sage from others, who do not learn to simply assist and preserve this state of naturalness and thus end up using their own privileged position or power to ruin it. This attitude of the sage toward naturalness embodies Laozi's theory of values.

The concept of naturalness is the core value of Laozi's system of thought; this is clearly illustrated in the relationship between people, heaven and earth, and the Way and naturalness. We read in chapter 25* of the *Laozi*:

> The Way is great; heaven is great; earth is great; and the
>   king is also great.
> Within this realm there are four things that are great, and
>   the king counts as one.
> People model themselves on earth,
> Earth on heaven,
> Heaven on the Way,
> And the Way on naturalness.[14]

People live between heaven and earth, and heaven and earth have their origin in the Way. The Way is both the highest and most basic thing in the universe and among the myriad things. What distinguishes the Way, though, is none other than the single word "naturalness." People take their model from the earth, earth takes its model from heaven, heaven takes its model from the Way, and the Way takes its model from naturalness. Therefore, while the Way is the ultimate reality, naturalness is the highest value or principle this ultimate reality embodies. If we arrange these five items along a spectrum we have the series: people → earth → heaven → the Way → naturalness. So although earth, heaven, and the Way are very important concepts in Laozi's philosophy, according to this presentation they are only transitional or intermediate concepts: they are necessary for expository and rhetorical purposes, but the emphasis really lies on the two ends of the spectrum—people and naturalness—and the relationship between these two. What this reveals is that people—and particularly the ruler—should emulate naturalness. The links of "taking the earth as a model," "taking heaven as a model," and "taking the Way as a model" are simply needed in order to strengthen the demonstration. The key to the message Laozi wishes to convey is that human society should develop naturally. In other words, naturalness permeates people, earth, heaven, and the Way, and is therefore both the most basic and the most ubiquitous principle. What is it to model oneself on naturalness? Wang Bi explains: "What is modeling oneself on nature? When placed in a square, be square-like; when placed in a circle, be circular. In this way the principle of naturalness will not be violated. When one says, 'naturalness,' one is naming nothing in particular and yet saying everything." Modelling oneself on naturalness is thus following along with the development and transformation of external things without interfering. Naturalness "names nothing in particular and yet says everything"; that is, when one refers to "naturalness" one is both referring to the beginning and pointing to the end—there is nothing more basic or more important. The Way, which is the source of the universe, is of course the most lofty of things, but the principle or the root of the Way is naturalness. To venerate the Way is thus really to bring attention to the principle or value of naturalness. This is why it is correct to say that naturalness is the core value of Laozi's philosophical system. With regard to this passage, some have read it:

People model themselves on what makes the earth the earth
On what makes the heavens the heavens,
On what makes the *Dao* the *Dao*,
On what is so of itself.[15]

According to this reading (which, of course, we do not necessarily have to adopt), the idea that people should model themselves on naturalness is even more clearly expressed.

With regard to naturalness, we also have the phrase in chapter 23: "To use words rarely is to be natural." Whether we put this sentence at the end of the preceding chapter or leave it at the beginning of this one, its relationship to the surrounding text remains quite unclear. Heshanggong's commentary reads, "Using words rarely is being sparing of speech, and being sparing of speech is the way of naturalness." Wang Bi's commentary reads, "Thus insipid words which are easily overlooked are actually the highest expression of naturalness." Neither of these explanations is entirely satisfying. Chen Guying et al., have suggested that "using words rarely" has the same meaning as "not uttering words lightly" (from the sentence "Hesitant, he does not utter words lightly") in chapter 17 and "wordless" (as in "the teaching which uses no words") from chapter 2, and is to be contrasted with "much speech" (from the sentence, "much speech leads inevitably to silence") in chapter 5. The surface meaning of "using words rarely" is to speak seldom or not at all; on a deeper level it means to not issue orders or directives.[16] Brief and to the point, eschewing governmental orders—this is according with naturalness. Looked at in this way, naturalness is here being advocated to the ruler or administrator.

Summarizing the import of the five passages in the *Laozi* where naturalness is mentioned, naturalness can be seen as the most important value when it comes to such things as the relationships between the ruler and the common people; the relationship between the sage and the myriad things; the interrelation of people, heaven and earth, and the Way; and the proper principles of administration. That is to say, naturalness serves as a fundamental value or principle, universally applied in dealing with the basic relationships between people and people, people and the myriad things, and people and the universe as a whole. We can thus without reservation view the concept of naturalness as a universal and basic value of the philosophical system of Laozi.

Other Ways of Expressing Naturalness

Since naturalness is the core value of Laozi's thought, it is clear that it finds expression in more than just this one concept (i.e., *ziran*). Other expressions which share some affinity with naturalness include such concepts as *zihua* ("transforming of one's own accord"). Chapter 37 of the *Laozi* reads:

> The Way never acts (*wuwei*) and yet nothing is left undone. Should princes and lords be able to hold fast to it, the myriad creatures will be transformed of their own accord. After they are transformed, should desire raise its head, I shall press it down with the weight of the nameless uncarved block. The

nameless uncarved block is but freedom from desire, and if I cease to desire and remain still, the world will be rectified of its own accord.

Transforming of one's own accord is thus simply the natural process of organic change. If the "princes and lords" (i.e., rulers and administrators) are able to respect and hold fast to the Way's principle of naturalness and *wuwei*, then the myriad creatures will be transformed of their own accord. This type of natural process of transformation is the most desirable, and should not be interfered with. If there are those who "wish to make a display of cleverness and artificial effort" (Heshanggong's comment), the princes and lords should press them down with the principle of "not acting" (*wuwei*), and in this fashion the myriad events and myriad things will once again return to their original peaceful and natural state. This is what is meant by, "The world will be rectified of its own accord." Laozi uses naturalness to signify what is "normal" or "proper"; therefore, "rectified" (*zheng*) can also mean "natural." Chapter 57 reads:

> I take no action and the people are transformed of
>   themselves;
> I prefer stillness and the people are rectified of
>   themselves;
> I am not meddlesome and the people prosper of
>   themselves;
> I am without desires and the people of themselves
>   become simple like the uncarved block.

The phrases, "Transforming of themselves," being "rectified of themselves," "prospering of themselves," and "of themselves becoming simple like the uncarved block" all describe a situation that develops spontaneously, without external force or intervention. They express the common people's yearning for and praise of a natural and satisfied life. This perfectly describes the principle of governing by means of *wuwei*. "Transforming of themselves" is the process of natural, organic change, learning, and development, and is the ideal form of social life advocated by Laozi.

In the *Laozi*, the word "constant" 常 (*chang*) also signifies naturalness. For instance, chapter 16* reads:

> Returning to one's destiny is called the constant;
> Knowing the constant is called discernment;
> Woe to him who willfully innovates
> Without knowledge of the constant.

Gao Heng 高亨 notes, "This means that returning to one's destiny is the natural way of things, that knowing the natural way of things is discernment, and that not knowing the natural way of things and willfully innovating leads to disaster." We also have the passage in chapter 52: "To see the small is called discernment, To hold fast to the submissive is called strength. . . . Bring not misfortune upon yourself—This is known as following the constant." Gao Heng's comment on this passage reads, "Following the constant means according with the natural." Similarly, the word "constant" in a passage from chapter 55, "To know harmony is called the constant; To know the constant is called discernment," also has the meaning of "natural." Gao Heng's explanation of the meaning of the word "constant" in these passages is for the most part correct.[17] When used as a noun, the word *chang* always describes a lasting and stable state of affairs or things. The state of naturalness is also a constant state—as long as it remains free from the intrusion of external force. Turning this description around, we can say that the state of constancy is the state in which things develop naturally or of their own accord. The word "uncarved block" (*pu*) also signifies naturalness. Consider a passage such as "If you are a valley to the world, then the constant virtue will be sufficient, And you will return to being the uncarved block" (chapter 28*). Ge Xuan's comment on the line, "Returning to be like the uncarved block," reads: "This means holding fast to naturalness"—that is, he directly identifies the uncarved block with naturalness. Heshanggong explains the uncarved block as being simple and unadorned, while Wang Bi explains that it means what is genuine. They all believe it to signify that which is originally so and that which is plain and simple, which is precisely the state in which things come about naturally or of their own accord. The phrase in chapter 19, "Exhibit the unadorned and embrace the uncarved block," also means to hold fast to naturalness.

The idea of naturalness runs throughout the entire *Laozi*, and many places in the text reveal more or less clearly Laozi's reverence for the value of naturalness, even when the word "naturalness" or similar words are not at all mentioned. For instance, chapter 38 never mentions naturalness, and yet is nonetheless completely infused with a reverence for the value of this ideal. According to the Dunhuang manuscripts, this is the first chapter of the *Laozi*, and its first line reads: "A man of the highest virtue does not keep to virtue and that is why he has virtue; A man of the lowest virtue never strays from virtue and that is why he is without virtue." Those with the highest virtue possess the noblest virtue. They do not take themselves to be virtuous—they are not dazzled by their own virtuousness, and feel it is merely happenstance that others credit them with possessing virtue. Seen from a modern perspective, this would seem to be aimed at teaching people modesty or humility. However, from Laozi's perspective, what is important is that one's personal character flows forth naturally and is not contrived or forced. Although this can certainly still be seen as advocating humility, this is not the main point Laozi wishes to emphasize. From a general point of view or from a Confucian perspective, an individual consciously pursuing some sort of improvement in personal character should be praised, or at least encouraged. In the opinion of the Daoists, however, all unnatural behavior is bad, or at least not ideal. This sort of critical standard is bound to be a little unforgiving, but it is nonetheless a true reflection of the Daoist tendency to revere naturalness.

Historically there have been many discrepancies in the exact wording of the lines that follow but these textual difficulties can be resolved fairly well if we make use of the Dunhuang manuscripts:

The [person of] highest virtue does not act (*wuwei*)
and does not have ulterior motives;[18]
The [person of] highest benevolence acts and yet does not
have ulterior motives;
The [person of] highest rectitude acts, but from ulterior
motives;
The [person of] highest ritual propriety acts, and when no
one responds, he rolls up his sleeves and resorts to
persuasion by force.

These four lines describe a progressive decline, and each line contains two items used to chart this decline. One item concerns external action (whether or not one acts); in Laozi's system of thought,

wuwei ("not acting") is clearly higher than *wei zhi* 為之 ("acting").
The other item concerns internal motivation (whether or not one is
motivated by cunning or by ulterior motives): "to be without ulterior
motives" or "to have ulterior motives." Clearly, Laozi feels that
"being without ulterior motives" (*wu yi wei*) is higher than "having
ulterior motives" (*you yi wei* 有以為). Of course, those of highest
virtue are the best in both respects: they "do not act and do not have
ulterior motives"—that is, they not only do nothing, but they are
also free from internal striving or ulterior motives. This distinguishes them from those who deliberately make a show of wanting
to be *wuwei* and intentionally affect a manner of transcendence.
More simply put, casual and entirely natural *wuwei* is better than
intentional *wuwei*. Another step down the scale are those of
the "highest benevolence" who—though they act—are not drawn
by thoughts of accomplishment or profit, and can therefore still be
without striving or ulterior motives. They "act and yet do not have
ulterior motives." Even lower are those of "highest rectitude" who
act and also have ulterior motives, which would seem to be the worst
possible combination. Yet even worse still are those of the "highest
ritual propriety" who not only act but want to compel others to
respond to their behavior. If these others do not go along willingly,
they then drag them along by force—leaving others with no choice
but to follow their lead. This is the sort of behavior generally
displayed by most people, and yet it draws from Laozi nothing
but scorn. Laozi reveres true transcendence and casual ease in each
individual, and opposes imposing one's values and modes of behavior on others. This is why he adds:

> Hence when the Way was lost there was virtue;
> When virtue was lost there was benevolence;
> When benevolence was lost there was rectitude;
> When rectitude was lost there was ritual propriety.
> Ritual propriety is the wearing thin of loyalty and good
>   faith, and the beginning of disorder.

Compared with the traditional values of virtue, benevolence, rectitude, and ritual propriety, the Way is the highest—and its value lies
precisely in the fact that "the Way takes its model from naturalness"
and leaves no traces behind. Those who cannot achieve this can only
emphasize the standard of virtue; those who cannot measure up to

virtue apply themselves diligently to the principle of benevolence; those who cannot measure up to benevolence must retreat to acting with rectitude; and, finally, those who cannot even manage to naturally put rectitude into practice must content themselves with grasping tightly to the formalized practices of the rites. The rites are external forms of behavior, and bring with them coercive social norms. The flourishing of the rites is thus always a direct result of a decay of genuine, internal spiritual principles, and not an embodiment of enlightened social cultivation. This is why ritual propriety is the result of a "wearing thin of loyalty and good faith" and is both a harbinger and initial stage of social decay (the "beginning of disorder"). The focus of Laozi's criticism is not on the rites themselves, but rather on the social problems that accompany the flourishing of ritual propriety. Laozi is targeting the tendency to value the external *form* of the rites and to overlook the actual virtue that should inform them. He is criticizing traditional, vulgar social standards and values, and advocating standards of value and social comportment that spring spontaneously and naturally from one's inner being.

The Significance of Placing a Value upon Naturalness

Naturalness is a concept with a wide range of uses; it can be applied to individuals, society, and the universe as a whole. Yet when all is said and done, the basic import of this idea is that *people* need to be natural—it is people who have a need to learn to live "naturally." The concept of naturalness is thus aimed primarily at human life and human society. For one to genuinely live a life in accordance with naturalness, it is necessary, on the one hand, to give up interfering with other people and things, and on the other hand to prevent other people and things from disturbing or interfering with oneself. In this regard, of course, the most important thing is that the rulers model themselves on naturalness, because it is the rulers who are most able to directly interfere in the lives of others. Actually, all human difficulties—with the exception of natural disasters such as flood and drought—basically result from the desire of some people to impose by force their virtue, ideals, values, interests, or beliefs upon others. Regardless of whether or not these things being imposed upon others are good or bad, the attempt to *impose* them always results in disaster. Even if we think that it is reasonable to impose things upon others as long as these things are good, who believes the things that they want to impose upon others are *not* "good?" If those with power and influence followed the principle of naturalness, human society would certainly be much more peaceful. So with respect to most people, the "natural" state of affairs is an ideal, a goal to pursue, a consolation, and a relief. With respect to rulers, however, the concept of naturalness is a type of demand—a restriction and a criticism. Therefore, the natural life is a standard of evaluation for the common people, a basic appeal to protect the populace's peaceful way of life. This is particularly the case in primitive agrarian communities. In these ancient times—free of the interference or disturbance of external influences—the people "rose at dawn and retired at dusk." This form of life comes very naturally to agrarian people, and from their point of view things like a powerful national political machine, government tithes and taxes, and the restriction of laws and regulations seem quite superfluous and unnecessary. Government interference inevitably brings with it inconvenience or disaster, and thus a reverence for naturalness is implicitly also a criticism of and restriction laid upon those engaged in government or management. Therefore, generally speaking, the concept of naturalness could be genuinely embraced by rulers only with great difficulty.

The reverence with which Laozi views the core value of naturalness can help us to resolve some difficulties and debates relating to various aspects of his thought. For instance, there are those who criticize Laozi's policy of "keeping the people in ignorance." In fact, no such policy can be found in the text of the *Laozi*—at least, not in the modern sense of the policies of keeping the populace ignorant pursued by contemporary repressive societies. In chapter 65* Laozi says:

> Of old those who excelled in the pursuit of the Way did not use it to enlighten the people but to make them ignorant. The reason why the people are difficult to govern is that they are too knowledgeable. Hence, to rule a state by means of knowledge will be to the detriment of the state; to rule a state by means of "no-knowledge" will be a boon to the state[19]. . . . Mysterious virtue is profound and far reaching; when things turn back it turns back with them. Only then is great conformity achieved.

Wang Bi's commentary reads, "'Ignorant' 愚 (*yu*) means to be without knowledge and to hold fast to genuineness—to accord with what
is natural"; Yan Zun's commentary reads, "The ancient emperors
and kings managed by means of the Way and virtue, transformed
the people by means of spiritual clarity, gathered purity and tenuousness, and venerated grand harmony. They did not try to lead the
people by promoting knowledge or taking action in an effort to
enlighten them. Rather, they sought to cover the eyes and ears of
the people and block up their minds. They tried to prevent the
people from becoming knowledgeable and to lead them back to a
state of naturalness. This having been accomplished, the people
were easy to govern and the world was at peace." With regard to
the term "great conformity" (*da shun* 大順), Lin Xiyi notes "Great
conformity simply means naturalness." The gist of all of these ancient commentaries expresses Laozi's philosophical inclination for
seeking to govern by means of naturalness. What Laozi seeks is
a situation where interpersonal relationships are marked by unadorned simplicity, naturalness, and peacefulness. He thus opposes
the sort of situation where discord, contradiction, and opposition
between people is created and fostered by making overly sharp and
finicky distinctions and judgments. Here *yu* ("ignorance" or "to make
ignorant")[20] certainly does not mean the clever taking advantage of
the foolish; it is simply advocating honesty, simplicity, and straight-
forwardness. One way in which Laozi's policy of "making the people
ignorant" completely differs from the later policies of totalitarianism
is that Laozi is advocating that both the rulers *and* the people
embrace "ignorance." For instance, we read in chapter 20*:

> The multitude all have more than enough,
> I alone seem to be in want.
> My mind is that of a fool (*yu*)! . . .[21]
> The multitude are clear;
> I alone am drowsy.
> The multitude are alert;
> I alone am muddled.

Clearly, this is pointing in the direction of a society in which those
above and below equally embrace purity and simplicity, and the
common people enjoy a peaceful existence. This ideal is entirely
unrelated to later policies which seriously try to "keep the people in
ignorance": where the rulers not only monopolize all political and

economic privileges, but also restrict the intellectuals' freedom of inquiry and prevent the common people from coming in contact with or learning anything about the outside world. In order to more fully appreciate Laozi's views on the art of governing, it is probably best to look at them in terms of his reverence for the value of naturalness, rather than criticizing them from the perspective of contemporary politics.

There are also those who criticize Laozi's ideal of reducing the size and population of the state as a historical retrogression. This is also a rather forced interpretation. Chapter 80 reads:

> Reduce the size and population of the state. Ensure that
>   even though the people have tools of war for a
>   troop or battalion they will not use them; and also
>   that they will be reluctant to move to distant places
>   because they look upon death as no light matter.
> Even when they have ships and carts, they will have no
>   use for them; and even when they have armor and
>   weapons, they will have no occasion to make a
>   show of them.
> Bring it about that the people will return to the use of the
>   knotted rope,
> Will find relish in their food
> And beauty in their clothes;
> Will be content in their abode
> And happy in the way they live.
> Though adjoining states are within sight of one another,
>   and the sounds of dogs barking and cocks crowing
>   in one state can be heard in another, yet the people
>   of one state will grow old and die without having
>   had any dealings with those of another.

Laozi is here expressing a yearning for a life in which everything happens naturally or of its own accord, and is criticizing the senseless strife that characterizes the social world. This attitude is one that finds expression in different forms even today, and thus certainly does not represent a "historical retrogression." The ideal of reducing the size and population of the state also embodies a strong antiwar sentiment. Yu Yue notes that "*shi bo zhi qi* 什伯之器 [implements for a troop or battalion] refers to implements of war"; the lines, "Ensure that even though the people have tools of war for a troop or battalion they will not use them" and "[Ensure that] even when they have armor and weapons, they will have no occasion to make a show of them" are thus both clear expressions of an antiwar, pacifistic sentiment, and evoke a memory of and longing for a style of small-village life where everyone exists contented and undisturbed. This represents a key element in the critique of contemporary culture—a reaction against the side effects of human cultural development—and should not be judged in political terms.

Laozi's antiwar sentiment is expressed even more clearly in chapter 31*:

> Arms are the instruments of ill-omen. Things detest them, and therefore one who has the way does not abide by their use. . . . When one is compelled to use them, it is best to do so without relish and to not glorify in victory. . . . When great numbers of people are killed, one should weep over them with sorrow. When victorious in war, one should observe the rites of mourning.

Going to war should be something that one is compelled to do. War should not be used as a tool to gain dominion or political power, or a means to win fame or glory. The sentiment, "When victorious in war, one should observe the rite of mourning," is quite profound, but something that most people would not understand or accept—with quite tragic consequences for the human race. It is foolish and cruel to view war as either a means of relieving the pressures of overpopulation or a purifying force motivating the advance of history. Laozi's opposition to war and advocacy of a natural, peaceful way of life is a position that is still quite valuable today. In contemporary society, where we now possess the means to wipe out the entire human race, it would seem to be still quite important to oppose war and the use of violence to solve problems. In a highly modernized society, there is such a high level of population density that people are forced to live crowded together, while at the same time these people, packed shoulder to shoulder, feel a strange sense of loneliness. Similarly, remarkable developments in information technology and transportation have linked together the farthest ends of the globe and reduced the barrier of physical distance, while at the same time the spiritual distance between people has grown. It is especially meaningful, in such a strange and contradictory world, to be able to look back and appreciate the reverence Laozi displays for the idea of the natural. Analyzing and evaluating the thought of Laozi from the standpoint of his reverence for the natural will allow us to better comprehend its profundity, and will serve to dispel many unnecessary and arbitrary appraisals of a politically motivated sort.

Because naturalness is the core value of Laozi's philosophy, it is necessary for us to analyze a bit more precisely the exact content and significance of this so-called "naturalness." Based upon this author's own research and analysis of this issue, if one considers all of the usages and explanations of the concept of "naturalness" in the *Laozi*, one can say the basic meaning of the term includes within it the senses of *ziji ruci* 自己如此 ("like this of its own accord"), *benlai ruci* 本來 ("originally like this"), and *shidang ruci* 勢當 ("like this in accordance with inclinations").

The sense of "like this of its own accord" focuses on the role of external forces or external causes: naturalness is a state that exists and develops without any need for outside input. In the line, "The common people all regard my rule as natural," the emphasis is on the lack of external or foreign influences—or at least on the fact that any such influences are not perceived by the people. This sense of "naturalness" implies a state that comes about spontaneously, either without external influences or with such small influences that they are of almost no account.

The sense of "originally like this" concerns change: naturalness is the calm continuation of a primordial state, and not the result of change. That is to say, naturalness not only excludes the interference of external forces, but also excludes a sudden transformation resulting from any cause. Therefore, the state of naturalness is by definition a steady or constant state. "Yet the way is revered and virtue honored not because this is decreed by any authority but because it is natural for them to be treated so" (chapter 51) means that things have always been like this. Naturalness in this sense is the continuation of an original state or the maintenance of a spontaneous state.

The sense of "like this in accordance with inclinations" concerns development: the natural state is one that includes within it the internal developmental tendencies inherent in all things and affairs. Unless spoiled by the intrusion of an external force, naturalness follows along with the overall, original evolutionary tendencies of things. These tendencies can be anticipated—they are not simply random changes—and the sage can therefore "help along the naturalness of the ten thousand things." Naturalness in this sense is thus the sustained and continuing inertial tendency of a primordial and spontaneous state.

To summarize the above, the "naturalness" spoken of by Laozi includes the ideas of spontaneity, primordiality, and continuity. The ominous phenomenon of social instability produced Laozi's faith in naturalness, and led him to the firm conviction that the continuation of a spontaneous, primordial state was the highest order in the universe. Now, one might ask whether or not naturalness can still be a sort of value or find a place in contemporary society, where technological development is advancing at an increasingly rapid rate, wars are becoming more and more destructive, conflicts are becoming increasingly violent and bitter, and the various nations and regions of the world are being knit more and more tightly together. Our answer is an unqualified "yes." The naturalness of the Daoists involves being spontaneous and not forced—remaining stable and not developing—and thus does not apparently accord very well with the tenor of our modern society. However, even in the midst of the development of contemporary society, it would seem that naturalness can still serve as a value of irreplaceable significance. Although things developed by natural means can encounter various problems, they are generally speaking seldom subject to large-scale disturbances or man-made disasters, whereas things contrived through the conscious effort of human beings are less stable: although they can expand quickly to encompass the globe, they can also fall apart in an instant.

Although naturalness is still useful as a value in a highly modernized society, it is nonetheless somewhat outdated. It is therefore necessary to redefine and reexplain the specific content of this concept. Contemporary "naturalness" should not be thought of in the same way as that of ancient society—the most basic difference is that contemporary naturalness should provide a definite place for human effort and development. A reformed conception of naturalness could be defined by the following four standards:

1. Interiority of motive force. This accords with the spontaneity of Laozi's naturalness, but does not preclude all human initiative, and leaves sufficient space for human effort.

2. Mediation of external force. This brings out into the open a latent problem in Laozi's naturalness; it does not preclude completely the application of external force, but places conditions and restrictions upon external forces and causal factors.
3. Mitigation of development. This accords with the primordiality of Laozi's naturalness, and is opposed to violent conflicts or dramatic changes of an internal or external nature, while still approving of development in general.
4. Even and smooth course of development. This accords with the continuity of Laozi's naturalness, but it does not deny change. It merely emphasizes that change should take a set form, and opposes radical alterations in modes of existence or development.

These four standards can be roughly summarized as two: interiority of motive force and stability of development. That is, in all "natural" phenomena the primary motive force of development should always come from inner needs and efforts—it should not be coerced by external forces—and the development process itself should not be marked by violent conflicts or sudden breaks or changes in direction.

Using this sort of standard of naturalness to evaluate life in contemporary society, we will find that there are some phenomena and things that are natural and some that are not, and some that are more natural than others or not natural enough. There exist different degrees of naturalness. The more the motive force for development comes from within, and the more the process of development is stable and gradual, the higher the level of naturalness. The reverse is also true. It is also the case that natural things are not necessarily entirely good, but in general we can say that the higher the level of naturalness, the lower the cost and the greater the vitality. Purely natural phenomena are relatively rare, as are things entirely without elements of naturalness. However, we can still distinguish in at least a general sense between things that have originated from natural development and those that have originated from unnatural development. Determining whether or not something has originated by means of natural development is an objective procedure, with its own unique standards. Whether or not these standards are directly related to standards of morality or theoretical principles is of no relevance, for these are entirely separate questions.

To summarize, then, we can say that Laozi's concept of naturalness can—after undergoing certain modifications—become a type of
value for contemporary society. Judging from the standpoint of
naturalness, modern technology, management, laws, and innova-
tions should serve to guide and channel the natural development of
affairs and society, and not become the conditions for the destruction of their natural tendencies.[22]

NOTES

1. Translator's note: Literally "non-action" or "not-doing." As these literal translations give the term an inappropriately passive flavor, it will be
left untranslated.

2. Translator's note: A Chinese therapeutic or martial arts technique.

3. Translator's note: For the sake of convenience, I will follow the translation and chapter numbering of D. C. Lau, *Tao Te Ching* (Penguin Books,
1963), except in those cases where Lau's interpretation clearly diverges
from that of Liu Xiaogan. In cases where I offer my own translation or
modify Lau's translation, the chapter citation that precedes or immediately
follows the passage will be marked with an asterisk.

4. Chen Guying, *Laozi zhuyi ji pingjie* 老子注譯及評介 ["Commentary on
and Critical Introduction to the *Laozi*"] (Beijing: Zhonghua Shuju, 1984),
132.

5. Chen Guying, "*Laozi zhexue xitong de xingcheng* 老子哲學系統的形成"
["The Formation of Laozi's Philosophical System"], in *Laozhuang xinlun*
老莊新論 [*New Discourses on Laozi and Zhuangzi*] (Hong Kong: Zhonghua
Shuju, 1991), 28.

6. Lao Siguang, *Xinbian Zhongguo zhexueshi* 新編中國哲學史 [*Revised
History of Chinese Philosophy*, vol. 1 (Taibei: Sanmin Shuju, 1993), 237.

7. According to the Dunhuang manuscripts, the *xia* 下 in *qixia* 其下 was
originally *ci* 次.

8. Chen Guying, *Laozi zhuyi ji pingjie*, 132.

9. Other editions read *Tianxia jie wei wo dao da* 天下皆謂我道大 ("The
whole world says that my way is vast"), see the Dunhuang manuscripts,
version A. (Translator's note: cf. Lau, *Tao Te Ching*.)

10. For *yue*, see chapters 14, 16, 24, 25, etc.; for *yun*, see chapters 57 and 78; for *you zhi*, see chapter 41; for *you yan*, see chapter 69.

11. According to the Dunhuang manuscripts, *er qi* 而器 was originally *shi* 勢.

12. According to the Dunhuang manuscripts, *xuzhi* 畜之 was originally *de* 德 *xuzhi* 畜之. (Translator's note: cf. Lau, *Tao Te Ching*.)

13. Translator's note: Cheng is here taking *ming* to mean "official rank" and Liu is taking it to mean a "summons."

14. The subject is different in the two phrases, "The king counts as one" and "People model themselves on earth"; for this reason, many commentators have changed one or the other of the subjects to make them accord. However, both versions of the Dunhuang manuscripts have two different subjects, as does Wang Bi's version, which suggests that no changes should be made. "The king" should be seen as a part or representative of "people"; "people model themselves on earth" can thus be seen as including the idea that "the king models himself on earth." There is thus no reason to amend the text.

15. Li Yue's theory; cf. Gao Heng, *Chongding Laozi zhenggu* 重訂老子正詁 [*A Correct Commentary on Rearranging the Laozi*] (Beijing: Guji chubanshe, 1957), 61.

16. Chen Guying, *Laozi zhuyi ji pingjie*, 157.

17. Gao Heng, *Chongding Laozi zhenggu*, 1–2.

18. For *wu yi wei* 無以為 ("does not have ulterior motives") other editions have *wu bu wei* 無不為 ("nothing is left undone"); some editions also add the line, "The [person of] inferior virtue acts and has ulterior motives." These alternate versions have been the cause of much debate.

19. For *yi bu zhi* 以不知 ("by means of 'no-knowledge'") some editions have *bu yi zhi* 不以知 ("not by means of knowledge"); this reading follows the Dunhuang text.

20. Translator's note: Or, as Lau renders it, "to hoodwink."

21. Translator's note: It should be noted that this line could also be translated, "How I deceive/make ignorant the minds of others!" (reading *yu* as a transitive verb), which would give this passage a more sinister twist. This is obviously not the reading Liu (or D. C. Lau) chooses to adopt.

22. It is the opinion of the author that the abstract concept of "the Way" (*Dao*) provides the value of naturalness and the principle of *wuwei* with a metaphysical basis, while the interdependence of thesis and antithesis of

dialectic theory provides naturalness and *wuwei* with a concrete proof. The author has discussed this subject in other works. Additionally, near the beginning of 1987, Ms. Gu Linyu 顧林玉, who was then working on an M.A. at the Shanghai Institute of Social Science, expressed a desire to write on the subject of naturalness as a value in Laozi's thought, and came to Beijing to discuss her ideas with me. I helped her to define a project that looked at Laozi's reverence for naturalness from the perspective of value theory. Her work discusses the issue from the perspective of epistemological value, moral value, and aesthetic value. It is not clear where or when this paper will be published. The opinions expressed in this article may have been influenced by the insights of Ms. Gu.

The Concept of *de* ("Virtue") in the *Laozi*

Philip J. Ivanhoe

Introduction

The earliest versions of the text attributed to the mythical Laozi[1] announce it as a *jing* ("classic") concerning two basic notions: *Dao* ("Way") and *de* ("power" or "virtue"). From the Mawangdui texts, we know that this twofold division even predates the first use of the title *Daodejing*. There is more general agreement about the importance and meaning of the term *Dao*.[2] But the notion of *de* has received remarkably little attention, in this, its Daoist *locus classicus*.[3] In the introduction to his elegantly terse translation of the *Daodejing*, hereafter referred to as the *Laozi*, D. C. Lau goes so far as to assert that in the text the term *de*, "is not particularly important . . ."[4] However, the word appears in sixteen of the text's eighty-one short chapters for a total of forty-three times.[5] This and the fact that it appears in the title of the earliest versions of the *Laozi* is prima facie evidence that the idea is central to the text's elusive message.

I will argue that an understanding of the concept of *de* is indispensable for a full appreciation of the philosophy presented in the *Laozi* and that the view of *de* that we find in this text shares several important characteristics with an earlier conception found in Confucius's *Analects*. I begin by presenting a brief account of the earlier Confucian concept of *de*, focusing on three characteristics. The first is the *attractive power* of the person with *de*; the second is the *distinctive effect* of *de* upon those who come into its presence; the third is the relationship between *de* and *wuwei* ("non-action") in government. After laying out the Confucian precedent, I will describe and contrast it with Laozi's notion of *de*. As we shall see, the Daoist notion is similar though distinct from its Confucian antecedent. I will then present a brief discussion of Zhuangzi's notion of *de* in light of my analysis and suggest some ways in which these different senses of *de* may be of interest to contemporary ethicists.

Confucius's Conception of de

In several of my works on the early Confucian tradition, I have developed a line of argument, first advanced by David S. Nivison, concerning the role of the concept of *de* in Confucian ethics.[6] My particular interest in the early Confucian concept of *de* has been the role it played in the development of an ethic of self-cultivation. In summary, my view is that in early Confucian writings, *de* took on a genuinely ethical sense. In its general use, it retained its older meaning of the characteristic function and power of a given thing: "virtue" in the sense of the Latin *virtus*. But in the specific case of the ethically cultivated individual it came to denote what I call "moral charisma," a kind of psychological power that accrues to virtuous individuals and allows them to attract and retain the support of others. Such power was particularly important for rulers, for it enabled them to attract loyal and worthy followers; it gave them a way to legitimize a noncoercive form of government. As we are told in *Analects* 2.1, "One who rules through *de* ('moral charisma') is like the Pole Star, which remains in its place while all the myriad stars pay homage to it." The "magnetic personality" of the ethically good person is the first characteristic feature of *de* we want to explore: its *attractive power*.

As noted above, the ability to attract and inspire people through the power of moral charisma was particularly important for the king. This view can be seen as a descendent of earlier beliefs regarding the king's unique responsibility to attract and gain the support of the spirits on behalf of the people within his state. In Confucian writings such power is thought to be characteristic of *any* cultivated person. For example, consider *Analects* 12.19, an exchange between a senior minister of the state of Lu and

Confucius, "Ji Kangzi 李康子 asked Confucius about government, saying, 'How about killing those without the Way in order to advance those with the Way?' Confucius replied, 'In your administration of government, why use killing? If you just desire the good yourself, the people will be good. The *de* of the cultivated individual is like wind. The *de* of the petty person is like grass. When the wind blows upon the grass it is sure to bend.'" In this and the passage quoted earlier, we see the second characteristic feature of *de*: its *distinctive effect* upon those who come into its presence. Moral charisma influences others to yield to, support and emulate the person who has it.

This is an extremely important feature of Confucian ethical thinking. It helps explain why Confucius and Confucians in general have such faith in the power of moral example. Morally cultivated individuals are thought to "transform wherever they pass by."[7] When, in *Analects* 9.14, Confucius expresses a desire to go and live among the nine barbarian tribes of the East, someone objects saying, "They are so crude." Confucius responds, "Were a cultivated person to live among them, what crudeness would there be?" Those in the presence of *de* come under its sway and are inspired to be virtuous themselves. Confucian *de* invokes a kind of psychological compulsion, to respond in kind to the treatment one receives. Kindness received elicits kindness from the recipient and thereby inspires them to become more virtuous. This idea is captured in a couplet which is now found in the *Book of Poetry, wu yan buchou wu de bubao* 無言不讎無德不報 ("There are no words that are left unanswered, No *de* ('virtue' or 'kindness') left unrepaid").[8]

In terms of the administration of government, the distinctive effect of *de* on others allows the ideal Confucian ruler to exercise his authority without ever having to order people about, much less threaten them with force. By rectifying themselves and assuming their proper ritual station, sage-kings rule, or rather reign, through *wuwei* ("non-action").[9] Though usually associated with Daoist philosophy, the first occurrence of this phrase is in *Analects* 15.5, "The Master said, 'Among those who reigned through *wuwei* ("non-action") there was Shun! For what did he ever do? All he did was maintain himself in a dignified manner and face to the south." This passage illustrates the third characteristic of *de* mentioned earlier: the close relationship between *de* ("moral charisma") and *wuwei* ("non-action"). A person who cultivates the right kind of *de* develops the moral charisma which both *enables* him to rule and *justifies* him as ruler. Since people naturally respond to the example of a morally good person, such a person need not employ force or any other form of coercion in order to rule. He rules through the power of *ethical authority*.

De in the Laozi

In the *Laozi* we see a related but significantly distinct conception of *de*. There are correlates to all of our three characteristics (and other similarities besides), but each of these has its own distinctive expression. For example, Laozi shared with Confucius the belief that those who possess *de* will attract others to them. But the *attractive power* of Laozi's sage differs in character from that of the Confucian. The Confucian draws people toward him through the power of his ethical excellence, which inspires similar behavior and attitudes in others. He is like the Pole Star or the wind—forces *above* the people to which they submit or defer. This explains the sense in which the properly cultivated Confucian gentleman is thought to be *wei* 威 ("awe-inspiring") to behold.[10] Laozi's sage also draws people to him, moves them to submit or defer, and influences them to behave in certain ways. But he draws people toward him and wins their allegiance by placing himself *below* them, welcoming all and putting them at ease. This is why one of Laozi's central metaphors for the Way is the valley:

> Know the male,
> But preserve the female,
> And be a canyon to the world.
> If you are a canyon to the world,
> Your constant *de* ("virtue") will never leave you . . .
> Know glory,
> But preserve disgrace,
> And be a valley to the world.
> If you are a valley to the world,
> Your constant virtue will be sufficient . . .[11]

Putting oneself last or below others increases and perfects one's *de*.[12] Another expression of the belief that placing oneself below others

draws them into one's embrace is the idea that extending unqualified love—even to those who wish one ill—has the power to relieve
their anger and even win them over. This is why the *Laozi* counsels
us to *bao yuan yi de* 報怨以德 ("Repay resentment with kindness").[13]
"The mother" and "the female," which are thought to conquer
through "stillness," "taking the lower position," "passivity," and
"compassion," are other central metaphors for this characteristically
Daoist ideal.[14] Only one who manifests such humble, accommodating, and nurturing "virtue" can legitimately rule. For only such a
person embodies in human form a dynamic witnessed throughout
Nature:

> The reason why the River and the Sea are able to be king
> of the hundred valleys is that they excel in taking the
> lower position . . .
> Therefore, desiring to rule over the people,
> One must in one's words humble oneself before them;
> And, desiring to lead the people,
> One must, in one's person, follow behind them . . .
> That is why the empire supports him joyfully and never
> tires of doing so.[15]

For Laozi, the draw of *de* is not the awesome power of the Pole Star
or the wind, but the natural tendency of things to migrate down
toward low, safe, and inviting, terrain. The *de* of the Daoist sage is
welcoming, accommodating, and nurturing—not awe-inspiring like
that of Confucius's sage. The Daoist sage "shines but does not
dazzle."[16] *De* is a power that protects all ("the sage always excels in
saving people, and so abandons no one; always excels in saving
things, and so abandons nothing")[17] and nurtures all ("The Way
gives them life; Virtue rears them").[18] Those who possess this kind of
virtue not only command the respect and allegiance of other people,
all creatures in the world find them attractive, "And so among the
myriad creatures, none fail to revere the Way and honor virtue.
But the Way is revered and virtue honored not because of some
command but because this is naturally so."[19]

    This last passage focuses our attention on another important
feature of Laozi's conception of *de*, one that further tends to distinguish it from that of Confucius. While the latter believed that virtue
was in some sense "natural" for human beings, he also held that the

particular excellences human beings manifest set them not only apart from but *above* other creatures. Related to this, Confucius seems to have believed that *de* affects people but not other creatures or things. While this last point is surely not true of all later Confucians, Confucius himself, at least as he is represented in the *Analects*, never talks of *de* affecting anything other than people. Laozi rejects this more anthropocentric understanding of *de*. For him the power that accrues to those who embrace the Way affects the whole world. Those who have cultivated an abundance of *de* "virtue" are protected from natural harms. Not only people, but other creatures as well will honor and respect their special "power."

> One who possesses virtue in abundance is comparable to
> a new born babe;
> Poisonous insects will not sting it;
> Ferocious animals will not pounce on it;
> Predatory birds will not swoop down upon it.
> Its bones are weak and its sinews supple yet its hold is
> firm . . .[20]

If a ruler succeeds in cultivating and maintaining such *de*, by "holding fast" to the *Dao*, his power will transform heaven and earth,

> Should lords and princes be able to hold fast to it
> The myriad creatures will submit of their own accord,
> Heaven and earth will unite and sweet dew will fall,
> And the people will be equitable, though no one so decrees.[21]

Let us now turn to our second characteristic of *de*, the particular effect it is supposed to have on those who come into its presence. We have already noted that unlike Confucius's *de*, which affects only other people, Laozi's "mysterious virtue" influences all of the myriad creatures and even inanimate natural phenomena. While these features of Laozi's view of *de* are worth extensive and careful consideration, given the purposes of the present study, we will concentrate on its characteristic effects on people.

In order to grasp the special effect *de* is supposed to have on people, it will be helpful to offer a brief sketch of what Laozi thought were the most pervasive and profound human failings. Put simply, he believed that humans err whenever they become overly reflective and "clever." This leads them to devise all sorts of artificial ways of being and deviate from their spontaneous tendencies and natural desires. This then carries them off in a vain pursuit of social goods like power, honor, wealth, and beauty and leads them to ignore and grow cold to the simple goods and basic natural desires which are the true source of satisfaction in life. Laozi's goal is to undo this process and return to a primitive agrarian utopia of small villages. Within states composed of such villages, people will pursue lives of simple pleasures. They:

> will return to the use of the knotted rope,
> Will find relish in their food
> And beauty in their clothes,
> Will be content in their abode
> And happy in the way they live.[22]

In order to reach this ideal, the Daoist ruler works to undo the damage of socialization. He eliminates and discourages technological innovation or any intellectual pursuits above those needed to carry out a basic country life. The Daoist path of spiritual improvement is one of paring away or relieving unnatural, distorting, and deforming influences and ideas and restoring original vitality and health.

> Therefore in governing the people, the sage empties their minds but fills their bellies, weakens their wills but strengthens their bones. He always keeps them innocent of knowledge and free from desire, and ensures that the clever never dare to act.[23]

Confucius's *de* seeks to draw the ethically deficient up toward the ideal example of the sage. While not everyone will be equal in their attainment of this ideal and the different social stations people occupy will require them to manifest virtue in a variety of ways, they nevertheless aspire to a common goal: becoming a *junzi* 君子 ("gentleman"). Confucius sought to *educate* and *develop* people. This is the very opposite of Laozi's model. Instead of inspiring people to strive to develop themselves, he seeks for a way to empty, unravel, and settle them. This is the only way to cure them of the malaise of inauthenticity. Thus, for Laozi *de* has what I call a "therapeutic effect" upon others. It helps to put people at ease and enables them to become aware of their inauthentic behavior and attitudes. Like bringing into a calm consciousness some repressed anger or undetected self-deception, such awareness helps the afflicted slough off the baleful influences of socialization and excessive intellectualization.

But the Daoist is not seeking a Sartrean-style authenticity, i.e., a self forged out of a series of free acts of will. Nor is the Daoist's final goal a Freudian-style "mature" awareness of the true character of one's motivations. Daoist authenticity entails allowing one's spontaneous, prereflective nature to operate unencumbered and guide one through life. The awareness of what we might call our false social self is a stage—not the final state—in a process of cultivation leading to such a life. The Daoist believes that such awareness carries off not only one's false social consciousness but any strong sense of (or need for) a self apart from the spontaneous patterns and processes of Nature. Once the reassuring ease and tranquility of the sage has relieved others of their social posturing, they will begin to unselfconsciously follow and rest in their own particular natures.

Like the natural attractiveness of the Daoist sage described earlier, this dynamic between sages and those around them is understood simply as a human analogue to a widely attested natural phenomenon. Laozi believed that whatever is "still" naturally has the *de* ("power") to settle and govern that which is agitated or restless. For example, "Restlessness overcomes cold; stillness overcomes heat. Limpid and still, One can be a leader in the empire."[24] The Daoist sage emulates this natural pattern of influence and response by cultivating an extremely ethereal, tenuous, and still state of mind, "Cultivate extreme tenuousness; Preserve complete stillness."[25] Anyone who achieves and maintains this state of peace and purity generates the special *de* ("power") to settle others as well.

If a ruler can cultivate such *de* he will be able to eliminate all strife and contention within his state. Everything will then run smoothly as each person "returns to" and pursues his or her individual task with a natural spontaneity. The ruler himself will be functioning in complete harmony with the Way, which accomplishes everything but does not self-consciously strive for any particular end. Here we see the third characteristic of *de*: the intimate relationship between *de* and *wuwei* ("non-action") in government. The ideal

Daoist ruler cultivates a still and tenuous state of mind. This generates *de*, which enables him to both attract others and move them to follow the Way. This however simply entails getting them to give up all the false beliefs and artificial practices that interfere with the spontaneous functioning of their natures. There is no additional work to be done above and beyond this:

> The Way always is *wuwei* ("without action"),
> Yet nothing ever is left undone.
> Should lords and princes be able to hold fast to it,
> The myriad creatures will be transformed of their own
>   accord.
> ... if I cease to desire and remain still,
> The empire will be at peace of its own accord.[26]

As mentioned earlier, Confucius too believed in an ideal *wuwei* ("non-active") form of government which was connected to his particular understanding of *de*. He believed the moral charisma of a sagely ruler enables him to reign through the power of ethical authority. In order for this to lead to the state of "non-active" rule, the sage must hold the attention of the people and inspire them to *develop* themselves into reliable ethical agents. In a state composed of such reliable ethical agents, the sagely ruler simply goes about his particular duties and allows others to pursue their respective tasks. He need not interfere (i.e., "act") in any direct manner in the administration of his rule.

The relationship between Laozi's notion of *wuwei* and his conception of *de* shares the general structure of the Confucian precedent but is quite different. The difference is largely the result of their dissimilar views regarding the character of human nature. Laozi believed that what people *really* needed in order to lead a happy and contented life were the goods associated with the simple agrarian utopia described above. Artificial social goals not only do not offer any real satisfaction; they spoil any chance for a happy and contented life. The social virtues so dear to the Confucians represent the decline of the Way. For the more aware and self-conscious the people become about what constitutes "virtue," the greater the possibility for deception and hypocrisy.

There is an obvious truth to this claim: for one cannot manipulate others by feigning virtue unless one understands *how* to do this.

And the greater one's understanding, the greater the possibility that one with such an aim will succeed. This helps us to understand why Laozi claims that the truly virtuous person does not consciously strive to be "virtuous" (i.e., in the normal socially sanctioned sense) nor does such a person need to self-consciously act in order to achieve. The virtue and actions of the sage are spontaneous and natural: like the flowing of water or the falling of timely rain. Any hint of self-conscious design or effort is a symptom of human cleverness and artificiality.

Of course, this picture of the ideal human life assumes that in the absence of striving, people will by nature gravitate toward the noncompetitive activities of the Daoist agrarian utopia and find these fully rewarding. But if we grant these assumptions, it is then easy to see why Laozi would believe that the process of spiritual cultivation leading to this ideal involves paring away and "returning" to an original, pristine natural state. We can also more fully appreciate the difference between this ideal and the Confucian developmental model of study and reflection:

> In the pursuit of learning one knows more every day; in the pursuit of the way one does less every day. One does less and less until one does nothing at all, and when one does nothing at all there is nothing that is left undone.[27]

These various and related beliefs also explain why Laozi describes the rise of a self-conscious understanding of morality as tracing the decline of genuine goodness:

> Those with the highest virtue are not "virtuous"
> And so possess virtue.
> Those with the lowest virtue never fail to be "virtuous"
> And so are without virtue.
> Those with the highest virtue never act
> Yet nothing ever is left undone.
> Those with the lowest virtue act
> Yet still have things to do. . . .
> And so when the Way was lost there was virtue.
> When virtue was lost there was benevolence.
> When benevolence was lost there was right.
> When right was lost there were the rituals.

> The rituals are the wearing thin of loyalty and
>   trustworthiness
> And the harbinger of chaos . . .[28]

The actions of the truly virtuous arise spontaneously from their nature. They are not so much *their* actions as they are the *Dao* acting *through* them. Such individuals have nothing they need to do (i.e., no personal goals to pursue), but this does not mean that they are inactive. When hungry they eat, when tired they rest. In spring they plant, in autumn they harvest. They move as their nature commands, in harmony with greater rhythms, and in so doing "nothing is left undone." Such a life generates an abundance of true virtue, which enables those who possess it to live safely and in harmony with all the world and bring peace and nourishment to all who come into their presence. This is the state from which the people have fallen and back to which the *de* of the sagely ruler is to lead.

We have seen that for Laozi, *de* is the "power" or "virtue" that accrues to those who attain a peaceful, tenuous, and still state of mind. In contrast to the Confucian process of self-cultivation, which consists of prolonged study and development, a person achieves the Daoist ideal by paring away the influences of socialization and intellectualization and "turning back" to a simple, agrarian way of life. Daoist *de* welcomes, accommodates, pacifies, and nurtures all who come into its presence. And so all creatures find it attractive and worthy of reverence. The primary effect of Daoist *de* on other people is therapeutic and purgative. The natural simplicity and contentment of the sage helps others to recognize and shed the artificial beliefs and practices that deform and interfere with their original, spontaneous nature. The *Laozi* claims even greater power for "mysterious virtue," for its influence extends out to all creatures and even affects the rain and dew.

The power of *de* enables the ideal Daoist ruler to rule through *wuwei* ("non-action"). While Confucian rulers can rule through a related form of *wuwei* it is different from what we see in the *Laozi*. The *de* of the Confucian ruler allows him to attract and retain like-minded subordinates who join and are inspired by him to realize the ideal Confucian society. The force of his virtue is very much centripetal, drawing people in and up in a common cause. The *de* of the Daoist ruler also allows him to rule over a peaceful and flourishing country but he relies upon a different dynamic. His virtue relieves the tensions within his state, which are generated by the artificial desires foisted upon his people through the insidious influence of socialization and human "cleverness." This allows them to return to those pursuits that represent their genuine or natural desires: the life found in scattered, simple agricultural villages. The force of the *de* of Laozi's sage is very much centrifugal. It turns people away from those social goods, the "goods hard to come by,"[29] which lead to competition, contention, and strife. It puts people at ease, brings them peace and allows them to settle down where they are. To "find relish in their food . . . beauty in their clothes, (to) be content in their abode, And happy in the way they live."

De in the Zhuangzi

The concept of *de* is by no means restricted to the two texts that have served as the focus of the present study. Though it is not emphasized by most interpreters, it is of considerable importance in texts like the *Zhuangzi* as well. For example, in the fifth chapter, "The Sign of Virtue Complete," we find characters such as Aitai Tuo 哀駘它, who is described as *quande zhi ren* 全德之人 ("one of perfect virtue").[30] Aitai Tuo is a terribly ugly man who appears to be without any remarkable gifts or skills. And yet, "When men were around him, they thought only of him . . . and when women saw him they ran begging to their fathers and mothers, saying, 'I'd rather be this man's concubine than another man's wife!'"[31] We also are told that when summoned to court, Aitai Tuo quickly won the favor of Duke Ai of Lu, who wanted to entrust him with the administration of his entire kingdom. In this story we see the first of our three cardinal characteristics of *de*: its attractive power. (

An earlier story in the same chapter illustrates our second characteristic of *de*: its effect on those who come within its presence. This story concerns Shentu Jia 申徒嘉, a man who had lost a foot as punishment for an undisclosed crime. Through study with a Daoist master, he had learned to accept his fate, something we are told only a "man of virtue" can do. At one point, Shentu Jia describes the effect his master has had upon him, "There were many with two feet who laughed at me for having only one, which would whip me into a rage. But when I reached the Master's place, my anger dissipated and I would return home. I do not know how he *washed me clean with goodness.*"[32] Here we see a poignant illustration of what earlier I called the "therapeutic effect" of Daoist virtue.

In these and other stories, Zhuangzi dramatically emphasizes the separation of true virtue and outward form. His sages are highly imperfect and undesirable from the point of view of society. But, like the sage described by Confucius and Laozi, Zhuangzi's exemplars have a spiritual "power" that arises from their special character. Aitai Tuo draws people to him and relieves them of their cramped, socially sanctioned opinions of what is attractive and who would make a good minister. Shentu Jia's master stills the boiling rage within him.

Zhuangzi's notion of *de* is very much like Laozi's in being primarily "therapeutic" in its effect. But in at least one way it is more like that of Confucius than his fellow Daoist. For both Zhuangzi and Confucius, other people are attracted to the sage as an *individual*. The sage we encounter in the *Laozi*—like the text itself—is anonymous.[33] Perhaps of greater importance, Zhuangzi's concept of *de* differs from either of our other two thinkers in having no direct connection with a theory of government through *wuwei*. Those with virtue—including Zhuangzi himself—are on several occasions *offered* control of the government, but they always turn away from these offers, often mocking such proposals.[34] Nevertheless, while such a direct "use" of virtue is explicitly denied, there is a clear sense that one with great virtue is preserved from natural harms, as was the case in the *Laozi*. In chapter 1, we find the following description of the Holy or Spiritual Man:

> This man with this *de* "virtue," is about to embrace the ten thousand things and roll them into one. Though the age calls for reform, why should he wear himself out over the affairs of the world? There is nothing that can harm this man. Though flood waters pile up to the sky, he will not drown. Though a great drought melts metal and stone and scorches the earth and hills, he will not be burned . . .[35]

A full account of Zhuangzi's concept of virtue is beyond the range of the present study. The preceding examples and observations are intended only to provide some evidence of the pervasiveness, importance, and richness of the concept of *de* among early

Chinese philosophers. This is a topic worthy of sustained and careful study.

Beyond the importance the concept of *de* holds for our understanding of traditional Chinese thought is its potential to contribute to contemporary philosophical discussions, particularly in the field of virtue ethics. Contemporary Western philosophers, even those who work on the issues of character and the virtues, do not have anything quite like the Chinese notion that we have been exploring.[36] We tend to talk about virtue in the sense of various excellences of character—not as a *power* that can affect others, arising from the possession of such excellences. Our attention has been focused, and often with good results, on the characteristics of various human excellences and how they fit together in a picture of human flourishing. We have not seriously considered how the example of such good people might affect the ethical lives of those around them and the communities in which they live. Such consideration might lead us to appreciate additional dimensions of value in traditional virtues.

Conclusion

We have described two different notions of *de*, each of which points to real and important aspects of what we might call interpersonal moral psychology. The Confucian notion of *de* as moral charisma is a phenomenon familiar to many people. Morally excellent people, e.g., a Gandhi or a King, *draw* people to them and are *inspiring* and *uplifting*. This makes perfectly good sense. An important part of what it is for something to *be* a virtue, in the sense of a human excellence, is that it attracts, inspires, and uplifts human beings. And most people, at least within a common community, understand *enough* of what makes virtue virtuous to feel some attraction to those who possess it in abundance.

The Daoist "therapeutic" understanding of virtue is equally illuminating. Once removed from its more dramatic metaphysical foundations, the core sense of Daoist *de* is not at all unknown to us—though like moral charisma genuine cases of it are quite rare (which is part of what makes it so valuable). In the presence of those who are at peace with themselves, who are humble and who are open to and caring of others, we can find the beginning of a cure for some of our deepest, self-inflicted wounds. People who accept us as we are (no matter how bad we might be) and offer reassurance and support, perhaps even love, create a psychological space for profound self-understanding and transformation. The experience of being in the presence of a person with such "virtue" can result in a greater awareness of how much of our attention and energy is dedicated to maintaining various social masks, defensive postures, and outright self-deceptions. Reflected in the stillness of such individuals we have the chance to see ourselves and our society more clearly and perhaps even alter the way we perceive and act in the world.[37]

-------------------- *NOTES* --------------------

I want to thank Bryan W. Van Norden, Paul Kjellberg, Mark Csikszentmihalyi, and Ted Slingerland for helpful comments and suggestions on earlier drafts of this essay.

1. I will use the name of the mythical author of the text in order to facilitate my presentation. I think there was no such person and that the text is clearly a composite, cobbled together by some third century B.C.E. editor. Nevertheless, there was someone who at some point brought these various passages together and fashioned them into a single text. Extending my original analogy, there was a cobbler and as cobblers make shoes (even from scraps of leather) editors make coherent texts (even with passages from disparate sources). So referring to an author (in the sense of a *creator*) of the text seems well warranted. I see nothing wrong with calling him or her "Laozi" (lit., "The Old Master").

2. This is evident from the simple fact that almost every translator of the text renders the term as "Way." There is some disagreement as to the exact sense in which it is understood as a "transcendent" principle underlying the observable phenomena of the world. These disagreements strike me as more concerned with the particular metaphysics one sees in the text, specifically the existence or strength of dualism. But in almost every case, the *Dao* is understood as the underlying and unifying *pattern* beneath the play of events. The one dramatic exception to this generalization is Chad Hansen, who understands the *Dao* as something akin to "discourse." The point of the text then is to *deny* that there is any universal principle or pattern underlying the phenomena of the world. All we have are various linguistic schemes for carving up the world. See for example his *A Daoist*

Theory of Chinese Thought (New York: Oxford University Press, 1992), 196–230.

3. The one notable exception to this is Roger Ames's essay, "Putting the *Te* Back into Taoism," in *Nature in Asian Traditions of Thought*, ed. J. Baird Callicott and Roger T. Ames (Albany: State University of New York Press, 1989), 113–144. As best as I can tell, Ames's view is radically different from my own. He seems to regard *de* as a metaphysical feature of all living phenomena. For example, he says that *de*, "denotes the arising of the particular in a process vision of existence" (125). He further claims that it unifies all particular phenomena in a way reminiscent of Huayan Buddhism, "any particular *de* when viewed in terms of its intrinsic relatedness entails the full process of existence . . ." (128).

4. D. C. Lau, *Lao Tzu: Tao Te Ching* (Rpt., London: Penguin Books, 1974), 42.

5. This number will vary slightly depending on which version of the text one takes as authoritative.

6. The most complete account of Nivison's views on *de* can be found in Bryan W. Van Norden, ed. *The Ways of Confucianism: Investigations in Chinese Philosophy*, (La Salle: Open Court Press, 1996): 17–57. My understanding of the concept can be found in my *Confucian Moral Self Cultivation* (New York: Peter Lang, 1993), 1–7.

7. *Mencius* 7A13. Cf. 7B25. Similar lines occur in chapters 15 and 32 of the *Xunzi*. Donald Munro provides a remarkably thorough and insightful account of the role moral examplars play in Chinese thought. See his *The Concept of Man in Early China* (Stanford: Stanford University Press, 1969).

8. *Mao* # 256. For a complete translation and the context of these lines, see James Legge, *The Chinese Classics*, vol. 4 (Rpt., Hong Kong: Hong Kong University Press, 1970), 514.

9. Herrlee G. Creel is the first to comment on the Confucian examples of *wuwei*. His analysis differs from the one presented here but contains a wealth of examples and insights on this important concept. See "On the Origin of *Wu-wei*" in *What is Taoism?* (Rpt., Chicago: University of Chicago Press, 1977), 48–78. An illuminating and more recent discussion of *wuwei* can be found in Schwartz's treatment of Daoism. See Benjamin I. Schwartz, *The World of Thought in Ancient China* (Cambridge: Harvard University Press, 1985), 186–254.

10. For examples, see *Analects* 1.8, 7.38 and 20.2 (2X). For a passage that evokes the awe-inspiring majesty of the gentleman with another meta-

phor that places him "above" the people (like the sun or the wind), see *Analects* 19.21.

11. Chapter 28. My translation. For other examples of the image of the valley, see chapters 6, 15, 39, and 41. See also the image of water in chapter 8, "Highest good is like water. Because water excels in benefiting the myriad creatures without contending with them and settles where none would like to be, it comes close to the way" (Lau, *Lao Tzu*, 64).

12. The idea that putting oneself beneath or humbling oneself before another *increases* one's *de* is a very old notion. In his discussion of an oracle bone inscription dating from around 1200 B.C.E. David S. Nivison describes how a Shang King puts himself beneath or at risk before the spirits. Nivison says, "In this rite in which the king as diviner-intermediary assists another person to get well . . . because of his willingness to put himself in danger on behalf of another, his *de*, 'virtue,' is magnified." See "'Virtue' in Bronze and Bone," in *The Ways of Confucianism*, ed. Van Norden, chapter three. The same dynamic can be seen in chapter 20 of the *Analects*. There we see King Tang pronounce to the spirits, "If I in my own person do any wrong, let it never be visited upon the many lands. But if anywhere in the many lands wrong is done, let it be visited upon my person" (Arthur Waley, *The Analects of Confucius* [New York: Vintage Books, 1938], 231).

13. Chapter 63. In *Analects* 14.36 this line is discussed. There Confucius rejects it and instead suggests one: "Repay resentment with uprightness and kindness with kindness." Compare these different teachings to the lines from the *Book of Poetry* quoted above.

14. For examples of the image of the mother, see chapters 1, 20, 25, 52, 59. For the image of the "female," see chapters 10 and 28.

15. Chapter 66; Lau, *Lao Tzu*, p. 128. See also chapter 32. Cf. chapter 7, "the sage puts his person last and it comes first, Treats it as extraneous to himself and it is preserved" (Lau, *Lao Tzu*, 63).

16. Chapter 58; Lau, *Lao Tzu*, 119.

17. Chapter 27; Lau, *Lao Tzu*, 84.

18. Chapter 51; Lau, *Lao Tzu*, 112.

19. Chapter 51; My translation.

20. Chapter 55; Lau, *Lao Tzu*, 116.

21. Chapter 32; Lau, *Lao Tzu*, 91.

22. Chapter 80; Lau, *Lao Tzu*, 142.

23. Chapter 3; Lau, *Lao Tzu*, 59. Cf. chapter 12 "the sage is for the belly, Not for the eye" (Lau, *Lao Tzu*, 68).

24. Chapter 45; Lau, *Lao Tzu*, 106. See also chapter 26, "The still is the lord of the restless" (Lau, *Lao Tzu*, 83).

25. Chapter 16. My translation.

26. Chapter 37; Adapted from Lau, *Lao Tzu*, 96. Cf. chapter 32 quoted above.

27. Chapter 48; Adapted from Lau, *Lao Tzu*, 109. See also the idea that the basic movement of the *Dao* is "turning back," chapters, 14, 16, 25, 40, 52, etc.

28. Chapter 38. My translation.

29. For this expression, see chapters 3, 12, and 64.

30. My translation. A complete translation of the story can be found in Burton Watson, trans., *Chuang Tzu: The Complete Works* (New York: Columbia University Press, 1968), 70–71.

31. Watson, *Chuang Tzu*, 72.

32. My translation. Both Watson and Graham have added a line immediately after the translated section which does not appear in the original and which changes the sense of the passage. Watson has, "I don't know whether he washes me clean with goodness *or whether I come to understand things by myself.*" Graham has, "I do not know whether it is the Master cleansing me by his goodness *or my own self-awakening.*" (Italics mine in both quotes.) See A. C. Graham, trans., *Chuang Tzu: The Inner Chapters* (London: George Allen and Unwin, 1981), 78. They both appear to be following the commentary of Guo Xiang, who glosses the original line to this effect.

33. But even in this regard, the similarity with Confucius's sage is not complete. For Confucius most often holds up *historical* exemplars while Zhuangzi's sages are clearly *literary* creations. In a way, Zhuangzi's exemplars stand somewhere in between those of Confucius and Laozi.

34. One of the most delightful examples of this kind of story concerns Zhuangzi fishing in the Pu River. See Watson, *Chuang Tzu*, 187–188.

35. Adapted from Watson, *Chuang Tzu*, 33.

36. In some earlier traditions within the West, the idea that one can be transformed by the virtue of another is evident and important. Of particular note in this regard is the notion of Platonic Love as seen in works such as Plato's *Symposium* or Dante's *Divine Comedy*.

37. In his profound and disturbing account of wartime experiences, J. Glenn Gray describes his chance encounter with an old Italian hermit who embodies many of the qualities I have tried to describe here as Daoist "virtue." Glenn tells us, "there was about him a rare peaceableness and sanity . . . I felt in him the strength of his close association with the things of nature . . . he seemed to possess a constancy, patience and endurance not often known . . ." See *The Warriors: Reflections on Men in Battle*, (Rpt., New York: Harper and Row, 1967), 240–241. See also 18–21.

Notes on Contributors

Mark Csikszentmihalyi trained at Harvard University (AB, East Asian Languages and Civilizations, 1987) and Stanford University (PhD, Asian Languages, 1994), and is currently an Assistant Professor of Religion at Davidson College. His dissertation treated the Han Dynasty phenomenon of HuangLao literature—texts associated with the Yellow Emperor and Laozi. He is a member of the Research Group on Newly Excavated Chinese Materials based at Tokyo University and is currently working on a translation of the Essay on the "Five Kinds of Action" discovered at Mawangdui.

Robert G. Henricks is Professor of Chinese Religions at Dartmouth College in Hanover, New Hampshire, where he has taught since 1976. He was trained at Penn State (BA, Religious Studies, 1965) and the University of Wisconsin (MA and PhD in Chinese Language and Literature, 1973, 1976). He is the author of numerous articles and three books: 1) *The Essays of Hsi K'ang: Philosophy and Argumentation in Third Century China* (1983); 2) *Lao-tzu Te-tao ching: A New Translation Based on the Recently Discovered Ma-wang-tui Texts* (1989); and 3) *The Poetry of Han-shan (Cold Mountain): A Complete Annotated Translation* (1990). He is currently working on early Chinese mythology while continuing his textual work on the *Lao-tzu*. Henricks is known to spend inordinate amounts of time and money on fly-fishing for trout and salmon when he is not doing research on ancient China.

Philip J. Ivanhoe received his BA (1976) and his PhD (1987) from Stanford University. He has published work on a range of topics in the fields of Religious Studies, Philosophy, and Asian Studies. He is the author of *Ethics in the Confucian Tradition: The Thought of*

Mencius and Wang Yang-ming (1990) and *Confucian Moral Self-Cultivation* (1993), the editor of *Chinese Language, Thought and Culture* (1996) and the co-editor (with Paul Kjellberg) of *Essays on Skepticism, Relativism and Ethics in the Zhuangzi* (1996). He is currently an Associate Professor in the departments of Asian Languages and Cultures and Philosophy at the University of Michigan, Ann Arbor.

Liu Xiaogan was in the first class to receive the PhD degree in modern China. He has been a lecturer and associate professor at Beijing University, a visiting scholar at Princeton, Harvard, and the University of Michigan, and is currently a senior lecturer in the Department of Chinese Studies at the National University of Singapore. He is the author of *Zhuangzi zhexue jiqi yanbian* 莊子哲學及其演變 (*Zhuangzi's Philosophy and its Development*, 1981), *Liangzhong ziyou de zhuiqiu: Zhuangzi yu Shate* 兩種自由的追求：莊子與沙特 (*Pursuing different freedoms: Zhuangzi and Sartre*, 1994), *Classifying the Zhuangzi Chapters* (1994), *Liangjihua yu fencungan* 兩極化與分寸感 (*Polarization and the Sense of Propriety*, 1994), and *Laozi niandai xinkao yu sixiang xinquan* 老子年代新考與思想新詮 (*Laozi: A New Investigation of Date and Thought*, 1997). He has also contributed to *Our Religions* (1993) and numerous other books and journals.

Bryan W. Van Norden received his BA from University of Pennsylvania (1985) and his PhD from Stanford (1991). His work appears in *Philosophy East and West*, *The Journal of Asian Studies*, *The Journal of Chinese Philosophy*, *International Philosophical Quarterly*, and *Midwest Studies in Philosophy* 21. He has also contributed several entries on Chinese philosophy to *The Cambridge Dictionary of Philosophy*, is the editor of *The Ways of Confucianism*, and is currently editing an anthology, *Essays on Confucius and the Analects*. He has taught at Stanford University, the University of Vermont, and the University of Northern Iowa, and is currently an assistant professor in the Philosophy Department and Asian Studies Program at Vassar College.

Isabelle Robinet is professor of Chinese History and Civilization at the University of Aix-Marseille. She has published extensively on the history of Daoism, most recently *Histoire du Taoïsme des origines au XIVe siècle* (*A History of Daoism from its Origins to the 14th Century*, 1991), *Taoist Meditation* (1993), *Introduction à l'alchimie intérieure taoïste: De l'unité et de la multiplicité* (*An Introduction to Daoist Interior Alchemy: Of the Unity and the Multiplicity*, 1995), *Taoism, Growth of a Religion* (1997), and *Lao zi et le Tao* (*Laozi and the Dao*, 1997).

Harold D. Roth is Associate Professor of Religious Studies and East Asian Studies at Brown University. He is the author of *The Textual History of the Huai-nan Tzu* (1992) and of a number of articles on the early history and philosophy of the Daoist tradition and on the textual history and criticism of classical Chinese philosophical works. These include: "Psychology and Self-Cultivation in Early Taoistic Thought," in *Harvard Journal of Asiatic Studies* 51.2 (1991), 588–650; "Who Compiled the *Chuang Tzu*?" in *Chinese Texts and Philosophical Contexts: Essays Dedicated to Angus C. Graham*, ed. Henry Rosemont, Jr. (1991); "Text and Edition in Early Chinese Philosophical Literature," in *Journal of the American Oriental Society* 113.2 (1993): 214–227; and "Redaction Criticism and the Early History of Taoism," in *Early China* 19 (1994): 1–46.

Tateno Masami received his BA (1977) and his doctoral degree (1982) from Nihon University. He has published on a wide range of topics in Chinese thought and culture primarily from a philosophical or psychoanalytic perspective. He is the author of *My Views on Ancient Chinese Thought* (1993) and co-author of *Qi Theory and the Concept of the Body in Ancient Chinese Thought* (1993). Among his published articles are: "Dao and Time: A Study of Zhuangzi's Way from the Perspective of Time" (*East Asian Religion* 82, 1993) and "Laozi, Dao and the Recluse in the Marketplace: The Context of Daoist Theories of Mind and Body" (*Thought* 864, 1996). He is currently an Associate Professor in the Department of Chinese Studies at Nihon University.

Zhang Longxi received his MA (1981) from Peking University and his PhD (1989) from Harvard University. He has published in both Chinese and English on many topics in Chinese and comparative literature, and he is author of *The Tao and the Logos: Literary Hermeneutics, East and West* (1992), which received honorable men-

262 Notes on Contributors

tion for the Joseph Levenson Book Prize in 1994, and *Mighty Opposites: From Dichotomies to Differences in the Comparative Study of China* (forthcoming). He is professor of Comparative Literature at the University of California, Riverside, and currently is also chair professor of Comparative Literature and Translation at the City University of Hong Kong.

Index to *Laozi* passages by chapter number

Name Index

Subject Index

spirit. *See xin*
spiritual practice, 20, 175–186
spontaneity, 4, 18, 26, 151, 214,
   233, 245–246. *See also ziran*
statecraft, 10–11
Stoics, 113
Straw Dogs (film), 187
śūnyatā, 11
suppleness, 38, 139, 174, 244. *See
   also* pliancy
Symposium, 256

taiji 太極, 13, 62
Taipingguangji 太平廣記, 101
Tanyilu 談藝錄 (Discourses on
   Art), 97, 121, 123, 126
ten thousand things. *See wanwu*
theology, 138, 141
therapy, 26, 43, 245, 249, 251–
   252
Thirteen Epistles, 125
Three Essays on Religion, 113
ti 體 (foundation), 133, 135, 140,
   142, 147, 152
tian 天 (Heaven), 129–130, 132,
   144, 151, 157, 169, 191, 194–
   195, 199, 203, 207, 220–222
Tibet, 65–67
tranquility, 19, 62, 69–70, 73–78,
   169, 246

uncarved block. *See pu*
unhewn. *See pu*
unmediated experience, 39, 52.
   See also pure consciousness

*Vimalakīrti nideśa sūtra. See
   Weimojie suoshuojing*
virtue. *See de*
vital essence. *See jing*
void. *See xu*

wanwu 萬物 (ten thousand
   things), 19, 51, 57, 76, 84–85,
   161, 163–164, 168–171, 175,
   222–223
war, 25, 153, 230–231, 257

Weicheng 圍城 (*Fortress
   Besieged*), 123
Weimojie suoshuojing
   維摩詰所説經, 105, 116
Wei Shu 魏書 (*Book of Wei*), 114,
   122
Wenxindiaolong 文心調龍
   (*Literary Mind or the Carving
   of Dragons*), 120
Wenzi 文子, 4–5, 7, 114, 118, 119
*Written on the Margins of Life.
   See Xie zai rensheng bianshang*
wu 無 (nothingness), 10, 21, 77,
   127, 136, 138–140, 143, 146–
   147, 151, 158, 170, 181–182
Wudeng huiyuan 五燈會元, 105,
   107
Wujing 五經 (*Five Classics*), 154
wushenglaomu 無生老母, 173
wuwei 無為, 8, 20, 23–27, 48, 79–
   80, 87, 145, 151, 164, 196, 198,
   201–202, 208–210, 211–215,
   218, 222–223, 225–226, 235–
   236, 240–241, 245, 247–249,
   251, 254
wuxing 五行 (five phases), 61

xiang 象 (image), 45, 139, 145
Xiang'er 想爾, 45, 48
Xiangshan quanji 象山全集, 122
xiao 孝 (filial piety), 9
Xie zai rensheng bianshang
   寫在人生邊上 (*Written on the
   Margins of Life*), 123
xin 心 (heart-mind, spirit), 145,
   150
xing 性 (nature), 145, 150, 162
Xintangshu 新唐書 (*New
   Chronicles of the Tang*), 122
Xishengjing 西昇經 (Scripture of
   Western Ascension), 50, 58
xu 虛 (void), 75–78, 137–139,
   146, 151
Xuanxue 玄學 (Mysterious
   Learning, Profound Learning),
   61, 156
Xunzi 荀子, 118, 254

yang 陽, 23, 53, 61, 112, 145,
  196, 198–203, 209–210
Yangism, 90
yi 義, 9, 35, 206, 225–227, 248
Yijing 易經 (*Book of Changes*),
  11, 18, 108, 118, 135, 148, 153,
  155–156, 158
yin 陰, 23, 53, 61, 112, 145, 196,
  198–203, 209–210
Yoga, 67–68, 178
yong 用 (function), 133–134, 140,
  147, 152
you 有 (existence), 127–128, 134,
  138–140, 143, 146–147, 151,
  158, 170
Yuanjuejing 圓覺經, 108

Zen. *See Chan*

Zhongdao 中道, 112
Zhonglun 中論, 105
zhuzi 諸子 (various masters), 10
Zhuzi yulei 朱子語類 (*Classified
  Conversations of Master Zhu*),
  111
Zhuangzi 莊子, 14, 18, 27, 37–38,
  46, 55, 57, 60–61, 66–68, 70,
  72, 77, 81, 86, 88–89, 92, 94–
  96, 103, 105–107, 115, 118,
  142, 144, 153, 155, 159, 162,
  170, 172, 206, 250
zihua 自化, 24, 222–223
ziran 自然, 20, 23–24, 27, 143–
  144, 146, 164, 195, 208, 211–
  237, 249. *See also* spontaneity
Zuo Commentary. *See Zuozhuan*
Zuozhuan 左傳, 215

d in the United States
VS00004B/243